D1825913

Speculations Transformations

Speculations Transformations

**Thoughts on the Future of
Germany's Cities and Regions**

Matthias Böttger, Stefan Carsten, Ludwig Engel

Lars Müller Publishers

Matthias Böttger, Stefan Carsten,
Ludwig Engel

Speculations Transformations
Thoughts on the Future of Germany's
Cities and Regions

Managing Editors: Matthias Böttger,
Stefan Carsten, Ludwig Engel

Associate Editors: Leona Lynen,
Matthias Heumeier, Tristan Biere

Scientific Support, BBSR:
Lars-Christian Uhlig

Concept and Support, BMUB:
Marta Doehler-Behzadi,
Michael Marten

Copyediting and Coordination:
Cordelia Marten, Katrin Sauerländer

**English Copyediting and
Proofreading:** Emily Votruba

**Translation (all texts except
Bouw and Swyngedouw):**
Christopher Jenkin-Jones

Graphic Design and Concept:
onlab, Nicolas Bourquin

Layout and Typesetting: onlab,
Floyd E. Schulze, Signe Vej Ugelvig

Cartography: onlab, based on data
provided by BBSR

Production:
Lars Müller Publishers, Martina Mullis

Printing and Binding:
Kösel GmbH & Co. KG
Am Buchweg 1
D-87452 Altusried-Krugzell

© 2016 Lars Müller Publishers, Zurich,
and the authors, photographers, and
their legal successors

No part of this book may be used or
reproduced in any form or manner
whatsoever without prior written
permission, except in the case of brief
quotations embedded in critical articles
and reviews.

Published by
Lars Müller Publishers
Pfingstweidstrasse 6
CH-8005 Zurich
www.lars-mueller-publishers.com

ISBN 978-3-03778-478-5
Printed in Germany

Speculations Transformations was
produced in the framework of the
research project "Baukulturatlas
Deutschland 2030/2050" commissioned by and conducted in collaboration with the Federal Ministry for the
Environment, Nature Conservation,
Building, and Nuclear Safety (BMUB)
and the Federal Institute for Research
on Building, Urban Affairs, and Spatial
Development (BBSR).

Contents

Preface

Analysis

Interviews, Theses, Essays

Maps

Speculations

Reflections

Transformations

Afterword

Appendix

How Do We Want to Live in the Future?

How do we want to live in the future? Who is "we"? Under what conditions will *Baukultur* be practiced in the future and how will our built environment change? The idea behind the more than three-year research project "Baukulturatlas Deutschland 2030/2050," on which this book is based, was to use future-oriented speculations to shed light on transformations latent in the present and possibly emergent in the future. For the organizations that commissioned the research—the Federal Ministry for the Environment, Nature Conservation, Building and Nuclear Safety (BMUB), and the Federal Institute for Research on Building, Urban Affairs and Spatial Development (BBSR)—creating a temporary "think tank" inside of which future developmental options for Germany's cities and regions could be investigated by interdisciplinary teams was a priority; or as Markus Eltges (BBSR) has put it: "It is also our job to think in alternative futures."[1] Therefore our treatment of the (highly German) concept of *Baukultur* and what it usually designates —visible surfaces, architectures, and infrastructures, precisely everything "built," in the light of its history[2]—took second place. Our concern was much more to discover what the catalysts and driving forces behind spatial developments might be and which societal arbitration processes lead to a particular built environment. Central here were the forward-looking questions: What developments will affect Germany and its inhabitants most powerfully and what impact will they have on the *Baukultur* of the country?

Rather than taking *Baukultur* simply to mean "built environment," we preferred to define *Baukultur* as "lived environment," thus broadening perspectives and at the same time the range of disciplines integrated in our investigations. The experts with whom we collaborated came not only from the fields of architecture, landscape architecture, urban planning, geography, and civil engineering, but also economics, sociology, demography, climate research, the cultural and political sciences, and information technology. They contributed valuable perspectives on the complex present within the context of our thoughts

1   Dr. Markus Eltges (BBSR) quoted by Michael Bauchmüller in "Datenrepublik Deutschland," *Süddeutsche Zeitung* (March 10, 2015), 6.

2   For a comprehensive treatment see Werner Durth and Paul Sigel, *Baukultur: Spiegel gesellschaftlichen Wandels* (Berlin, 2010) and the Bundesstiftung Baukultur with its publications and reports on *Baukultur*.

on the future of Germany's cities and regions, providing us with as exhaustive a picture as possible of what are generally taken to be the current realities with which we live.

A corollary to this extended concept of *Baukultur* was a self-imposed ban on images. We wanted to escape the all-too-familiar repertoire of images of past utopias and futures to which almost every relevant illustration of the future resorts, especially when what is at stake is "the city of tomorrow." Nonetheless, our subject is utopian in Ernst Bloch's sense. Utopia for Bloch was no bold dream of a better tomorrow, but a seismograph of potential latent in the present: "Utopian consciousness wants to look far into the distance, but ultimately only in order to penetrate the darkness so near it of the just lived moment, in which everything that is both drives and is hidden from itself. In other words: we need the most powerful telescope, that of focused utopian consciousness, in order to penetrate precisely the nearest nearness."[3] Pursuing this idea, the thoughts set out in this book may be understood as "currently thinkable futures," as social negotiations of a tomorrow today. The chapter entitled "Analysis" sheds light on Germany and its *Baukultur* from different angles and approaches to dispel the "darkness so near." Documented in interviews, essays, statements, and maps, these approaches to the present and its recognizable challenges, developmental driving forces, and potential build a foundation for the future scenarios described in the chapter entitled "Speculations." Participants in our workshops addressed the question: In what ways, given the present state of knowledge, might Germany change through the year 2050? In a first step, positing different initial societal starting points, the speculations ran through various population scenarios. We took not only possible immigrant figures into account here, but also German society's response to the changing composition of its population—a topic the scale of whose present relevance could not be foreseen at the time of the discussions. In further workshops, these scenarios were discussed, elaborated, and adapted together with local experts in regard to six specific cities or regions—Hamburg, Offenbach, Kitzscher, the Saale-Orla-Kreis, Ludwigsburg, and Völklingen. The speculations focus "utopian consciousness" by amplifying the

3   Ernst Bloch, *The Principle of Hope*, vol. 1, no. 12. Translated by N. Plaice, S. Plaice, P. Knight
(Cambridge, MA: MIT Press, 1986). (Translation slightly changed.)

weak signals of already existing developments; or, as Armin Grunwald put it in response to our first drafts of speculative scenarios: "Are not these scenarios already reality today in the way we describe current conditions and developments? Some see the green-communitarian paradise as already at hand (Integralland); others see social division and the de-solidarization and fragmentation of society as already under way (Wattland); and the networking of society in infrastructures (Netland) is today already part of our self-descriptions."[4]

The contributions in the chapter entitled "Reflections" mirror and extend our procedure from an external, international perspective. Finally, the chapter entitled "Transformations" brings together present-day approaches of which we became aware in the course of our research in talks, presentations, and discussions, as well as in the context of our workshops. The three big topics—quality of life, value creation, resources—were a central strand unifying the whole process and are brought together here in a deliberately normative, condensed form. They thus describe basic directions that, according to our investigations, are central to the social transformations currently experienced as pointing the way forward. The three paradigms—"Alternative Prosperity," "Decentralized Production," "Renewable Energies"—are, therefore, starting points that are rooted in the present and from which we can reengage with the question: How do we want to live in the future? Ideally, they will stimulate an open and fundamental encounter with the future design of cities and regions.

4   Armin Grunwald, e-mail to the authors, November 1, 2013.

Analysis

How do things stand in Germany with respect to *Baukultur*? What factors, developments, and actors have the biggest impact on the lived environment? Interviews, theses, and essays with experts give an overview of the present challenges to German cities and regions and identify the major factors influencing possible futures. The analysis is supplemented by maps based on BBSR data comparing different indicators for current geographic situations.

Klaus Hurrelmann

"The young generation must live with a high degree of structural uncertainty and accept economic, professional, and climatic risks that can have a substantial impact on their lives."

Your Shell Youth Study[1] research shows that the generation of 12- to 25-year-olds today takes a very realistic approach to current living conditions. What is the source of this pragmatism?

Today's young people view the situation they live in extremely intuitively and weigh up what their environment means for them personally. Accordingly, they're strongly inclined to ask what the current economic, social, cultural, media, and climatic situation entails for them. The core question is invariably: What does this mean for me? For this reason we have named today's young generation the "pragmatic generation." They have to adapt to a situation currently marked by the fact that not everyone may get a job, that it's difficult to predict when—and whether at all—they'll be able to learn a profession, under what conditions this will take place, and the position that they'll finally take on. The young generation must live with a high degree of structural uncertainty and accept economic, professional, and climatic risks that can have a substantial impact on their lives. And for all that, they have to keep telling themselves that somehow or other *I myself* will make it, and *I myself* will find my way.

Interestingly enough, a particularly strong version of this attitude is found among young women, who are more flexible and shrewd in dealing with these uncertainties than young men. Their approach to their own lives and biographies is far more entrepreneurial: they experiment more. Having abandoned the traditional women's roles of mother and housewife, they demand new, combined roles. Young men are still a long way from this and rate correspondingly poorly in terms of performance.

You have said that some 20 percent of young people, mainly from socially underprivileged classes, often with a background of migration, constitute a severely disadvantaged group. What are the future expectations of this group, not least in the face of insecure economic developments?

The pragmatism of which we're speaking applies to the mainstream and it reflects the attitude of the majority of young people. It is not possible to state the exact size of this group. Our research puts it at around 80 percent. But distinctions also need to be made within the group. Of this 80 percent majority, only around 40 percent are in a genuinely good position, while another 40 percent lag behind this basic level with various deficits.

The remaining 20 percent experience growing division and inequality. These young people are unable to maintain the pragmatic basic assumption, with positive, constructive elements: the assurance that somehow or other they will make it, whether through flexibility, investment in education, or simply good, concentrated, healthy life conduct. And this group, compared with that of the previous generation thirty years ago, is worse off. Without completing secondary education, they have almost no chance on the job market today. That was different thirty years ago. In this sense, the current latent German crisis situation affects this group particularly strongly.

This group feels extremely disadvantaged. It consists primarily of young men from socially underprivileged classes. Around half of them have a migratory background, though what is important here is not ethnic or religious factors but social disadvantages: the financial resources of parents and the low level of family education. This group dares not protest, however, because they feel overwhelmed by the 80 percent, who, in their eyes, react to the increasing uncertainties with ever-growing optimism and investment. Some of them have already given up on themselves. They have health problems, tend to political extremes, no longer believe in the political system or even in democracy sometimes. This group seems to constitute itself anew year for year: 7 to 8 percent each year don't complete secondary education; a further 7 to 8 percent complete no vocational training; plus several percent that fall by the wayside. So each year one arrives at just short of 20 percent.

How is this group geographically situated?

The group is heavily segregated. Its geographic distribution, generally speaking, also correlates powerfully with the wealth and prosperity of the respective region. Demographic maps show where the members of this group are found: primarily in the east German federal states and in the poorer west German municipalities.

Who or what do these young people hold responsible for their situation? Family, politics … or is it more that they suffer from a lack of self-confidence?

In principle, one can say that the young generation has no great faith in politicians. They prefer to get involved themselves. Up to a pre-political point they're certainly prepared for social commitment. But the discrepancy between the groups ensures that as young people descend lower on the social ladder, it becomes more difficult for them to see a way out of their adverse situation. They neither trust politicians nor have any self-confidence themselves. The result is combined despair and resignation.

● 90

● 86

77 ●

82 ●

1   Since 1953 Shell Germany has commissioned independent research institutes to document views, moods, and expectations of adolescents and young people.

How do you see the role of the new information and communication technologies in this context? Do young people know how to exploit the new technologies, not just to make themselves heard, but to use new forms and possibilities of participation so as to play a part in political, social, and economic discourses?

Yes, with the proviso, though, that the ones who succeed stand on a firm footing and are conversant with media so they can apply these tools to their own interests and for their own development. The socially weaker and educationally disadvantaged fail here, and one sees a more destructive use of media. Members of this group consume passively, let themselves be controlled, even exploited, by the media—it is not going too far to compare it to drug use. Social divisions between the groups ramify extensively in these areas as well.

Will new spaces develop to provide new educational opportunities for socially disadvantaged young people?

I'm convinced they will. Developing the educational and training infrastructure is certainly one of the proven strategies for strengthening this group. Giving young people a space, allowing them a hand in the shaping of spaces, and thus giving them self-confidence that they could not develop in other areas, is a good option.

The Campus Rütli[2] pilot project in Berlin is a good example of how educational activities can be integrated into such structures so that education functions as an incentive toward strengthening, facilitation, and empowerment, and not as a set of external demands made on children and adolescents. But we must await the results, because unfortunately what counts in the last analysis is whether there are fewer dropouts and more school students with better grades. That ultimately is what determines one's later professional opportunities and whether one is among the 20 percent or not.

What factors will effectively shape the future of today's children and adolescents?

I don't think one needs to look too far here. What counts is, and will remain, the structure of economic opportunity. The opportunities for young people to be professionally active, to earn money, and thus to secure their own lives—that, as I see it, continues to be the first and foremost component, and it exerts a strong influence on all the others.

Of course, in today's extremely extended pre-work phase, young people have vast opportunities for self-development and they experience a wide range of cultural and media influences that can act as catalysts. Whether this will remain the case, though, is uncertain. Should demographic changes modify the economic situation and the young generation shrink in size as a result, so that they are in

high demand, leading again to drastic shortening of training phases to speed up integration in the labor market—then it could be that this entire sector of leisure, media, education, social networks, and so on, loses a certain amount of ground again.

Do you tend toward optimism, pessimism, or, like the majority of young people, pragmatism concerning the future?

In answering this question, one needs to look at Europe as a whole, because mutual interrelations are strong. Moreover, many European countries have the same demographic developments as in Germany. Against this backdrop, I would say there are grounds for moderate optimism despite the current extremely tense, crisis-ridden situation. The chances are also moderately good because Germany's experiences in labor market reforms from the Schröder–Fischer government will lead to similar developments in other European countries.

To summarize: Positive conditions are also always positive for young people and hence positive for the social fabric of Germany. Poorer, pessimistic conditions have a corresponding impact on young people.

And young people are so intuitive, sensitive, and in this respect expertly perceptive that they transmit this to a very high degree.

93 ●

● 91

2   In the wake of problems of violence at the former Rütli School in the Neukölln district of Berlin, the school was transformed into a pilot project unique in Germany. The objective was to create a new and effective concept of education as well as a communal social space within the neighborhood.

Gerhard Bosch

Residual social security expenditure has risen in recent years as a result of growing poverty. This expenditure is met primarily by municipalities. Changes in income distribution in recent years have increased the importance of residual social security systems such as Hartz IV support, basic old-age pension, youth assistance, and other provisions. These social security systems are not financed by social security contributions but through taxes, so that because of income inequality among municipalities, investment in many regions is being replaced by social security expenditure.

● 76

It is a fatal development, because municipalities are Germany's biggest investors. However, there are big differences between municipalities. There are scattered municipalities in Germany that are not even able to preserve their assets. We're living from our substance. Further, negative net investment is a danger for the future because the burden of social expenditure is crushing many municipalities and they are no longer able to maintain their infrastructures. Average public net investment in Germany has been negative since 2006. Solidarity between affluent and poor communities and federal states is decreasing. Welfare state support is also declining if one is dependent on social transfers despite long-term gainful employment. Lowering pension levels could prove an additional explosive factor.

● 94
230

● 82

Lecture: "Die Stadt von Übermorgen: Ökonomie und Arbeit," part of The City of Tomorrow: Trends and Possible Futures in Urban Development in Germany, a documentation expert panel at the Federal Ministry for the Environment, Nature Conservation, Building and Nuclear Safety (BMUB) and the Federal Institute for Research on Building, Urban Affairs and Spatial Development (BBSR), Bonn, December 11–12, 2013.

Frauke Burgdorff

"I have a dream, it goes like this: maximum individual responsibility without deregulation. In other words, to put confidence in each and every citizen and to stick to that, because only then can we retain one of Germany's essential qualities, namely, its middle-class orientation and permeability."

How do you rate the status quo in Germany? And against this backdrop, which topics are particularly relevant for the country's *Baukultur* and the lived environment?

There is one topic related to planning and building that I think is urgent: the regional housing market disparities and the increasing social divide; and related to this, whether more housing in densely populated areas means land consumption in one place and more open land in another. What possible means of regulation is there apart from the labor market? That for me is a big question.

Moreover, what shape will coexisting neighborhoods in a culturally segregated society assume in the future? That's a politically relevant urban-planning question. This is particularly clear at present in the case of east European migration. It's easy to talk of heterogeneity as a goal, but people tend quite naturally to organize themselves with their likes. The question is what this will entail for urban systems.

What specific spaces in particular are worth observing?

Pressure is high in the prime locations, the 1A and 1B areas;[1] only people with capital are found there. Wealthy, educated people with social capital can act out heterogeneity well because they are homogeneous in one particular—their affluence. In the 2A and 2B areas, where people have less money, define themselves by status, and are subject to middle-class fears, there will be more mobility in the future. Most of these areas are residential with a relatively low percentage of house owners, or areas with low-market-value single-family homes. The development trends of the other areas, the central 1A and the C areas, are less open to mobility.

What are the main grounds for the lower middle classes being at risk today?

The opportunities for upward and the risk of downward social mobility have increased—not that I can substantiate that statistically. The banking crisis has further exacerbated the situation: life for those without property is more precarious. The job market is relatively stable again at present, but the deep-seated fears initially triggered in 2008 are still very much with us. And when people with fears of this kind live side by side, then segregatory movements are likely to occur.

Would this have consequences for the lived environment?

Not necessarily, given that we live in an exceptionally low-violence society in Germany. The rules of the game in densely populated urban spaces—one definition of cities—differ from those in more relaxed spaces. This has to do with the sociology of closeness. In densely populated spaces, increasing numbers of homogeneous groups might segregate themselves. That need not always lead to violence. Some withdraw into cheap gated communities; those who can afford it, into expensive ones. They see to it that they stick together, because within these communities they can organize safety, networks, and mutual support.

The problems begin at the edges of these areas. T. C. Boyle's novel *The Tortilla Curtain* deals with just such a segregated community in the suburbs of Los Angeles. The question for us planners, of course, is whether we design these edges to be in some sense permeable, peaceful, and socially fertile, or whether we draw up walls at the periphery. Enabling people to coexist in a mixed Italian, Romanian, Turkish, Bulgarian community, for instance, is a pretty big challenge. Either one says it's worth the effort—it's the European, and the German, model, which I personally support—but it's also possible that we find ourselves involved in fighting against phantoms. I think both approaches are legitimate.

Spatially, one would need different areas in the city, some living here, others there; and then one has to make sure it all functions peacefully. We need to take care, though, that groups don't opt out of the legal framework and start developing their own subjurisdictions.

What conditions and possible courses of action will most influence these aspects of Germany's lived environment in the future?

Global migration and the relation of Europe to its borders. Are we to reinforce our external borders by means of Frontex, or will waves of migration become a new part of European history? How are we to deal with the newcomers? How can we integrate them into society? Where will their dwellings be? How will they live in public space? Other countries, the Commonwealth nations, but also France, have had completely different experiences that we lack in Germany. There's also no acceptance of what is coming: massive global migration, whether we want it or not. And not only from eastern Europe.

73
76
70
88
76
70
114

---

1   Real estate is distinguished according to centrality of location, layout, and environment, 1A indicating the best location. However, the scale is not used uniformly.

That fits in roughly with what Doug Saunders defines as the basis of arrival in his book *Arrival City*: the opportunity to acquire property.
That precisely is a basis. It's also entirely possible that we are faced with a situation where the financially strongest inhabitants of a city no longer come from the classical native German middle class. That will also be reflected in the real estate and housing markets and will lead to a far more colorful and vital culture of planning and building.

Some spaces undergo a great deal of change and others none at all.
When it comes to stability and fragility one can also be way off the mark. An astonishing example in recent years is Emsland. Emsland was one of Germany's poorest regions for many years. Suddenly, a new factor came into play: wind power. Emsland today is one of the wealthiest regions. For decades, Emsland was said to be sinking in inertia. That changed entirely in a short space of time. So I wouldn't tie urban spaces down either—add to which, cycles of reproduction and change in the markets have grown shorter in recent years.

Which factors will only come into play in the middle and long term?
Education and training have always influenced equality of opportunity in social spaces. We have simply neglected to channel much energy into the locations that are not doing as well. So deliberate investment in locations and social spaces where there are currently fewer educational opportunities might conceivably have a big impact in the next ten years. For this to happen, municipalities will have to act very focusedly and also take the risk of wealthier locations profiting less as a result of redistributions.

Will extremism play an important developmental role?
Definitely. It doesn't matter whether it's a Grey Wolves mosque, a right-wing football club, a Pius Brothers church, or an evangelical parish: all extremist developments are the same. This trend to go to extremes, because the world has become too unsafe, worries me enormously.

The Constitution might be said to represent a kind of guiding culture in the sense of ideas that we wish to uphold as a community and for which we're prepared to fight. Such ideas include enlightenment, humanism, the Constitution, the rule of law.
And I think this is a good situation for many in-migrants. There are seven nationalities in our team; I notice how, for many, being able to operate here in Germany with the backing of our Constitution is a great gift. I also think many in-migrants would be prepared to stand up for it, but no one dares open the debate. Many immigrants come to Germany for precisely these reasons, not just because they are being persecuted, but because the economy works. I think it's crazy only to allow people in if they're being persecuted. We also claim the right to go where life is better.

What might the future look like for Germany? Will it differ significantly from today?
Taking the extremes of growth and negative growth, one future scenario as far as the lower- to middle-middle class is concerned is that there will be a strong trend toward segregation. This will occur on a large scale, because the gifted immigrants, no less than the gifted Germans, of course, are highly mobile and will move out of poorer regions, while the poorest immigrants, those with the least social and cultural capital, will stay in these shrinking regions because they are least mobile. Comparable developments could also occur within both the expanding and the shrinking locations.

What are the causes, or the catalysts, for this continually growing divide?
The day-to-day and relocation mobility that is demanded by the economy. You can only succeed in today's job market if you are unbelievably flexible and well-trained or educated, even in the middle or lower-middle classes. You must be able to react rapidly when the job market changes. And job markets will be changing rapidly, too.

It's said that conventional job structures are altering because the Internet and other communication technologies facilitate local yet global work. It's fascinating when you think that our generation still places great value on person-to-person communication, being accustomed to it from a pre-Internet age, but that this might change with a generation that has grown up with the Internet.
Yes, it's true: having an impact no longer depends necessarily on the urban context, which I actually find very reassuring. The people relocating to the country today, or back to their roots, tend to be the older generation who are tired of moving around so much.

What we consider far too little is that we Europeans, on the Isle of the Blessed, might one day be forced, as economic refugees, to migrate. One's not allowed to say it, but when one looks at developments in the Indian, Chinese, and Arabian markets, then a scenario for 2050 ought definitely to include this possibility.

How ought Germany to look in the year 2050? What positive aspects should be reinforced and what negative aspects avoided?
I have a dream, it goes like this: maximum individual responsibility without deregulation. In other words, to put confidence in each and every citizen and to stick to that, because only then can we retain one of Germany's essential qualities, namely, its middle-class orientation and permeability. The eternal disqualification "We can't let them participate—they won't join in anyway" is a self-fulfilling prophecy that never fails to make me furious. Let's have confidence in people and open doors rather than shutting them with DIN norms[2] and fear of taking risks.

90
24
88
66
80
92

---

2   The German industrial standardization agency Deutsches Institut für Normung.

Claus Leggewie

Cities need not fear the increasing number of immigrants. Statistics of the Federal Employment Agency (Bundesagentur für Arbeit), for example, have made it clear that Bulgarians and Romanians, against whom society tends to be biased, are on average less frequently jobless than other foreigners. The jobless rate among them is higher than that of the native German population with no migration background, but lower than that of other foreign groups. They also receive fewer total social transfers than most of the other foreign groups that have been living in Germany now for a considerable time. And so-called problem areas—Duisburg-Marxloh is often cited—have stabilized out again thanks to their own niche economies, thus reanimating the urban environment.

● 70

● 94

    What we need for the future is a genuine culture of welcome for migrants. Towns and cities can benefit from immigrants and will require financial resources to allow them to take suitable measures to realize open urban and spatial developments and/or to support community-building groups. Financially and institutionally, municipalities must be put in a position not just to manage crises but, together with civil society, to improve the quality of life in towns and cities.

● 88

● 94

Lecture: "Die Stadt von Übermorgen: Aus der Sicht Soziales," part of The City of Tomorrow: Trends and Possible Futures in Urban Development in Germany, a documentation expert panel at the Federal Ministry for the Environment, Nature Conservation, Building and Nuclear Safety (BMUB) and the Federal Institute for Research on Building, Urban Affairs and Spatial Development (BBSR), Bonn, December 11–12, 2013.

Julian Petrin

In the future, broad sections of the population will claim participatory rights, rights to potentially contribute to planning and to self-planning options. Along with this development, classical urban planning instruments will cease to be effective, and political and planning structures may gradually become communitized.

The chief characteristic of a communitarian model of society based on common interests as the cell of society is the transference of the formative power of politics to local players. Hence, as urban organization becomes increasingly local, the importance of national levels of influence in urban affairs will decline.

● 28

Against this backdrop, a supranational unit of control is conceivable, organizing European cities in the context of a Europe of metropolitan regions. What might such a Europe look like in forty years? Do we perhaps really have something like a Europe of metropolitan regions with widespread deregulation, nation-states a mere historical-cultural framework, where foreign policy has shifted to the European level? While a new constellation of city-states arises in the European context, cities organize themselves at the regional level into communities of responsibility that are decentralized, local, and interest-based.

● 50

We are currently experiencing an atomization of interests; no longer are there three or four big social milieus. For every interest there is a counterinterest, and then another, and then a pro-interest, which mainly blocks decision-making. The contemporary disenchantment with politics is likely the result of this. Generally, though, the political sciences speak of a repoliticization. Seen thus, the present passivity in standardized political processes is less the expression of a general disenchantment with politics than it suggests that people are no longer able to relate to existing political forms and institutions. The desire to participate, to play a role in planning and shaping, to shape oneself, won't vanish in a hurry.

● 82

Lecture: "'Gutes Regieren' in 20 Jahren," part of The City of Tomorrow: Trends and Possible Futures in Urban Development in Germany, a documentation expert panel at the Federal Ministry for the Environment, Nature Conservation, Building and Nuclear Safety (BMUB) and the Federal Institute for Research on Building, Urban Affairs and Spatial Development (BBSR), Bonn, December 11–12, 2013.

Stefan Bergheim

"The big question for *Baukultur*, then, is whether the social narrative changes—either through broad-based social discussion, or not until Europe has experienced a yet deeper economic crisis."

By the year 2050, the trend toward post-materialistic lifestyles under way for decades now will have advanced yet further. Based on sound economic development, priorities in the cultural sphere (satisfaction, self-determination, etc.) will broaden, and people will call for rights to be extended and institutions (freedom, an effective state, codetermination) to be improved.

New standards for social prosperity being worked out around the globe will meet this trend and complement the classical gross domestic product. They should enable societies to be guided along the lines of these modified priorities. The trend is substantiated by international projects (the OECD Better Life Index), national projects (the National Well-being Programme in the UK and the German government's strategic Gut Leben in Deutschland program), regional projects (Tasmania Together), communal projects (Jacksonville Indicators, or Positive Futures—Forum for Frankfurt), and even corporate projects (Global Reporting Initiative). What all these share is that they take a wide range of aspects concerning quality of life into consideration. They attend not only to economic factors, but also to health, education, the natural environment, community life, safety, art, and culture, no less than administrative issues and politics. Specific quantification ranges from percentage population overweight to the number of school students absent more than twenty-one days, or the homeless rate.

As for *Baukultur* in Germany, it is worth taking a look at quality-of-life projects in municipalities, not least because the migratory trend to big metropolitan conurbations will presumably continue. In our modern knowledge-based society people want to move to where there are many other people, where there is a wide range of cultural activities and educational facilities. Decades of air-quality improvement in cities are undermining the old "life in the country" argument. The 1994 Charter of European Cities and Towns Towards Sustainability already made quality of life among urban populations a central concern.

According to surveys, however, people in the metropolitan conurbations in and around Munich, Frankfurt, or Cologne today are not those who are most satisfied with life. Monetary incomes there are highest, and cultural activities and educational facilities plentiful. But, at the same time, anonymity is high in such cities—and with it trust in others is relatively low. Rents are high, and long commuting and work hours lead to stress and neglect of personal interests. The bottom line: life satisfaction is not especially high.

Life satisfaction among those in medium-size urban areas such as Osnabrück, Siegen, or Ulm tends to be higher. Taking into account all relevant aspects such as life satisfaction, trust, life expectancy, unemployment, birth rate, and income, the quality of life is found to be particularly high in the two Danube-Iller regions in and around Ulm, in East Württemberg (Schwäbisch Gmünd, Heidenheim), Osnabrück, Bielefeld, Neckar-Alb, and Oldenburg. A great challenge for *Baukultur* and urban development will be to identify the qualities of these medium-size areas and to introduce them into growing metropolises and conurbations. Populations will assert their right to these qualities and partake in realizing them through civil and civic engagement. Politicians will increasingly pay attention to and base their actions on this broadening conception of quality of life.

While many people in Germany are already living an alternative, post-materialist lifestyle, the discourse of society since the mid-1990s continues to stress concepts like "competitiveness," "world export champion," and "industrial base," which reflect the interests of the export industry yet bear little relation to the broader concepts of life quality. Furthered by interest groups on both sides of the political spectrum, this narrative has led to massive negative developments. The decades-long structural transformation from industry to services ground to a halt in Germany in 1995. The revenue from profits rose sharply, while workers' real wages stagnated. At the same time, the German export surplus rose hugely, and (constrained by the mechanics of economic balances) had to be invested in deficit countries such as Greece and Spain, thus contributing to the current debt crisis. The profits from high productivity in the export industry were not passed on—as would have been sensible—in the form of higher wages. Consequently, prices of these goods remained low, leading to imbalances. In many countries life quality and life satisfaction are higher than in Germany (Denmark, Sweden, Canada, Holland, etc.) and the share of industrial production in value added is significantly smaller.

The big question for *Baukultur*, then, is whether the social narrative will change—either through broad-based social discussion, or not until Europe has experienced a yet deeper economic crisis. If German society succeeds in forging a communal vision of life quality and in launching its implementation, it would be connected with an enormous structural transformation—for many parts of the country a catching up—away from industry to the service sector. Further factory closures would accelerate the influx into metropolitan service centers with their attendant problems. Should this transformation not take place, then the future of Germany will continue to be plagued by euro and bank crises.

The second challenge for German society is to develop a new approach to old age. People in Germany continue to retire at around the age of 61. This value has remained more or less constant for fifty years, although the further life expectancy of a 61-year-old has doubled from ten to twenty years—with predictable consequences for the pension funds, from which pensioners are now to receive benefits for twice as long as they used to.

Society still operates with statistics like "fit to work until 65," implying that at 65 one is unfit to work. At the same time, we live longer because we remain healthy longer. And after decades of discussing pension funds, also in companies, we have still not

103 ●

● 228

74 ●

56 ●

● 72

● 54

56 ●

● 80

93 ●

90 ●

succeeded in developing an alternative approach to age. If we manage to keep older people (a trove of experience in the knowledge-society) in gainful employment and honorary work longer and more flexibly, then we can relax more about the future. If in addition we create a child-friendly society, as in Denmark, Finland, or France, then Germany will also have very good long-term prospects. But to achieve this, society as a whole will have to exert itself to make many changes, from the mere "presence culture" in many offices to standard marital-status relief and the childcare system (lack of all-day schools).

The third challenge consists in facilitating a thriving, prosperous coexistence among the different income groups, ethnic groups, religions, lifestyles, world-views, and age groups, a plurality that is presumably going to increase. It is not a question of assimilation and leveling, but the segregational tendencies of recent decades may have gone a bit too far. What is needed is to strengthen mutual responsibility and understanding and to retain or create social centers and meeting places—the modern metropolitan equivalents of the marketplace and the village church. Here, too, *Baukultur* has concepts to offer that can point the way forward.

● 84

234 ●

Heinz Bude

"It is just not true that the welfare state leads to people dropping out, but it is true that there are people who work hard fifty hours a week and take home a net income of 800 to 1,200 euros. This is a significant problem."

What processes are currently shaping Germany?
Germany is going through an interesting transformational process that one might describe as a switch from an extensive to an intensive growth model. It is not the case, though, that a postgrowth society is looming on the horizon in Germany. It is more a change from one type of growth to another type. It is evident in a comparison of the technological policies of Airbus and Boeing. Take, for instance, materials reusability, energy use, or the use of plastic elements and you immediately see that the USA is still in the phase of extensive growth. The European model—with Germany by all accounts in the leading position—pursues the idea of intensive growth. It is driven by a different awareness, different materials, different technologies, and it operates with different, inclusive managerial policies.

This model incorporates two major elements found in export-oriented, high-productivity companies such as Airbus. The first is the inclusion of older staff members in mixed-age teams. Effective old-age policies are indispensable, both in respect of tacit knowledge and in maintaining the intergenerational transfer of experience. The second element is women. Packages have already been

developed that implicate biopolitically organized jobs with reference to the care of children and older family members.

However, these positive trends are not met with in all companies. A postindustrial proletariat is developing in the sphere of simple service-industry work. It is just not true that the welfare state leads to people dropping out, but it is true that there are people who work hard fifty hours a week and take home a net income of 800 to 1,200 euros. This is a significant problem because this group must shoulder the entire burden of childcare, support of elderly family members, etc. Moreover, they are in no position to bargain with their employers.

231 ●

● 227

235 ●

Because processes of deindustrialization are on the rise?
Deindustrialization in particular sectors. The shortage of skilled labor is a big problem for companies in the high-technology export sector because no new young engineers or skilled workers are forthcoming. The question is what political repercussions this has on the urban context, whether it will define new lines of segregation—because segregation need not necessarily be a problem if it can function as a springboard. That's the American logic: segregation

56 ●
74

as a road to integration. For us in Germany it is often hard to understand this. But, in more recent debates, favelas are no longer seen as an expression of a problem but as an opportunity.

Negative segregation, on the other hand, occurs when sections of the population are forced to occupy neighborhoods that we believe are no longer suitable for urban development. And precisely these people will be the losers in the three big areas of social division in Germany in the future: security, education and training, and health.

Security in the sense of social security, old age security, or also a sense of safety?

We won't see gated communities watched over by armed guards in Germany. But we will find people having to do something themselves toward maintaining and improving the environment in which they grow old. Citizens will become involved in keeping the peace in neighborhoods and city districts. Which, after all, is also something positive. I think public goods today are experiencing a wave of reconsideration. High-income earners will be prepared to pay higher taxes for public goods. Politically as well, public goods will become principal—particular services, for example, such as local public transport. In Switzerland, for instance, there is a postbus in every valley, no matter how many inhabitants the valley has. That is the principialization of a public good. And there is still too little of it in Germany.

What gender-specific developments are important? How do you see the role of women in contemporary society?

Since 1999 there have been more women than men at German universities, and they tend to have better grades. Of course, there's a bottleneck problem. But trajectories are altering. Life choices among well-educated women have become more complex: under no circumstances do they wish to forgo having children. The birthrate in Germany is no longer falling, and, at bottom, the better-educated women are responsible for this. There are more women with more than two children—that is significant.

What is too little researched is the fact that these women don't want to shift child education away from the family. They want support, but the family is to remain the control center. More and more people are affirming that the family, as Engels put it, is the cell of social life. As society becomes unclear, family becomes a substitute concept for society. It is one response to this lack of clarity. One sees, but does not feel, the crisis. So one seeks to salvage idylls of survival, and family is one such model concept.

The large generation born between 1954 and 1964, the baby-boom generation, will soon be reaching retirement age. The 1968 generation is of no interest at all now. We know that the poverty rate for this generation will increase in old age as a result of atypical employment; at the same time, there are those who are highly privileged. When the baby boomers reach retirement age, or when they drop out of the job market, all will be better, and pensions for the subsequent generations will become more stable.

Does that also mean that future prospects for today's students are good?

Today's 20-year-olds will have to take care of a generation that is not much larger than themselves. Today's 30-year-olds will have a generation to take care of that is significantly larger than they are. This means that we can't expect people to take labor-intensive jobs for which they earn 1,000 euros, knowing full well that in old age they will end up in poverty. Nor do I think everything can be regulated through taxes and contributions. There is also a joint liability.

Is there a tendency today for men to orient themselves less on career and money and to focus instead more on family and children, on the body and health?

Needs such as commitment and connection have always been women's subjects. But it is in fact true that hysteria is no longer just women's concern but increasingly that of men as well. Headaches, a classical symptom of hysteria, are increasingly frequent among today's men. Needs for commitment and connection are growing. Children alone create commitment and connection—the classic non-terminable relationship. Men are taking this more and more seriously. The classical model of motivation comprising career promotion and switching between job markets is becoming increasingly difficult. But I know of no society that is more productive than Germany is at present.

If my diagnosis that we're heading toward an intensive growth model is correct, then part-time labor can be considered entirely unproblematic. From the labor-sociological point of view we know that one works as hard in twenty-five hours as otherwise in thirty-five hours. Germany is a competitive society with high competence in dealing with insecurity. A colleague and I compared Japan and Germany in terms of subjective feelings of vulnerability. The result for Germany: the older one grows, the more vulnerable one feels. In Japan it is the exact opposite: the younger people are, the more vulnerable they feel.

What are the reasons for this, do you think?

Japan is a highly education-based society—if you fulfill certain educational conditions, you need not worry for the rest of your life. And precisely this is no longer the case today. Young people in Japan are entirely unable to cope with the situation. Skills in dealing with insecurity in Germany are much more advanced than in Japan. That means that the theses in Ulrich Beck's *Risk Society* have proved true.

Meaning, we live in increasingly hybrid structures, we combine increasing numbers of attitudes and needs within ourselves, and we try to play with them?

Both our competence and options in dealing with situations are growing. The whole question of individualization of skills leads to a readiness to intensify work. But it is difficult without inner guides for orientation. The topic of burnout is in today, but it touches on an important point. If you look at the answers in questionnaires of burnout victims, you

● 19
94

● 237

87 ●

● 86

● 84

● 90
93

see that a driver for a logistics company and a middle manager of a big corporation use the same words to speak about the problem. The ways exhaustion is structured are applicable to all classes.

We've covered many topics that are especially acute in cities. What about rural spaces in Germany?

Of all the social landscapes in Germany the most postmodern is the country. The country as such no longer exists in Germany. There is a division of different influxes coexisting there. There is a dramatic rural exodus in Germany, on the one hand, for instance in Mecklenburg–West Pomerania. But on the other, educational projects are exerting an influence. There are scattered towns in Brandenburg that are prospering as a result of having parent school projects. That is to say, you can work in the country and do something for children. And there's a generation of German Democratic Republic 60-year-olds. Everything exists simultaneously in the country. I'm tempted to speak of our social landscape in terms of fragmentation. Medium-size cities such as Chemnitz or Krefeld tend to stand as symbols of negative depopulation.

In other European countries rural depopulation is a bigger problem. In the Canal du Midi region of France, for instance, rural depopulation in the past thirty years has reached almost 50 percent. And what has happened? The English have come, bought houses, taken over businesses, and created an entirely new infrastructure. This was only possible, though, with low-cost airlines. Which brings us on to the energy question.

What are your scenarios for the year 2050? Are you optimistic or pessimistic concerning the future of German society?

I'm more optimistic than pessimistic. However, I see financialization as a problem. I'm not sure whether we ought not to opt out of certain growth models. The problem will be that expectations in relation to pensions and savings are becoming increasingly insecure. The entire field of private retirement insurance is linked to the capital markets. When interests drop then inflation will soar (medium-term), resulting in loss of capital. And against this backdrop I'm not sure whether that will be so pleasant in Germany.

● 50
70

Gerhard Bosch

Incomes of the broad political center have only been secured through the regional pay contracts customary in Germany. Because of the erosion of wage contracts, the low-pay sector has grown more rapidly in Germany than in any other EU country. The minimum wage only corrects income distribution in the bottom quarter of the income hierarchy. Germany today is no longer one of the countries with above-average opportunities for advancement.

The deregulation introduced by the Hartz laws[1] was linked to the promise that it would facilitate entry to the world of work and social advancement. But today it is clear that opportunities for advancement in Germany have declined. The polarization of income and wealth, then, is coupled with declining upward mobility, both within and between generations, and leads me to fear a "refeudalization" of society. This would also have far-reaching consequences for the future forms of urban society. The future of society does not come about of its own accord. It is shaped by a plurality of political and economic decisions at a variety of levels.

Depending on the kinds of decisions taken, our social and economic system can develop in completely different directions. It can become yet more unequal and move further toward the U.S. model of a polarized society decreasingly capable of long-term political as well as corporate planning. Society is then profoundly segregated, with ghettos for the poor and luxury enclaves for the rich. The alternative is the "Scandinavian way"—restoration of the social balance and minimal income inequalities through high investment in education and infrastructure. The future city here would be just what we want: integrative, multicultural, open.

If investment in education and training is not substantially increased, the expensive combination of consolidated long-term unemployment and chronic shortage of skilled labor is inevitable. The jobless rate among the low-qualified workforce is 20 percent, while 80 percent of low-wage earners are professionally qualified. The cities will have to take on the challenges of the education and training sector. Costs for minimal employee training continue to increase. German companies in the past—in contrast to many other countries—invested in trained skilled workers. Up to more than 90 percent of core personnel in Germany today have a university qualification or vocational training.

● 94

● 90

1   Laws modifying the German labor market system, in particular the unemployment benefit system.
     The first of these laws came into effect in 2003; the last, known as Hartz IV, in 2005.

This is very different in, for instance, France or the USA. In both of those countries 40 to 50 percent of workers have no professional training. Meanwhile, the majority of even simple jobs in Germany are occupied by professionally qualified workers. "Muscular," near-mute jobs have largely vanished. Core workforces tend to be trained personnel. This has serious consequences for the organization of work. Work in Germany is much more decentralized than in France or the USA.

Aging of the working population represents another risk. ● 90 The central challenges of aging in the working world are regional non-simultaneities, the variable vulnerability of industrial sectors and businesses (good and well-known companies and sectors will have no recruitment problems), employment rate differentials at the end of the working life (employment till 67 is for many not possible), work changes related to extended working lifetimes, productivity and innovation of older workforces, and the shape of immigration in the open EU job market where developmental scope is limited.

Lecture: "Die Stadt von Übermorgen: Ökonomie und Arbeit," part of The City of Tomorrow: Trends and Possible Futures in Urban Development in Germany, a documentation expert panel at the Federal Ministry for the Environment, Nature Conservation, Building and Nuclear Safety (BMUB) and the Federal Institute for Research on Building, Urban Affairs and Spatial Development (BBSR), Bonn, December 11–12, 2013.

Tanja A. Börzel

"On the basis of democratic EU majorities we can expect a future strengthening of intergovernmental cooperation, that is, of collaboration between national governments."

How do you rate the underlying political conditions in Germany?

As a political scientist the thing that interests me most here is the basic framework of political and legal institutions. This framework is being increasingly defined by the European Union. But at what political level are the decisions being taken in elaborating this framework of political and institutional conditions? Because of the Federal Republic of Germany's federal structure we have three governmental levels: the states, the federation, and then the EU. If we take a look at developments over the past fifty or sixty years, we see that the states' level has progressively declined in importance, while that of the EU has grown progressively. True, the federation has also surrendered competencies, but it is compensated by being able to play a significant role, via the federal government, in decision-making at the European level and is also responsible for implementing decisions made. The big losers are, above all, the state parliaments. The states—as the CDU (Christian Democratic Union—the main conservative party in Germany) politician Helmut Lenz put it forty years ago—have become little more than regional notarial offices for the ratification of decisions taken at the EU or federal levels.

What role do cities play in this three-tier system?

The cities are an interesting point. The sociologist Daniel Bell's so-called sandwich theory states that the national level—which lies between what occurs at the global or European levels and what occurs at the local level—will become progressively insignificant until it finally disappears. In the 1980s, when a "Europe of regions" was being discussed, this argument was crucially important for the institutional organization of the EU. Cities and municipalities played a major role here, because in many other member states the regional level is not so important; instead the municipalities have the competencies. Unfortunately, at least as far as the basic political and institutional conditions are concerned, none of this materialized.

Governments have denied the European Union direct access to regions, townships, and cities. Then as now, they have succeeded in functioning as gatekeepers and to a large extent in controlling the access of regional and local players to the EU level. Nevertheless, freedom for maneuver still exists at the communal level, if less in the areas of formal law and politics than via the question: What EU subsidies can be obtained for particular social projects? This freedom for maneuver varies greatly. It's always a question of who is currently the top mayor. Interesting in this context are so-called policy entrepreneurs. These are entrepreneurs conversant with all three tiers of the political system—they have the European level and its

opportunities systematically in focus, and, with the aid of the central players in their township or city, are also able to grasp and to implement specific opportunities.

Is the multitier model—also with reference to the Lisbon Treaty—capable of efficient action?

I'm somewhat pessimistic there. In my view, the frameworks of formal institutional conditions stipulated by the treaties are of limited political relevance at the local level. Only the Bundestag makes little use of the contractual competencies that it is guaranteed because Bundestag members are often overtaxed by the provisions and there are also few incentives to exploit them. So you can imagine how this works out at the local level. Who exactly is present locally, their resources, networks, and connections are far more important. It is not simply a question of money but also of social capital.

Aside from efficiency, a far more important topic here—the one after all that led to these reforms—is the issue of democratic legitimation. The local level is especially important here because it is the grassroots level. Yet the regional parliaments are among the losers. How much individual citizens get thus depends heavily on the local administration. It also depends on whether they are in the right networks. Unfortunately, these networks are incredibly untransparent.

Are these also reasons why people are disenchanted with politics in the Federal Republic?

The disenchantment with politics is a much bigger problem at the national level. The function of the parliaments, in particular, has shifted to implementation and away from formative politics. They ought really to function more as mouthpieces for citizens, feeding their interests into the decision-making processes at federal and EU levels, and to communicate what is to be, or already has been, decided there. This is the only way to ensure that citizens feel they understand what is actually happening. People today don't feel that they are being informed any longer about what is being decided where, about who is deciding and why.

What significance does the financial crisis, and the euro crisis, have for the political system of Europe?

It needs to be said first that the financial crisis is the biggest crisis the EU has experienced to date. Crisis analysts are pretty much unanimous in viewing it as threefold: it is a debt crisis, a banking crisis, and a growth crisis. But naturally all these are in some sense interconnected. And where at least the experts, and I believe also the politicians, are pretty much unanimous is in seeing the cause of the crisis as having already been laid down in the Maastricht Treaty, insofar as the institutions it established are insufficient to structure a currency union. Discussion concerning the necessity of strengthening European institutions is rife, whereby most of the measures, whether the so-called Six Pack or the fiscal pact, aim at strengthening domestic political control at the European level.

And the lessons for the future?
On the basis of democratic EU majorities we can expect a future strengthening of intergovernmental cooperation in particular, that is, of collaboration between national governments. And that means no strengthening of the European Commission, no strengthening of the European Parliament, but instead a strengthening of the collaboration between the European Commission and the European Court of Justice perhaps in the sense of more efficient or effective implementation of what governments enact in the sphere of fiscal policies.

I see neither a fundamental upgrading of supranational players, nor do I see where any fuller inclusion of nonstate players is to come from. I have never heard anyone say that the crisis results from a failure to consult business or civil society; on the contrary, what we see is a reanimation, a strengthening, of national governments, of the governmental level. This trend will continue in the next few years.

Will the federal structure of Germany undergo modification?
The federal states of Germany will continue to exist, unless we give ourselves a new Constitution and repeal the principle of a federal country, subject to the eternity clause set out in Article 79, paragraph 3, of the Basic Law. The problem pertains not so much to the nature of the federal state as it is one of democracy. From the point of view of effectiveness, i.e., the idea that states participate in decision-making, because they have to implement the decisions, this works very well. But as in the relation of the EU to member states, so too the federation and its states: it is the governments that are actively involved and not the parliaments. Parliamentary control is extremely weak. Regional parliaments play practically no role at all in European affairs.

Will there be alliances in future between cities like Berlin, Paris, and London, which then promote their own developments, acquire their own resources, and set their own priorities?
This could very well work horizontally. On the part of the government, this is much easier in Germany than in France. The French government has a hard time allowing its communities and regions to cooperate across borders. Among other things, this is a question of formal law. German communities have no such problem. Things are organized so that communities are relatively, I won't say independent, but there is room for freedom of action that they can exploit, also transnationally.

But there are also limits here. Especially when transborder cooperations of this kind attempt to exert direct political influence, they can only emerge as lobby groups competing for influence at the European level with hundreds of other interests. Formal law prohibits them from acting as political representatives except in regional committees. That, of course, can dampen initiatives involving regional or urban players.

● 50
103

● 50

Michael Krautzberger

"*Baukultur* presupposes a *culture* and with it a certain consensus in relation to planning and building issues within society. And we don't have that in Germany."

What role does *Baukultur* play in Germany?
Baukultur plays no very great role in Germany. We're relatively uninterested in the subject, and I see no real reason why this should change in the long term. *Baukultur* here has been completely liberalized—anyone can do what they want. *Baukultur* presupposes a *culture* and with it a certain consensus in relation to planning and building issues within society. And we don't have that in Germany. Since reunification at the latest, a deregulation of *Baukultur* has been prosecuted that tries to answer what and what not to do in building-policy terms exclusively through competition. Competition is important of course, but it's a method and not a goal. On top of which, *Baukultur* does not involve the people—its processes simply take place over their heads.

Which spaces in the inhabited environment are particularly important today or do you see as being problematic?
The real problem in spatial development is urban sprawl, which, like many other countries, we're not managing to get under control. That I see as a big issue. We've been lamenting it for decades, but the process of suburbanization simply goes on. Space cannot be controlled through planning because planning can only ever be policy-oriented. Instead we need to create economic incentives in order to effectively intervene in controlling space. But all the initiatives so far—business development, house-building support, etc.—have been geared to expanding space still further, and everyone knows that that's wrong.

The other area in which we are challenged is in the shaping of public space. The design and maintenance of public space is seriously neglected in Germany. In Italy or Spain you immediately notice how much value is attached to public spaces—from their design as inhabited centers to their safety and cleanliness. With us what we see are disorganized and messy places. But the healthy organization of public space is important for people, especially when it comes to accepting and coping with higher-density spaces, because these are certainly going to increase. In the wake of demographic change, older people will be moving back into the denser areas—for the well-known reasons that they are safer and better looked after there. Younger people live there anyway because most of the jobs are there, so we'll see a drying up, a thinning out, of the country. This will radically alter rural areas and landscapes.

This leads on to another fascinating issue: How, given the energy transition, are we going to deal with landscape as a resource? Rural areas are actually the biggest problem sector. For some twenty years we have been prioritizing energy over landscape. It began with wind turbines, continued with biogas plants and now transmission lines. There are good reasons for all of this, only we need to take care that we don't lose the power of the landscape. Germany is a beautiful country rich in natural resources that also need to be taken great care of. The energy transition is no doubt inevitable, but that doesn't mean it has to occur as cheaply and brutally as possible. That would be this primitive capitalist approach again—with green trappings, but at root the same. Why not lay the transmission lines underground? It may be more expensive, but that way we save the countryside. If this doesn't happen, rural areas are certainly going to alter radically, and not for the good.

How is climate change going to make itself felt for us? How are we going to have to react here?
Phases of warming are going to increase. In Berlin, for instance, there is a danger that the Spree will likely have dried up in twenty years' time. These are serious changes. What will happen when a city like Berlin no longer has a river? The consequences of climate change, of warming for instance, will create health problems for older people. We are going to have to green our cities and provide for fresh air. This means pretty major interventions that cost money and call property claims into question. Strong and clear planning vision is essential here.

A big role will be played by public transport, which is already well developed in Germany and will further increase. If growing numbers switch to public transport, alternative models can also develop—more local, flexible car sharing, for instance, though this will need to be reorganized. All this costs money, especially the public authorities. Public participation will be necessary again here along with efficiently functioning administrative structures.

Are there things that will only come into effect, say, in thirty years' time, things that simply need longer to become relevant?
The relation between the sexes. This area is far from having been exhausted. Complete equality between men and women, in every respect, in the family, professionally. This is still a predominantly traditionally structured area with us and could lead to very big changes.

The other point is that we are likely on the way to becoming a completely areligious society. Religion, in the majority of people's minds, is an outdated model. A small number of people will occupy themselves with religion but it will cease to shape society. That has numerous consequences; think of views on abortion, for instance, or genetic research. One needn't share the church's opinions here, but it's good that there are churches and that they raise these questions. Churches critically challenge society.

● 58
206 ●
236 ●
● 234
231 ●
● 92
● 60
207
● 52

Is modernization really going to proceed to the point where we can do without the church? Might not other, populist—and even more questionable—ideas come along to fill this gap?

Indeed, you see this clearly in the USA. Abstruse notions like Genesis are being integrated into the school curriculum. Is society so strong that it can go its own way without having God in the background? And in times where dangerous challenges face us? And democracy—is it sufficient that we have democracy? Or is it a question of results? Or Europe—one has to keep on convincing and winning it over. Issues of democracy have been discussed too little in recent years. A constitution isn't a life insurance policy. One has to keep campaigning for it and convincing people.

What significant differences can we foresee today? What will be radically different?

There will be depleted spaces and a population living in cities. We are going to see a large number of buildings being deconstructed—big settlements and single-family oases. I don't think the latter have any future. One sees prices dropping in the urban hinterlands because nobody wants to move there anymore. I feel pretty sure these are soon going to be fallow lands, open spaces. Cities, on the other hand, will continue to flourish. Training and education are still on the increase. Migrants will also make their way into the middle classes, just as all immigrants do. The number of museumgoers has risen sharply. More museums will be built. You used to be pretty much alone in museums; today you have to stand in line.

● 54
84

What will or ought to have changed in Germany by the year 2050?

Because of the dwindling workforce, we will strive for full employment of women, as in the GDR. I see issues such as childcare as having been solved. This will entail new infrastructure—there's no way of avoiding it, and to a large extent this will have to be financed by taxes. The relation between men and women will also change, becoming more of a partnership.

Further, we should use the strength we have to involve people more in political processes. As things stand, the population participates only peripherally via elections. Incentives need to be created for people to take things into their own hands in everyday life. From hospices to urban commitment, citizen participation is a vast resource that has hitherto remained untapped. Much can be changed here—the sleeping populace needs to be awakened. Planners don't want that, because they don't like what they consider to be interference. The bureaucrats are the same. They are always afraid and fail to notice that it's a gain. Ultimately, it's a question of strengthening links with community when social and religious structures are being eroded. It's a matter of developing social cohesion and solidarity. Citizen participation is the most neglected resource in Germany. We have an active citizenry, we have the people who can do it. The level of education in this country is high and that we don't involve citizens is simply a matter of culpable neglect.

● 82

Armin Grunwald

"The transition to renewable energies is a social transformation and not just the replacement of old technology by new technology."

What are the Office of Technology Assessment at the German Bundestag's main spheres of interest as far as *Baukultur* in Germany today are concerned?

Our primary concern is new and emerging science and technology, in particular nanotechnology, synthetic biology, and human enhancement, where technological options for optimizing human beings are central. These are immensely attractive fields, both for politics and business. They are also of interest to German feature pages, because apart from their technological and scientific aspects, they also touch on cultural, anthropological, and socio-theoretical issues. These areas have recently been supplemented by Industry 4.0, data mining, and robotics, subjects in the field of digitization. We must also bear in mind wholly new mobility technologies that will likely be realizable in the future. An end to personal automobility in urban systems would doubtless have consequences for the built environment.

How open is German society to new technologies?

I don't think there's any aversion or hostility toward technology in Germany. There are well-known problem areas such as nuclear energy and green gene technology. Otherwise society is very open. The situation is different with German industry. German industry is very conservative in its dealings with new technologies. It isn't that people are afraid of new technologies and industry is the pioneer—if anything the reverse is the case.

To what extent is your research concerned with the energy transition?

By and large, energy systems to date are understood as synergies of power stations, supply lines and pipelines, energy stores, and outlets. What is overlooked is that we are dealing with an infrastructure that is linked up with all social processes, and that one cannot simply isolate individual parts.

We can observe how infrastructures are converging increasingly right now. Unlike in the nineteenth century, when infrastructures were unrelated—electricity, transport, information, communication, etc.—today, in the transition to renewables, we see how everything is linked via the Internet. Electromobility will bring transport and energy together. Some people talk of the emergence of a mega-infrastructure with the Internet as its nervous system. That's a completely different infrastructural world from the old one we are familiar with.

The field of infrastructure so far still has a remarkably national character. This is especially evident in the energy transition. We ran an international workshop on the subject of transition management. It transpired that Austria, the Netherlands, and Denmark are already thinking beyond their national borders. And yet still everyone is working far too individualistically. The extent to which Germany and other countries look to themselves and think they can deal with problems of sustainability and service security on their own is an anachronism.

So the transition to renewables doesn't just consist in replacing nuclear power stations with wind turbines, but in grasping it as part of a transformation affecting the whole of society. The transition to renewable energies is a social transformation and not just the replacement of old technology by new technology.

Which areas do you see as presenting the biggest challenges?

Whether the fluctuation and unequal distribution of electricity is best solved by more power lines or by building more energy storage facilities is a moot point. Otherwise, I think there are many things in the social realm that are not understood or that are simply accepted without being sufficiently examined. Electromobility, for example. Since World War II we have been accustomed to living in an automobile culture, even though mobility is clearly changing as a result of smartphones and modern information and communication technologies. Yet I wonder if society hasn't internalized this automobile culture to a point where switching to, say, electric cars is going to present a far greater obstacle than many experts and politicians suppose, simply because electromobility demands different operating principles and different types of behavior for which a cultural and developmental leap is required.

Will climate change, the question of resources, and new lifestyles lead to demographic shifts?

Centralization as a phenomenon exerts a powerful effect in Germany. Cities such as Berlin, Munich, and Stuttgart are exceptionally attractive, while rural areas are gradually emptying out. Young people move away, and the lack of value creation in the country will augment this in the future. There has already been a countermovement though: the dream of a house in the country, the longing for nature and landscape. Just now we are experiencing strong centralization. These processes come in waves, and we don't know what it will be like in the year 2050.

To whom would you assign most responsibility for facilitating positive scenarios?

Politics takes first place because it is everybody's environment that is at stake. Politics, an externalization in society's eyes, is responsible for public duties. Ultimately, it is up to us to adjudicate this system of people and institutions. I would like to see politics being powered far more by the people. This was considerably more the case in the 1980s

203

253

78
209

92

52

211

and 1990s. Not only was the Green Party founded then but many young people with new, ecological ideas joined the various parties, with the result that nearly every party developed its "greenness." Their demonstrations showed that they were in a position to point the way. The political system needs to be powered more in this direction so as to create the appropriate underlying conditions with a framework of incentives and regulations.

Konrad Götz

"Highly complex procedures are employed to compute minute CO₂ reductions instead of thinking about ways of getting rid of oil."

Your main sphere of research at the Institute for Social-Ecological Research in Frankfurt/Main is "mobility and urban spaces." Where do you see this overlapping with the lived environment?
Alongside cities and mobility, the subject of space is part of practically all our research activities—space here is not just urban space but also other space-related phenomena such as water infrastructures, risk analyses, energy, and climate protection. In a highly applied interdisciplinary working environment the category of space is always a pivotal factor.

Why do you think multimodal mobility has experienced what seems to be a breakthrough recently?
Competition in this field is intense right now. We transport-researchers have been advocating multioptional mobility for the past twenty years. Companies and public transport associations have just woken up to the subject. It is indeed an exceptionally dynamic one because forecasters and market researchers in companies and corporations have grasped its significance and are communicating this internally to an increasing degree. Major changes are occurring in the field of mobility: everything that we, the onetime "ecos" predicted

is coming true. Greenness has escaped its industry-hostile context: models such as the green city and green future have arrived at the core of society.

So mobility concepts are really nothing new?
Far from it! One need only open the drawer, take out some of the old reports, and fit them to the present. Many concepts were simply not compatible with the mainstream a few years ago. Now there's a different generation and different information technology. Moreover, climate protection is on the global agenda now—it's no longer an issue that makes you an outsider.

The demand for new mobility services depends heavily on supply. Why didn't this supply exist ten years ago?
Apps are a significant developmental factor here. Convenience has also always played a big role. The apps, geopositioning, and mobility options have all facilitated a significant step forward. Suddenly, the new ideas are attractive to large numbers of users. Intermodality has become concrete and visible.

● 78
236

Are you optimistic about mobility options such as car-sharing, or will the culture of car ownership prevail in the future?

I'm optimistic. These issues receive full press coverage and we specialists are asked more and more what new kind of generation of mobility users with new needs is actually emerging. These young people fly to Australia, live in two metropolises simultaneously, but they don't buy their own cars. Once this trend extends to a more upmarket sector, then owning one's own car that stands around at home as a constant source of expense will lose interest. Large sectors will make use of alternatives. Following the Deutsche Bahn, the ABG, the biggest housing company in Frankfurt/Main, has entered the car-sharing market. ABG has understood the trend and is planning city districts with integrated car sharing. These developments are materializing at a good pace with double-figure growth rates—they are stable and will prove lasting. Alongside this, we know that there is also a large group that finds owning one's own car attractive.

Is the next step integrated offers, where car sharing is just one module alongside local public transport, intercity transport, and other types of local mobility?

Yes, I think so. Combining the two factors of data-cloud ubiquity—in other words the omnipresence of data and information flows—and device flexibility, this will lead to a networked supply system. Options such as the most beautiful, fastest, cheapest, or most ecological route can then easily be implemented.

What are the social groups behind these developments? Is it young people with a playful approach to mobility, or older people who want to live more ecologically, perhaps with an eye on their children's and grandchildren's living conditions?

If you look only at those who are not fixated on cars, then it's the older, underprivileged, and young people who need to save. But if you look at who actually is using the new options, like free-floating car sharing, then it's mainly the better-educated people living in the major cities.

Do you use any particular city as a benchmark for orientation?

As far as amenity value, the development of common goals, and the promotion of integrated working methods are concerned, we've learned the most from Zurich. The Zurich department of public works plans shady paths with drinking fountains along the river; they take into account public toilets; pedestrian mobility is always part of the plan, and they ask people what they find attractive—the approach to mobility in Zurich is extremely well thought out. There is always a common goal in Switzerland and that helps everyone involved in the process of urban construction to orient themselves.

Although in Germany a start has been made toward enhancing the quality of urban life, the priorities of urban politics are still not really attuned to this goal.

We're currently experiencing a negation phase in Germany. Having discovered that a large number of constructions and amenities from the postwar period were badly or incorrectly planned, we are now faced with what to do with these buildings and streets. Many of Germany's public squares are good examples. They consist of rectangular arrangements, visual axes, and designs straight from the drawing board. In France, squares are irregular and asymmetrically planted with plane trees; masses of small public and private spaces have high amenity value. But the subject is finally reaching Germany. The Bockenheim cultural campus in Frankfurt is currently being redesigned with the active involvement of local residents. And a host of new questions are arising. Some people want to preserve the 1960s buildings, others want to demolish and reconstruct. Then there are financial problems. It would cost more to renovate than to build from scratch. The question "What is spatial planning and building?" is a hot topic of discussion at the moment.

● 258

Are planners in a position to shape these processes in line with the new demands?

Yes, these developments are being factored in, not least because of a new generation. But Germany has certain traditions and prescribed codes that contribute to laying down lines of conflict: progressive vs. reactionary, beautiful vs. ugly, authentic vs. artificial, historical vs. the new. A dispute along precisely these lines of interest is observable in Frankfurt where direct opposites have come into conflict. How the juxtaposition and coexistence of medieval and 1970s architecture is perceived is also a question of perceptual constructions, and they are open to influence. We shouldn't underestimate the aesthetic qualities that various historical phases coexisting in urban space have to offer.

● 211

How is mobility changing in rural space?

One thing is certain: if cars continue to exist in the future, then they will do so in rural space. Intermodality, car-sharing concepts, etc., need to be thought out in more detail in these spaces. It's one thing to provide cars at stations and bus stops; the next step would be to bring the cars to users' homes. Though intermodality in these regions is still pretty much in its beginnings, there too it will continue developing in future. Many of the innovations in rural areas are occurring in regions in east Germany, which shows that they are no longer problematic; rather their potential and attractiveness are slowly being discovered.

78 ●
80

● 234

What might our mobility culture look like in the year 2030, or even 2050?

The future will be powerfully transformed by large numbers of private initiatives because far less big capital is going to be available. Apps will play an important role. Sharing and the appropriation of spaces will gain in importance. Bicycles, whether one's own or on a share basis, are also inexpensive and space-friendly.

And driverless cars?

That might be the car's rescue—time could then be put to dual use in the car, as with rail travel today. To begin with this is presumably going to occur in only a privileged sector, but in time it will extend to the small-car range. It could also solve the problem of how car-share vehicles reach their users in less densely populated areas.

And electromobility?

Large-scale systems such as highways that generate energy and charge cars are regular topics of discussion in the electromobility field. The problem today is the lack of financing options for these megaprojects. What we need instead are decentralized systems, which today are feasible, such as the free-floating car-share concept in Stuttgart. It has been clear for a while now that electric cars need to be charged intelligently. This works best with fleets. We know, further, that electromobility only makes sense with small, light vehicles. This also accords with what the car-share fleet has to offer. Semipublic services of this kind can also see to it that vehicles are charged exclusively with green electricity. But developing the charging infrastructure invariably impacts public space. Nonetheless, a ten-year time frame is right for thinking about electromobility, because our first priority must be to reduce our oil dependence. People are forgetting this again. Highly complex procedures are employed to compute minute CO_2 reductions instead of thinking about ways of getting rid of oil.

Independent initiatives, decentralized energy systems, and sharing concepts are all plausible future scenarios. High-speed trains and optimized airplanes are further possibilities. The big transport infrastructures and highways will continue, though they won't cut through the middle of cities as they do now. The things that were built in Stuttgart, Frankfurt, or the Ruhr area in the 1970s are simply crazy. What we need instead is attractive urban space combined with basic mobility that is good, rapid, and flexible.

● 262

● 210
236

Ralf Schüle

"We're so preoccupied with crises and related events that we're finding it difficult to see beyond them to the old and instructive question: How do we want to live? But it is highly important for structuring and organizing political discourse."

What changes or improvements have there been in the sustainability debate?

In Germany a great deal has changed. In the field of energy, a range of European Directives has been implemented—the Buildings Directive (EPBD), for instance, or the Renewable Energies Directive. Packages of measures have been implemented at federal, regional, and municipal levels; businesses are committing to emissions reduction and are introducing environmental management systems. Developments in recent years have been impressive.

After long years of relative quiet, we are experiencing a climate protection renaissance at the community level. There are local reasons for this since, aside from the climate-protection aspect, more and more municipalities are recognizing the added-value and cost dimension of commitment to regenerative energies and energy-efficiency technologies. Another reason is that the national energy transition is increasingly supporting activities at the local level, for instance in the form of support programs.

All in all, though, but above all globally, it has not been possible to significantly check the dynamics of environment and resource consumption, either in Germany or internationally. Economic and social forces continue to ensure that resource consumption is still cheaper than protecting the life cycles of the products we consume. A basic set of conditions needs to be created at the European or national level laying out incentives for curtailing resource consumption.

207 ●
● 39
213

Discussion of cities and urban models and concepts is rife. However, 60 percent of the German population live in cities of less than 50,000 inhabitants. What developments do you see occurring in rural areas?

In a range of subject areas we have noticed that a city's size—the size of its administration and the division of labor this entails—has a big influence on how systematically sustainability-related topics can be tackled. Strategic topics such as climate protection can be addressed far more systematically by the administration of a big city. Precisely in the case of small cities and towns there comes into play the additional level of districts and district-related communities with correspondingly scant resources to tackle the more general issues.

Nonetheless, the number of regions and rural districts aiming at zero emissions by 2050, for example, is increasing. More than 140 have committed to this goal so far. It presupposes a suitable political will in these regions, and also the ability to determine and coordinate on an intermunicipal basis the specific path to take in the fields of climate protection and energy transition. Activities in the Steinfurt district, for example, are exciting because the approach to climate protection adopted there is ambitious and thus boosts innovative and developmental potential throughout the area. But only a minority of the approximately 11,000 communities in Germany are pursuing such approaches. Then there are smaller and medium-size communities that have established administrative structures and departments to engage with urban development issues including regional structural change, demographic change, and climate protection. The cities of Arnsberg and Ludwigsburg are good examples of how smaller cities can create the right structures and conditions within their own administrations for strategy development to tackle new areas such as climate change adaptation.

How do you rate the chances and potential for these communities reaching zero emissions by the year 2050? After all, local populations, de facto mobility, and companies active in particular places all play a role.

The German Federation also plays an important role. It all depends on whether the transition to renewable energies succeeds or fails, and whether all players at all political levels act in coordination. The important position of municipalities is clear, although of course they also need regional and federal support since otherwise their potential for action is limited. Local communities have an important function as focal points and also as transmission points. It is their task to implement transregional, national goals using local players, to inform citizens, to involve small and medium-size companies in energy consultations, and so on.

However, the conditions under which shrinking spaces and expanding spaces can reach zero emissions are utterly different. Continuous population decline and industrial migration out of shrinking spaces will lead to appreciable emissions reductions and thus, from the climate-protection point of view, they are desirable. Only how these "stress factors" are to be reduced in communities and climate protection brought under control while simultaneously coping with regional economic structures or demographic changes poses a big strategic challenge for municipal development.

In which of the following fields do you see the greatest need for action: energy, climate, or transport?

The major initiatives in current political discourse concern energy, and related to them, the climate sector. One reason for this is the heavy investments pending in the power-station sector in the years ahead, and utility companies will be attending very carefully to how and in which directions power-generation mixes are to be modernized. Despite its share of energy-consumption, the transport sector lags relatively far behind—it is still a political taboo and generally gets discussed from the point of view of preserving the existing infrastructure.

But here, too, we must think a step further. Because even if we succeed in effecting significant reductions in energy consumption in the next ten to twenty years, sooner or later the climate-protection resource issue will arise, namely: What materials are we to use to insulate buildings? Where will the rare materials necessary for electronic devices, but also for wind power stations, come from?

How do you see the activities of the German Federation relative to the impact of the energy transition, for instance in the areas of land use and land conflicts?

The energy transition with its flexibilized forms of energy provision will create new energy landscapes.

There is already a whole range of studies in developmental planning, land use planning, regional planning, and state planning around the question of how climate protection and the energy revolution can be further accelerated. And climate protection as a goal and area of consideration is also meanwhile firmly anchored in the German Federal Building Code.

Nevertheless, many cities continue to expand, new industrial and residential areas are designated, and it is proving all but impossible to meet the Federal Government's thirty-hectare target for reducing land use by 2020. Land use conflicts are among the major key issues in flourishing conurbations. Given the tense financial situation of the municipalities, however, I hardly see how the logic of land designation can be broken. And we ourselves together with our lifestyle encourage this trend: average per capita living space in Germany has risen continually in recent years.

What does this entail for the concept of sustainability? What sort of indicators do we need in order to structure sustainability?

Sustainability as a normative, political, and scientific concept is extremely important for our work both as experts and politically interested citizens, yet it provides no answers to the questions that concern us in this interview: How do we want to live in the year 2050? What qualities of society do we aspire to and wish to see materializing within a generation or a lifetime? The concept of resilience—in the sense of the enhancement of the durability of technological, economic, and social systems and modification of dynamically developing basic conditions—is currently flourishing. The idea of resilience offers players an interesting perspective for action because, in all fields of activity,

● 205

● 52

● 126

208 ●
● 214

● 205
58 ●

● 54

it conduces to defining criteria and properties that a robust society will need to fulfill in the future.

I understand what you're saying qualitatively, but quantitatively I have my difficulties, especially in the context of our discussion of basic technological preconditions in 2050. How can we judge today what technological properties are going to be relevant?
I think having a goal and being goal-minded are highly important. We have problems thinking in positive futures. We're so preoccupied with crises and related events that we're finding it difficult to see beyond them to the old and instructive question: How do we want to live? But it is highly important for structuring and organizing political discourse. I think science has an important contribution to make in integrating goal-related thinking and what it entails for action into political discourse.

And I also believe that we must take leave of the big technological energy-transition utopias of climate and resource protection. Given the current underlying conditions, it will always be a question of searching for the right sustainable technologies to be used. But relevant criteria can already be formulated here: reversibility and correctability, resource and energy efficiency, social compatibility.

I'm also skeptical about radically innovative processes. I can think of remarkably few successful examples. Is this how you see it?
Climate protection and the energy transition are being talked about today primarily as technological utopias. On the one hand, technological approaches are required. However, there's a tendency to think all we need is a few photovoltaic roof units, block heating plants in basements, electric cars, and a bit of network infrastructure, and the problems are solved. But that is a very limited perspective. We can't say what the solution to the problems will look like right now. It is very hard to judge just how radical the effects a desired energy reduction of 80 to 95 percent within the next forty years would be. What's clear, though, is that a completely different society is required, with a different relation to nature. We must think much more in social categories because it is evident in both climate protection and the energy question that we're increasingly coming up against social limits. We are witnessing social polarization processes and growing social and spatial inequalities. Given which, to consider climate protection from an exclusively technological point of view is very one-sided.

What about the suburbs and small towns that lie just outside cities and administrative urban structures? And to contrast this with an exaggerated example: What about the small towns being impacted by massive shrinkage?
In very few regions will the situation remain stable. Polarization of social space in Germany will continue. Greater city areas such as Berlin, Munich, Frankfurt, Düsseldorf, Hamburg, and their peripheries will continue to grow with predictable social and spatial consequences.

This can be seen, for instance, in expanding cities that decide to stop expanding. This leads to conurbation population pressure being transferred to outlying communities. But there will also be urban and rural regions heavily influenced by demographic changes. The results are already visible in some places. There was a pilot project in the district of Nordfriesland in Schleswig-Holstein, for example, in the context of the Federal Ministry of Education and Research's "Masterplan Daseinsvorsorge" [Public Services Masterplan]. Ongoing regression of the social infrastructure, for instance hospitals, social care, swimming pools, schools, etc., is expected in the outlying coastal regions. In all likelihood, the existing buildings will become obsolete, and falling real estate prices will lead to heavy capital depreciation. These are grave problems, and we will have to think about how the inevitable regression in shrinking communities and their infrastructures can be dealt with in socially responsible ways.

During a meeting in the region, I myself experienced how property and landowners demanded that representatives from the planning office hinder these developments. The head planner replied that he hadn't the leverage to prevent these gradual processes. Examples like this show that there is no way of getting around organizing the regression of infrastructures and communities along socially compatible lines. The International Building Exhibition Urban Redevelopment Saxony-Anhalt included shrinkage as a specific subject area on its agenda.

Do we require new kinds of conversion spaces?
Yes. They can be green corridors or the utilization of peripheral space. We may be thinking too little in terms of interims and interspaces, the wild edges of our cities, as Benjamin Davy once put it. What the Ruhr area teaches us is to study industrial landscapes in the process of their transformation. They can be urban yet at the same time highly rural, for instance with a horse paddock in the middle of town, or townships between the central towns in the area, agglomerations of old warehouses and factory buildings, industrial and residential estates, and green areas that have been forgotten. Interspaces like this still offer plenty of opportunities for urban development.

So you see positive scenarios. And yet here, too, some regions will be winners and others losers—whereas in the negative scenarios there will be a strong division between the few successful metropolitan regions and a broader basis of losers?
The British sociologist Zygmunt Bauman once spoke of the deep ambivalence of modernity. That is to say, along with its positive elements, every innovative development also has its shadow side. At best we will succeed in implementing the energy transition and in allaying the imminent social dislocations and polarizations in social space—that's the positive vision. In the international context, though, we are currently talking of climate scenarios with an average temperature rise of 6°C by the year 2100. We are further than ever today from reaching the 2°C target. Even if the energy transition is successful at the national level, we will still

72 ●

76 ●

● 212

206 ●

be up against the international consequences of climate change.

What is important for you relative to *Baukultur* in Germany?

For decades the energy supply played no appreciable role in *Baukultur*, and it took more than four years after the first oil crisis in 1973 before the first energy directives were enacted as laws in the building sector. In five years' time, new buildings will be meeting low-energy standards. Energy infrastructures will also have changed by then, because despite political resistance to the Renewable Energy Act and the big electric-line systems I don't think it's possible to halt the ongoing decentralization and flexibilization of the energy and heating supply networks. The advent of the LED strongly influenced our aesthetic experience of lighting and lamps—new building materials, new structural usages, new sustainable urban development standards will have similar effects on *Baukultur*.

But I think energy and energy supplies will remain a marginal issue for planning and building, an unloved child, because people have tended so far to see it as restrictive rather than as being enabling. The dire antagonisms between the high priests of *Baukultur*, on the one hand, and the energy modernizers, on the other, reflect this over and over again—yet the debate has clearly become more productive.

When thinking about cities, specialist and research groups in construction and technology especially tend only to take into account the visible city. I would welcome more interest from climate protectors, energy specialists, architects, and urban planners in engaging with the concealed trends underlying these processes. What factors influence a building? Not only insulation thicknesses and Reconstruction Loan Corporation subsidies, but also demographic change, housing requirements, existing buildings, aspects of *Baukultur*, and cultural heritage.

I would very much welcome specialists and experts whose job would be to lay bare the various strata involved here. This would open a window on the invisible and dynamically evolving city that needs to be developed in sustainable directions.

● 52

Thomas Auer

"Any kind of 'eco-dictatorship'—i.e., sustainability by fiat—is guaranteed to fail. If a desirable and economic lifestyle can emerge from the various sustainability goals, then social change can take root."

In addition to political, economic, and demographic developments, global warming is significantly influencing inhabited building culture in Germany. The European Union's "Carbon Roadmap 2050" stipulates the emissions reductions that are to take place in different sectors. According to the road map, buildings sector CO_2 emissions are to be reduced by 90 percent of their 1990 value by the year 2050. This applies to all inhabited buildings. Such buildings are responsible for around 40 percent of CO_2 emissions, which is why the construction sector is so important. This is an enormous challenge that will not only impact technology but will also modify our built environment. Definition of targets has so far been primarily informational. In reality, in the case of Stuttgart, for instance, CO_2 emissions have been constant since the mid-1990s, so the gap between target and reality is continually growing. Moreover, climatic conditions are changing (rising summer temperatures), which will put further strain on and affect above all the urban centers.

The 90 percent CO_2 emissions reduction target in the construction sector can certainly not be met by heat insulation alone, on top of which public criticism of external thermal insulation systems is increasing. The whole area must be considered far more holistically. Among other things, carbon budget limits need to be revised. Apart from building-related energy factors, an infrastructure is needed, especially in the urban context, to facilitate intelligent energy exchange between, for instance, housing and industry. Personal energy and carbon budgets, as in the Swiss "2,000-Watt Society" model, need to be examined. This would involve computing, aside from a building's running costs, the total energy consumption (or CO_2 emissions) of its users divided by the number of persons in each household. American Department of Energy statistics show that commercial high-rises in the USA consume over 50 percent more energy than lower buildings. If, however, one looks at energy consumption per user, it is the other way round. Not that this means that high-rises are usually more efficient in terms of personal energy budgets, more that they are primarily located in urban centers. Because of high rents, the average number of people working here per square meter exceeds that in suburban low-rises. Increased density inevitably leads to higher energy demands, but above all it shows how misleading area-based energy ratings can be. Per capita living space is rising constantly in the Western world. A personal energy budget would deal with this phenomenon no less than with energy demands for home–work commuting. If the distance is 30 or more kilometers—using a private car—then the energy standard of the building ceases to be relevant.

Increasing outdoor summer temperatures are another challenge. Urban spaces in particular often suffer from the so-called heat island effect. Urban overheating is largely caused by solar radiation being absorbed by sealed areas and buildings that retain heat during the night, resulting in limited and insufficient nocturnal cooling. Temperature records of Paris

in the record-breaking summer of 2003 indicate that the temperature of downtown Paris was 1° to 2°K higher than in surrounding areas during the afternoons, but 10°K higher at night. If we fail to reduce urban overheating, we will be forced to equip buildings with air conditioning, which will take us yet further away from the Carbon Roadmap targets.

In the context of the 2,000-Watt Society model, Switzerland has defined the interplay of efficiency, consistency, and sufficiency as the key to significant CO_2 emissions reduction. Apart from energy efficiency and the transition from fossil fuels to renewable energy sources, lifestyle is also coming under scrutiny in respect to sufficiency. A holistic view comprising extended carbon budget limits and a personalized approach to all energy-related aspects of life will certainly do the subject far greater justice.

With regard to buildings in general, the heat-insulating properties of building envelopes must be improved and/or heating-supplies efficiency and CO_2 emissions optimized. Provision must also be made for aesthetic and planning-and-building-cultural aspects. Aesthetic considerations—apart from listed buildings—are urgently necessary, particularly in extended inner-city contexts. Just as entire architectural ensembles are listed, buildings whose facades and materials contribute to the appearance of a city or city district (e.g. clinker brick facades) must be defined. Debate here sometimes takes on an uncalled-for, dogmatic tone. In addition to interior thermal insulation, the heat-transfer properties of windows, roofs, and basement components need to be optimized without their significantly affecting building design.

In densely built, mixed-use districts, energy exchange—above all heating—between users is an option. The waste heat from a computer center or bakery, for instance, can be used for heating apartments. As waste heat temperatures tend to be low, energy must be deployed near the producer, otherwise the energy demands of the pumps quickly exceed any benefit gained. Seasonal heat reservoirs or geothermal probe fields (near-surface geothermal energy) allow combinations with solar thermal or PVT (photovoltaic with integrated solar thermal collector) and can offset seasonal demand fluctuations. Supplementing seasonal heat reservoirs with block heating plants and fuel cells, if necessary, is economically and ecologically interesting. High efficiency can thus be achieved by means of a customized mix of technologies and integrated local resources.

The large-scale deployment of photovoltaic and wind energy is leading to increasing load fluctuations on the electricity grids. This will grow substantially in the next few decades. Big load fluctuations are more frequently producing short-term power grid surpluses. The buildings sector with its inertia can serve as a reservoir here, either through short-term absorption of large quantities of surplus power (power-to-heat) or by switching off big energy consumers such as heating or cooling (load management). Action such as this leads

● 35
213

214 ●

209 ●

68 ●

● 80
67 ●

to potential synergies between the power grid and the existing architectural substance and is an interesting alternative to the current purely passive concept of improving the energy efficiency of buildings. To exploit this potential, overhaul of panel heating and cooling systems combined with geothermal heat pumps must be accelerated and the energy conservation regulations amended to cover this option.

Inadequate new housing construction in urban centers in the past two decades, together with increased per capita space demand, has led to the populations of our major cities falling perceptibly compared with the 1980s. At the same time, daily commuters are growing in number. The only answer here is to increase affordable living space, whether in the urban or suburban context. Urban mobility cannot fail to change for all types of transport. Extending local public transport will be as necessary as continuing to develop cycle path networks and the infrastructure for other—possibly hitherto unknown—means of transport.

Statistics indicate that, in the West, the per capita kilometers traveled are already falling, if only slightly to date. This decline would increase as a result of, for example, work becoming yet more flexible. Consequently, cities could reduce or dismantle car-related infrastructures and control traffic flows.

As a result of rising summer temperatures, public space will have to be used far more intensively to regulate the urban climate (microclimate). Surface radiation reflectivity (from streets, roof areas, etc.), shade, as well as green areas and bodies of water will become increasingly important. Studies here indicate, though, that green spaces exert a quantifiable effect only on their direct environment. It will be necessary to vegetate entire urban areas much more intensively. The ratio of tree-shaded urban space will become an important index in calculating the heat island effect. A tree canopy cover index has already been introduced in the USA.

This needs to be combined with the planning of appropriate-size buildings. Wind gaps must ensure that cities receive sufficient fresh air in summer. Similarly, on hot days, buildings will be able to channel wind into public urban space from higher strata of air. Part of the space needed will come from the deliberate dismantling or reorganization of transport infrastructures. Private spaces outside architectural structures will also be able to make central contributions. As a consequence, many boundaries between public and private exteriors will merge perceptibly. Inner-city fruit and vegetable cultivation—urban farming—can also contribute positively toward regulating the urban summer climate.

The promise of economic prosperity will inevitably attract increasing numbers to the cities. The resultant population densities would create benefits in energy efficiency (infrastructure) and mobility (fewer commuters, city of short paths). Locally dense populations, if successful, can potentially enhance urban quality in city districts, right through to the polycentric city.

Yet this clashes with the need for extra green areas for climate regulation, and with the fact that many major cities have a dearth of open spaces. These conflicting goals mean that post-densification of population must either occur in suburban space or as a result of increasing the height of buildings, which again would alter the aspect of our cities. From the urban planning point of view, both are conceivable and feasible. Compared with a post-densified city center,

suburban space—particularly after 2030—will be able to react more flexibly to demographic change and possible population decline.

The success of the Carbon Roadmap 2050 will depend on whether we can give sustainable shape to everyday life. Any kind of "eco-dictatorship"—i.e., sustainability by fiat—is guaranteed to fail. If a desirable and economic lifestyle can emerge from the various sustainability goals, then social change can take root. Architecture and our handling of *Baukultur* in the developing human context will be crucial factors here. Architecture defines living space and is thus in a position to pinpoint sustainable forms of life and suggest solutions for the demands of the age in which we live.

● 236

● 80

● 78
262

● 233

● 214

Fritz Reusswig

"All in all, the transition to renewable energies impacts the countryside and the functionality of land. We need to discuss the subject of a new land culture."

What are the central discourses shaping contemporary society in Germany? What developments can we expect up to the year 2050?
Starting off with the fields of energy and ecology, of course the energy revolution is the big topic in Germany today, and the year 2050 is the relevant horizon in this respect. At present we are still witnessing heavy fossil-fuel dependence, but a wide range of attempts are being made to bring about the transition to renewable energies. The question will be whether it can actually be done.

As things stand, our ability and chances of reaching these goals are good, though it won't be easy. A tricky issue for renewable energies, apart from the question of acceptance, is buildings. In the buildings sector, thanks to European and other regulations, it is conceivable that new buildings will have arrived at today's Passive House standards by 2020. I would like to say here that the German energy conservation regulations (EnEV), experienced by some architects as "technocratic harassment," are technologically open and allow plenty of room for architectural maneuver. From the point of view of energy efficiency and climate protection we have to tackle buildings. And, as we know, a whole host of planning and building as well as social challenges lurk here.

Which spaces in the lived environment are of particular significance for the transition to renewable energies?
Given the current state of technological developments, our energy system is at a bifurcation point. An energy system that remains centralized might assume two different forms. Either it retains a high proportion of fossil fuels and only slowly do we move in the direction of renewable energies, the energy mix resembling what it is now. Or a system run primarily by the big energy corporations and grid operators offers a relatively high proportion of renewable energies. The dual strategy of some energy providers, who have split into conventional and renewable sectors, points in this direction.

But a relatively decentralized energy system with a high percentage of renewable energies is also a possibility since renewables have the technical potential for decentralization. Is this what we want, politically and organizationally? If an energy shift with a large share of renewables entails a different approach to energy—decentralized distribution and control—then we must ask ourselves whether and to what extent we are prepared to see ourselves as "prosumers" and to commit to a give-and-take energy deal.

Moreover, climate-friendly cities and urban districts represent important experiential spaces in the energy transition, because it is here that the pulse of the ensemble of energy technology, buildings technology, built environment, infrastructure, and inhabited urban praxis can be taken. We see here that what is at stake is not only energy but also a particular model of society. It is interesting in this context, I think, to ask which variants of capitalism we actually want and which are sustainable. I see this in the offing, boosted by a range of phenomena such as demographic change, insecure pensions, old-age poverty, also financial capitalism reemerging after the last financial crisis, concomitant effects on the real estate markets, and so on. Given these trends, it cannot be ruled out that we are heading for a segregated model of society that no longer has a great deal to do with the founding ideas of the Federal Republic; the idea, for instance, of a social market economy as the basis of a functioning democracy.

Which factors and players will influence the inhabited built environment particularly strongly?
From the macro point of view, the influence of markets and companies on urban structures is important. The underlying questions here are: What culture of capitalism do we want or is democratic society in Germany and Europe able to achieve politically? What return assumptions are normal, and how will returns be distributed? If you expect high returns, then particular forms of company cease to be competitive. But this is very important for urban development, precisely in regard to anticipated land and rent prices. As I see it, return assumptions need to be restricted so that the public authorities, when distributing land, take into account other models with lower returns—their social value being higher, for example, or because they can make important ecological contributions to urban society.

Technology is also an important force, construction technology for instance. I'm a sociologist, not an engineer or construction specialist, but as I see it, the exorbitantly high costs of building, whether for new buildings or for renovation and refurbishment, requires more research and investment with a view to developing cheaper and better materials. If not only industry is allowed to research, but also science with its broader focus is encouraged to invest in small innovative ideas, much can be achieved in the sphere of environmentally friendly (e.g. regenerative) building materials. Many changes can be made in the field of construction costs and technology, I believe, both ecologically and in terms of cost minimization—in other words not just high-tech plus add-ons but also linked to recycling-economic ideas. Thought based on principles of recycling is flourishing today and we have developed a highly technological, dual system. But we still have no genuine recycling economy. Article turnover and the metabolism of society are still heavily geared to disposables and the industrial recycling of certain basic materials or commodities. But there are already examples, for instance, of prefabricated wooden elements being used to build

228 ●

76 ●
88 ●

● 60
205

255 ●

aesthetically attractive buildings both ecologically and quickly—and at competitive prices. The entire "circle of players" involved in building (builders, planners, architects/engineers, users, disposal contractors) needs to be addressed. In this area, too, the prices don't yet "tell the truth."

What about indirect consequences of the transition to renewable energies? For instance, will the countryside be radically transformed by increasingly local production of foodstuffs and energy?
Every technological culture has implications for the countryside, and this holds of course for the transition to renewables too. Wind power plants transform the countryside; they also impact the ecosystem. To some extent planners are already taking these things into account. There remains the issue of public acceptance. People's reactions vary widely. For many in north Germany, these power plants have become part of normal daily life. But others, especially in southern areas, protest vigorously and block projects. Such protest has to be taken seriously and investigated to see what underlies it. It may be that people want better participation procedures, financially for instance—this has to do with our basic orientation in the process of energy transformation, about which we already talked.

What I see as being more critical is the use of biomass energy. Here, at least with the current generation of fuels, land competition with foodstuff production often occurs. This in my opinion is ethically untenable. The situation is different if we achieve technical progress in ways such that it is not edible parts of plants that are being used for energy.

All in all, the transition to renewable energies impacts the countryside and the functionality of land. We need to discuss the subject of a new land culture. And yet this needs to be done on a factual and comprehensive basis—the implications of the different energy systems, including their spatial implications, must be brought out into the open, no less than the historical details of land preference transformation.

When it comes to land use in Germany, it is generally assumed that there will be a reduction, due among other things to demographic change and shrinkage in rural areas. How will climate change affect Germany?
I don't think the really serious, large-scale effects of climate change will have become visible by midcentury. The observable effects won't be so dramatic for most of us. Temperatures will rise somewhat, drought will increase. We developed a 2050-scenario for Berlin-Brandenburg with visible effects—a doubling of hot days, for example, and an increase of heavy rainfall days. But by 2100 there will be a marked increase in extreme weather phenomena that will have an impact on everyday life.

Hence, on top of shrinkage in many rural areas, especially in east Germany, municipalities and regions will be faced with considerable challenges. We will have to think more intensively about cost-efficient adaptation measures. Canalization systems, for instance, will have to cope with increased heavy rainfall, but also with fewer paying users. Developing

them at great expense in order to protect communities against flooding is not an option. But we can consider the role played by streets, squares, and green areas in rainwater management. Costs here are lower, yet it necessitates a lot of rethinking on the part of administrations and urban corporations.

Conferences with titles like "The Chances in Climate Change" are already being held in north Germany. Touristic upgrading of the North Sea and the Baltic is already in the cards. An entirely new tourist landscape will need to develop when more people visit these regions; target groups and prices will change.

● 60

What ought Germany to look like in 2050? What positive aspects can be enhanced, and what negative aspects forestalled?

● 207

My wish is for us to develop in the direction of a socially responsible and environmentally friendly national economy. That means growth in certain areas, shrinkage in many others, and, by and large, institutionalized thinking as to what we need and where we want to go. Simply continuing a dynamic of growth will lead to disaster in the long term. If we could shift profit-seekers' goals by making real capital more attractive and rewarding while investment in finance market products and real estate speculation declines, then restructuring the industrial system and built infrastructure could be raised from 1 percent to 2 to 3 percent annually. The process could then be made more climate friendly. Incidentally, I find this less utopian than it still was only a few years ago, although as a political undertaking it is certainly not easy.

● 66

● 62

I see our cities as spaces where model experiences are possible. A lot of people think that the energy transition will be decided in the country: wind turbines, networks, solar parks, perhaps biomass. Cities, according to this view, are drains: here consumption reigns, not least of energy. On the basis of our experiences with urban projects—the integrated climate protection concept for Potsdam, for instance, or the "Climate Neutral Berlin 2050" feasibility study—I hold this view to be false, or at least a distortion. Cities have considerable potential to generate and to efficiently distribute renewable energies: the surface of a city can support large quantities of photovoltaic; combined heat and power, district heating with higher regenerative components, surplus power, hydrogen, methane, electromobility, car-sharing concepts—all these ideas indicate that the city of the future will be increasingly able to satisfy its own needs. Moreover, this also takes the pressure off the surrounding regions and helps reduce conflicts there relating to the development of renewable energies—especially, of course, if we live not only more efficiently but more sufficiently.

207 ●
67/53/69/63 ●

Might a more anti-consumerist model establish itself so that more is undertaken for later generations?
Whoever has followed the consumption and growth-critical debates of recent years will be inclined to answer this question affirmatively. If you look at a regular shopping mall in this republic at Christmas, for instance, or just let two or three

TV ads work on you, you can't help but conclude that advertising is totally out of touch with reality. The fact is that the consumption and growth critique oriented to sustainability is real: it addresses spontaneous feelings and thoughts that many people have over and over; and yet it is a marginal reality. Another fact is that modern consumer society only developed as the result of a relatively long historical process and that it has repeatedly changed. So our hope is for gradual (more or less rapid) transformation of modern consumer society, heightened awareness among sections of the "mainstream," consumer unlearning and relearning, added importance of social niches and experiments plus political support for such niches enacted by political players, for instance at the communal level.

Finally, I would like to challenge a conventional view that one hears again and again in this context. According to this line of thought, the "standard-bearers" of a sustainable future are the upcoming generation, in other words our children and grandchildren. But one glance at their daily lives, characterized by the pressure to achieve and by digitally fueled social-network-and-amusement stress, and one can't help but feel that there is hardly a generation that attends, or could attend, less to their own and to society's future. One does keep meeting, on the other hand, old people—digitally and analog networked, and free of the worries of professional life—who are genuinely concerned about a future that is worth living. My conclusion here: Let's not just think about child parliaments, but also about new forms of councils of elders.

Claus Leggewie

Cities need a matter-of-course, regularized, and sustainable culture of participation in order to become the living hub of urban society again. Participation of this kind requires that in all relevant projects those locally and directly affected are able to articulate and bring into play their needs and points of view. Consultative and participatory procedures are part of the urban planning process where professional state participants, market players, and the urban population come together. Participation must not confine itself to the "usual suspects"—a certain degree of representation needs to be aimed at, also in the direction of nonparticipating elements of the population. The interests of future generations (children and grandchildren of those alive today), insofar as they can be anticipated, must also be included in appropriate ways.

● 82

Following a phase of privatization, urban space needs to be more strongly influenced once more by thinking based on the idea of the commons. In neighborhoods, districts, and regions we-identities form, and demands are articulated for cities to be understood and used as a commons beyond market-based privatization. Common areas (such as public squares, green corridors, and open spaces) are protected by communities of users. Collectives and neighborhood and tenants' associations require financial resources to give these demands firm and enduring anchorage.

● 94
238

Lecture: "Die Stadt von Übermorgen: Aus der Sicht Soziales," part of The City cf Tomorrow: Trends and Possible Futures in Urban Development in Germany, a documentation expert panel at the Federal Ministry for the Environment, Nature Conservation, Building and Nuclear Safety (BMUB) and the Federal Institute for Research on Building, Urban Affairs and Spatial Development (BBSR), Bonn, December 11–12, 2013.

System and Design of the Maps

How can statistical data be represented and localized to facilitate a better understanding of the present? Using ongoing geographical and spatial observation materials gathered by the BBSR we have brought together a range of indicators in order to view Germany from different perspectives. The graphics in this publication present complex interrelations uniformly and pictorially and make them easily legible. The basic principle underlying the diagrams is a grid that allows extremely diversified data to be formally systematized. The fuzziness inherent in the grid-format of the maps makes harmonization of heterogeneous data sets possible. The macrospatial contrasts and tendencies that are brought out in this way provide a macroscopic view of Germany in its entirety.

The scale of the maps is 1:3,870,000, so that Germany is depicted in 7,269 squares measuring 2 × 2 mm, each of which represents an area of approximately 7.7 × 7.7 km. The data of the maps is represented by dots, semicircles, and lines of different density and size.

Cities with more than 100,000 inhabitants

Depending on the data presented, one dot per square (frequency 5/cm) or four dots per square (frequency 10/cm) are used.

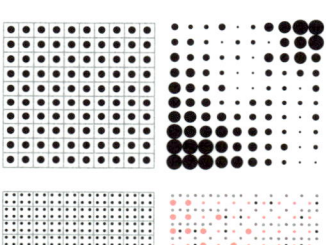

Accordingly, different map data can be depicted by two semicircles or four different dot sizes.

The different dot sizes express different densities of data. Additional levels of content are depicted within the basic grid-format by means of lines.

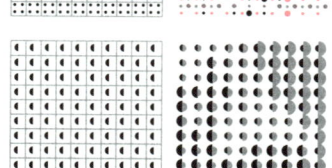

The graphic representation of reliefs is likewise based on a dot-format of frequency 20/cm. Thus, topographical and quantitative data is displayed in one and the same grid-format.

The extracts from the maps show selected regions in detail (200% enlargement, standard 100 km diameter). The symbols are likewise enlarged by 200% and hence not related to the key for the main map

Maps

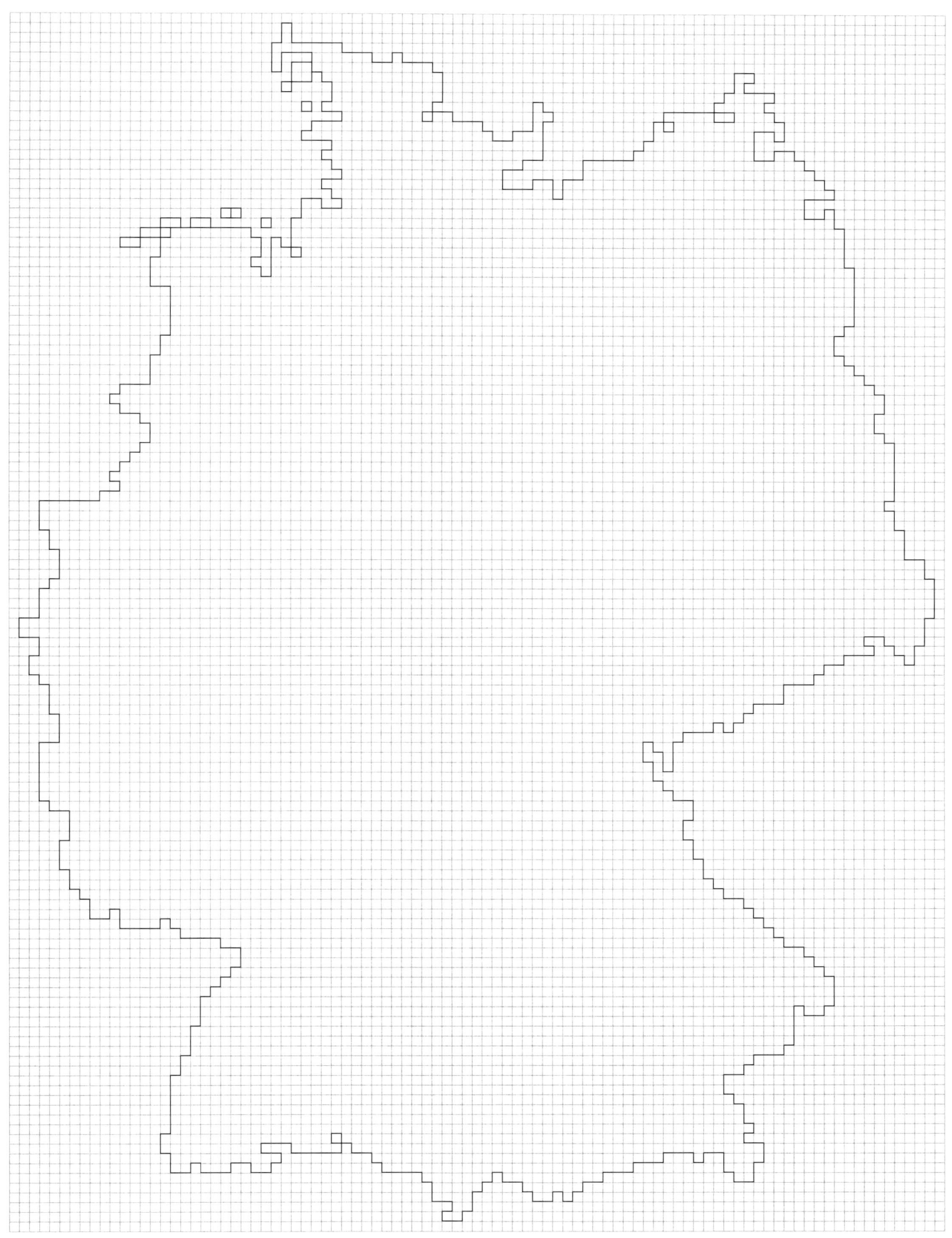

Topography and Water Surfaces

100 km

Population Distribution

Communities with more than 20,000 inhabitants

Population density

Inhabitants 2012 per km²

‹	20,000 to	50,000
‹	50,000 to	100,000
‹	100,000 to	500,000
‹	500,000 to	

˙	to	100
›	100 to	200
›	200 to	500
›	500 to	1,000
▸	1,000 plus	

Given the conditions set by the transition to renewable energy, new value creation processes, and models of prosperity, will Germany retain its polycentric structure? ● 25

What effect would a reduction in the number of federal states have on geographic distributions? ● 29

Will the metropolitan regions assume a superordinate political position in the future? ● 21
29

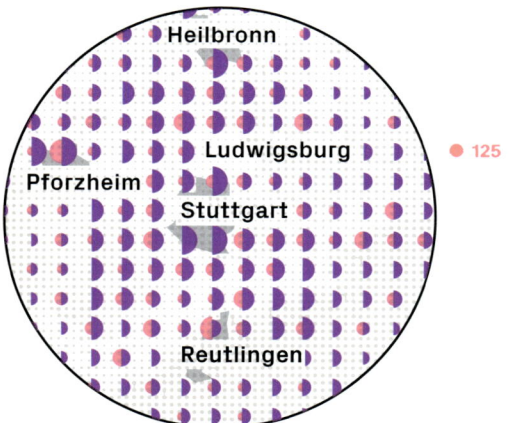

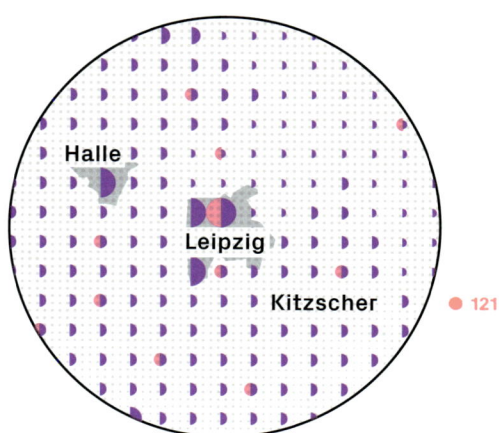

200% / ⌀ 100 km

100 km

Transport and Energy Axes

Transport routes **Supergrid**

─── Express highways   ─── 380 kV line
━━━ ICE rail network   ─── 220 kV line
─── Navigable waterways

How will infrastructures change as a result of the energy transition and new patterns of mobility?   ● 32
    38
    99

What prioritization will rural regions pursue: energy, country-side, agricultural production?   ● 36
    208

What international interdependencies are manifested in the infrastructures?   ● 104
    136

Hamburg Metropolitan Region
● 117

Saale-Orla-Kreis
● 129

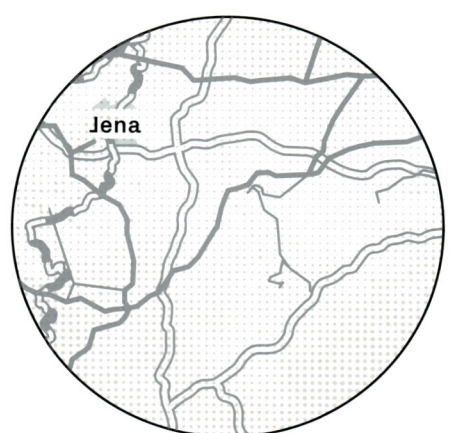

200 % / ⌀ 100 km

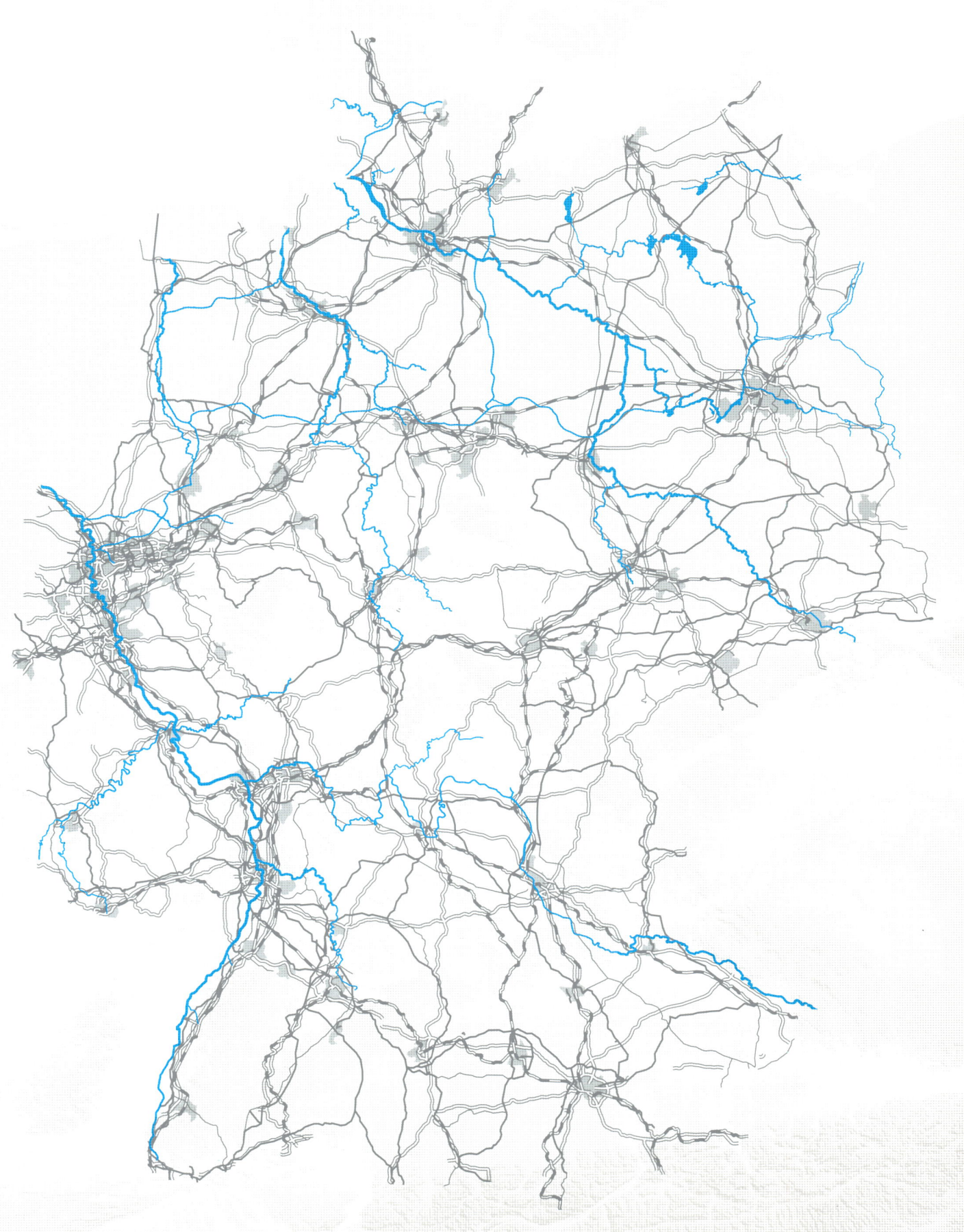

100 km

Population Development

Average age 2030

Population development

Changes in population numbers
2010 to 2030, in percent

50.5	plus	
49	to	50.5
47.5	to	49
46	to	47.5
44.5	to	46
	to	44.5

	to	-20
-20	to	-10
-10	to	-3
-3	to	3
3	to	10
10	plus	

Population prognoses are subject to constant change, which
is particularly evident in the Berlin region.

What will the next population prognosis look like?   ● 31

Are today's areas of shrinkage the growth areas of tomorrow?   ● 22
                                                                  231

Must peripheral infrastructures be cut back to make these   ● 36
regions viable for the future?   260

Population development 2030

Base 2012

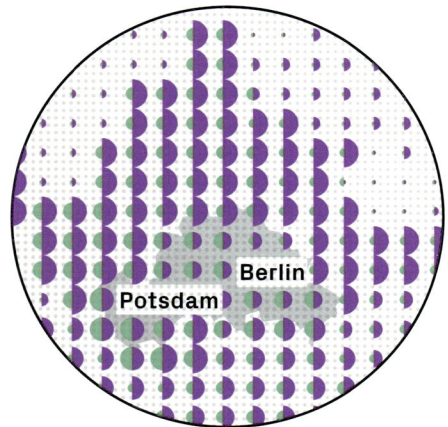

Population development 2035

Base 2014

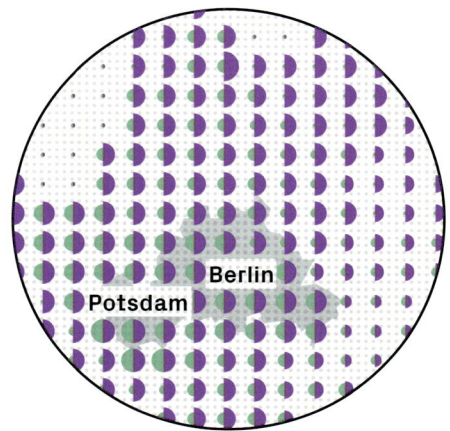

200% / ⌀ 100 km

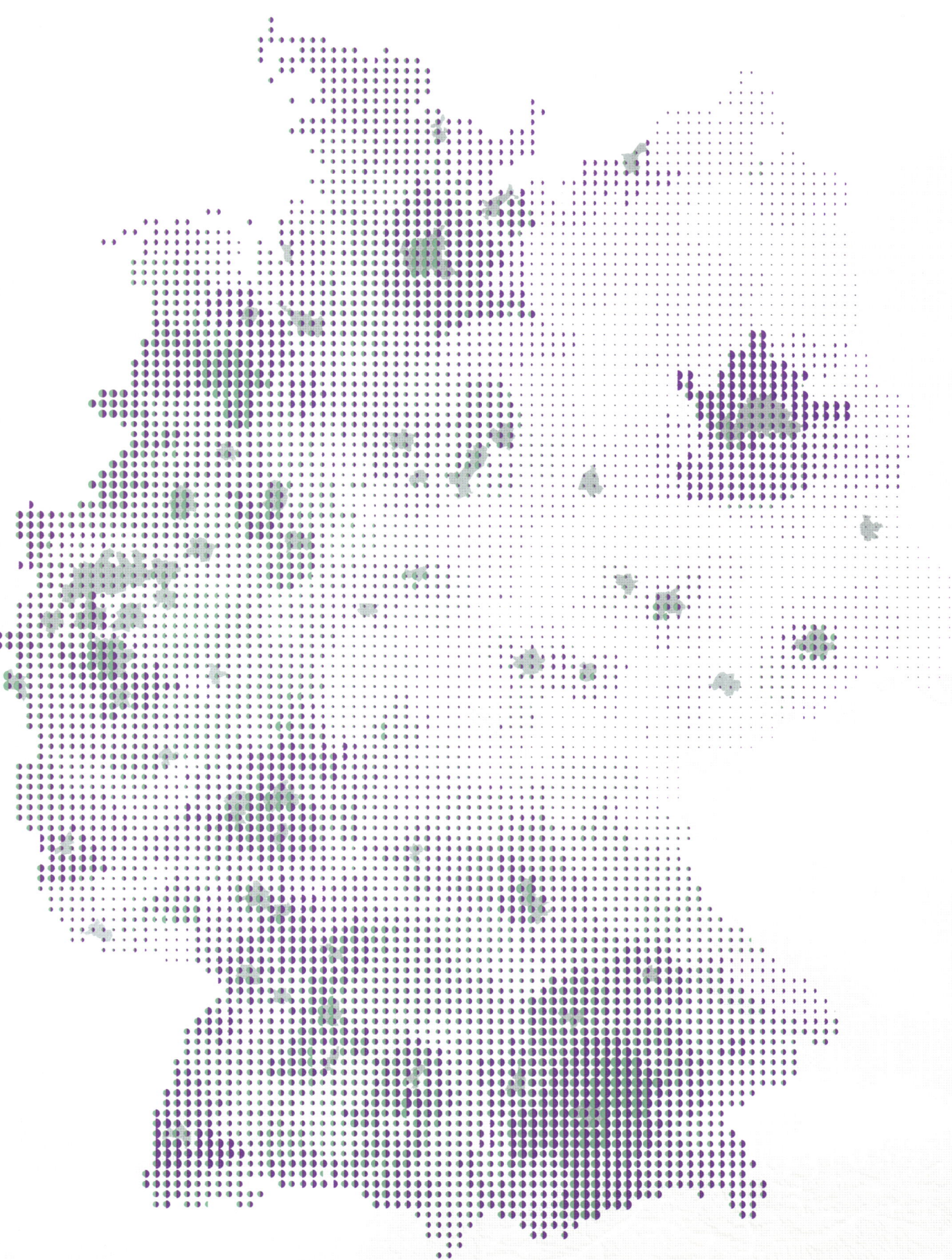

100 km

Employment Patterns

Secondary-sector employment

Employed in secondary-sector (WZ 2008) per hundred employed, 2012

	to	25
25	to	30
30	to	35
35	to	40
40	plus	

Tertiary-sector employment

Employed in tertiary-sector (WZ 2008) per hundred employed, 2012

	to	55
55	to	60
60	to	65
65	to	75
75	plus	

Will digitization lead to decentralization and deterritorialization, and hence to a renaissance of the countryside as against cities? ● 260

Will digitization change the north-south distribution of industries and services? ● 254

Will Germany experience a phase of deindustrialization? What geographic effects would this have? ● 22
24
256

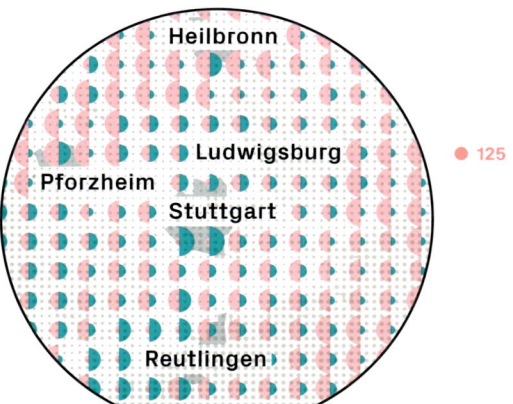

● 125

Hamburg Metropolitan Region
● 117

200 % / ⌀ 100 km

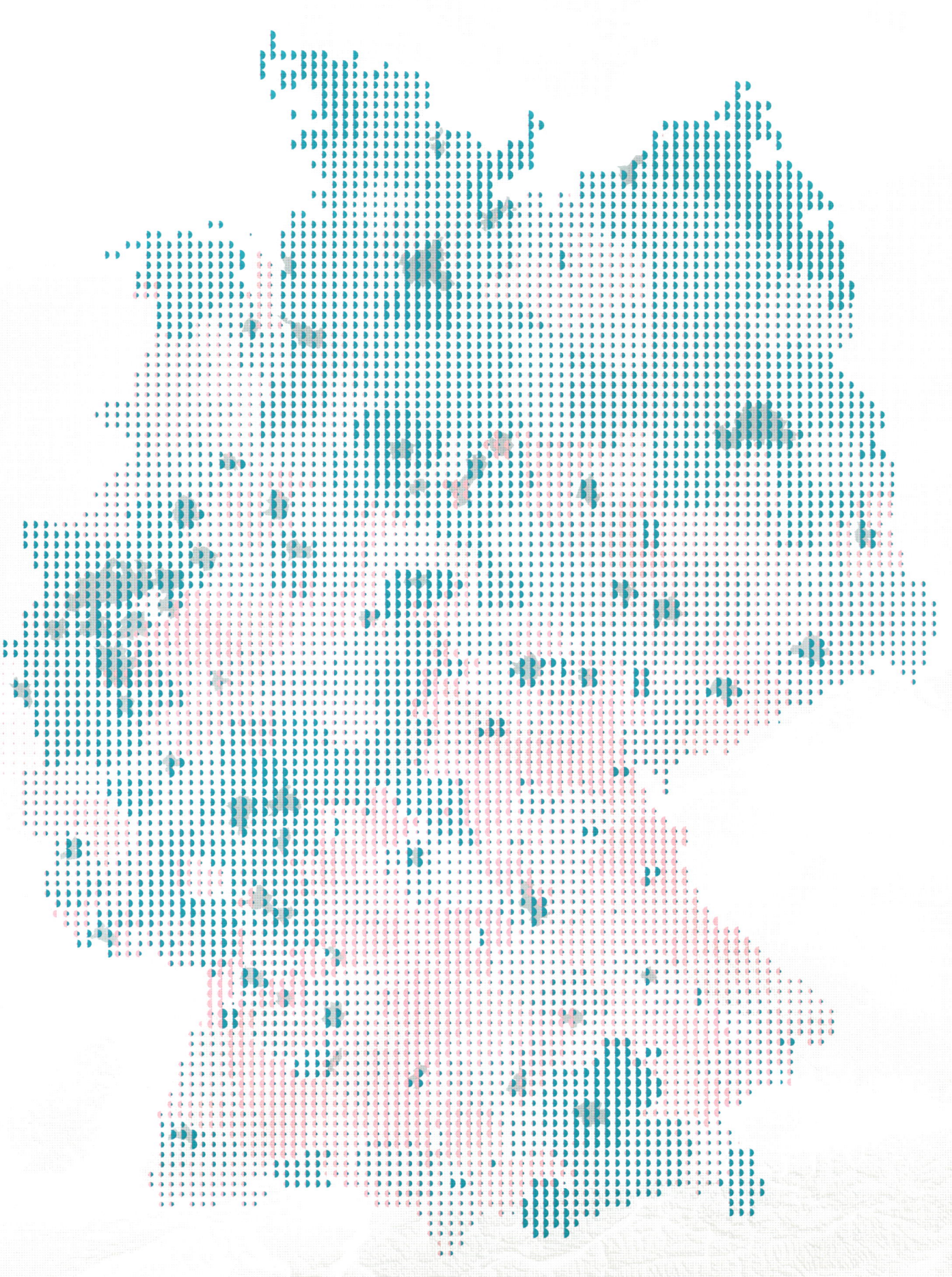

100 km

Impervious Surfaces, Woods and Forest

**Settlement and
transport surfaces**

Proportion of grid 2013, in percent

·	to	10
‹ 10	to	20
‹ 20	to	30
‹ 30	to	40
‹ 40	plus	

**Woodland and
forest areas**

Proportion of total area 2013,
in percent

0.9	to	14.2
14.2	to	24.4
24.4	to	32.7
32.7	to	42.9
42.9	to	64.4

Given the scarcity of financial resources in cities, will it be
possible to restrict land use to thirty hectares per day? ● 30

Who will protect the countryside as a resource? ● 36
206

Will impervious areas in urban regions decrease as a result ● 262
of reduction in transport infrastructures, for instance?

Saale-Orla-Kreis
● 129

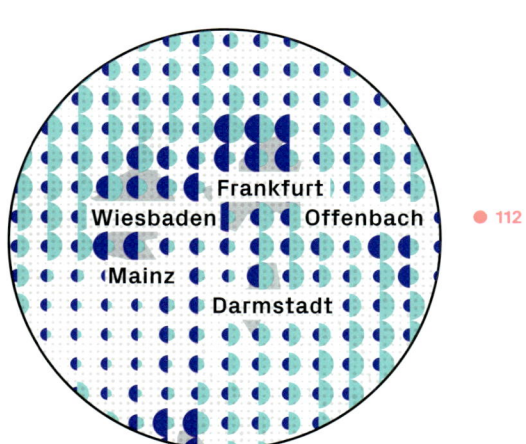

● 112

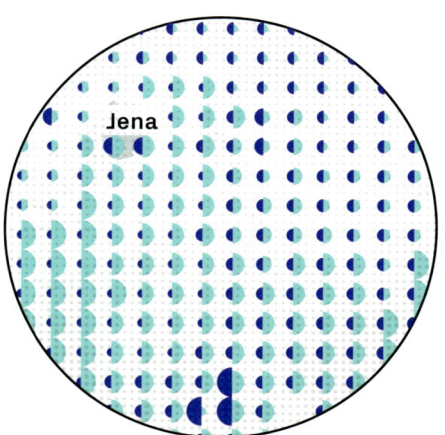

200% / ⌀ 100 km

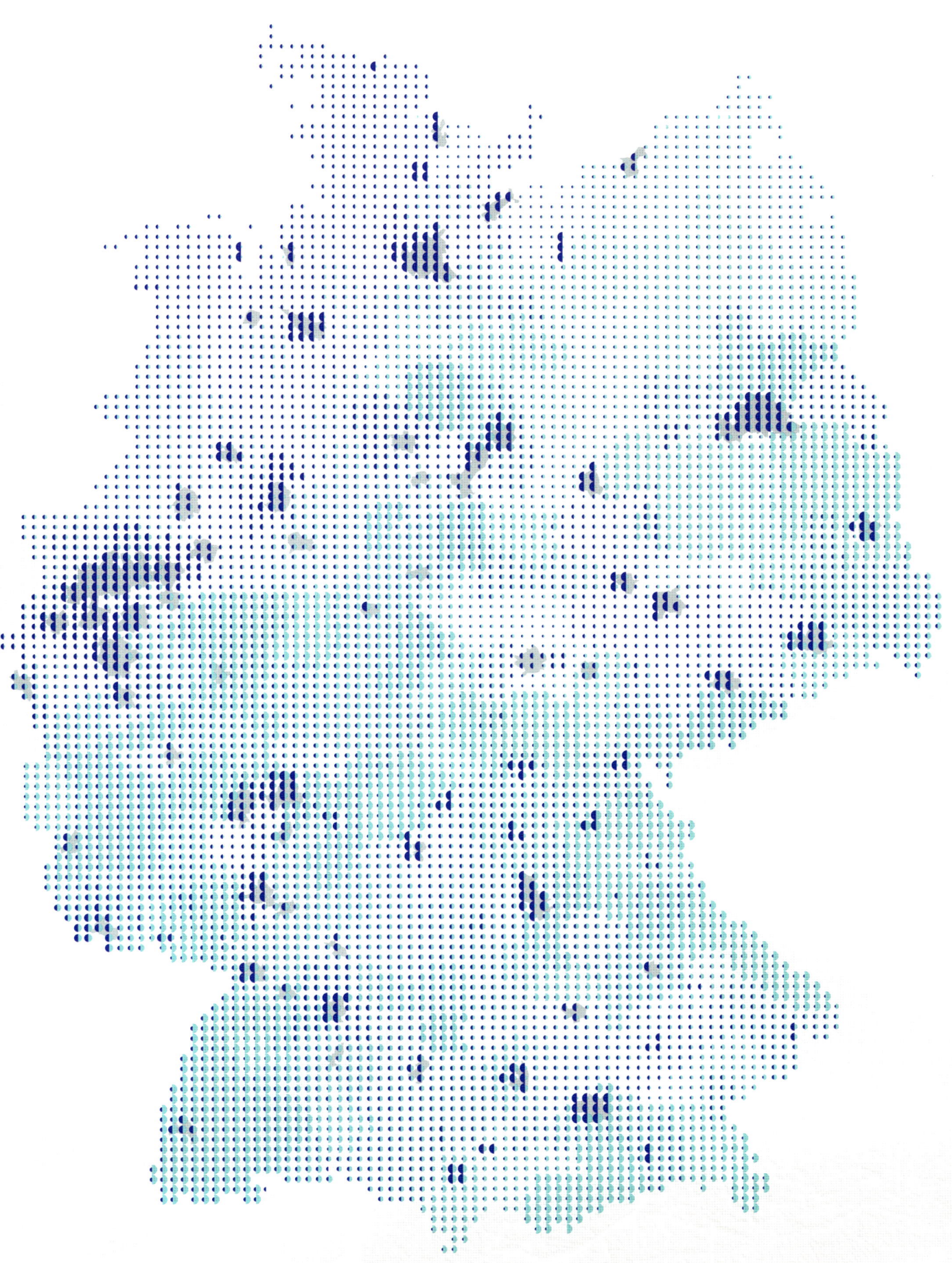

100 km

Potential Renewable Energies

Energy potential: biomass

In GJ per hectare

- ·   to   5
- ·   5   to   15
- • 15   plus

Energy potential: solar

In kWh/m²

- ·   to   900
- ·   900   to   950
- ·   950   to 1,000
- · 1,000   to 1,150

Energy potential: hydro

In kW/km

- · Low
- · Medium
- • High

Energy potential: wind

In percent of reference gain

- ·   to   60
- ·   60   to   100
- • 100   plus

How will the countryside develop once the potential for renewable energy is exploited?

- ● 30
  42
  207

How will supply be organized when energy production has been decentralized while customers live centrally?

- ● 41
  205

Is renewable energy production a must in the cities?

- ● 42
  134
  211

Allgäu

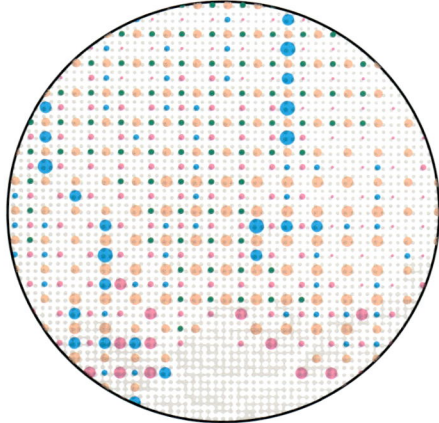

200% / ⌀ 100 km

Saale-Orla-Kreis

● 129

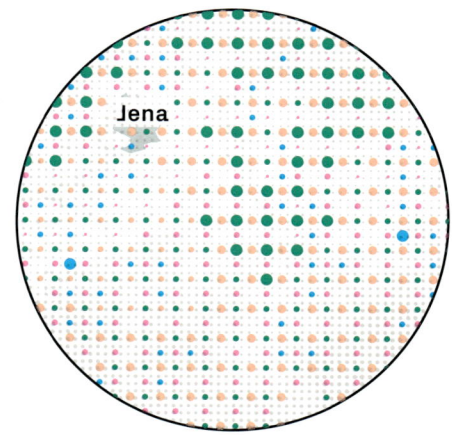

Jena

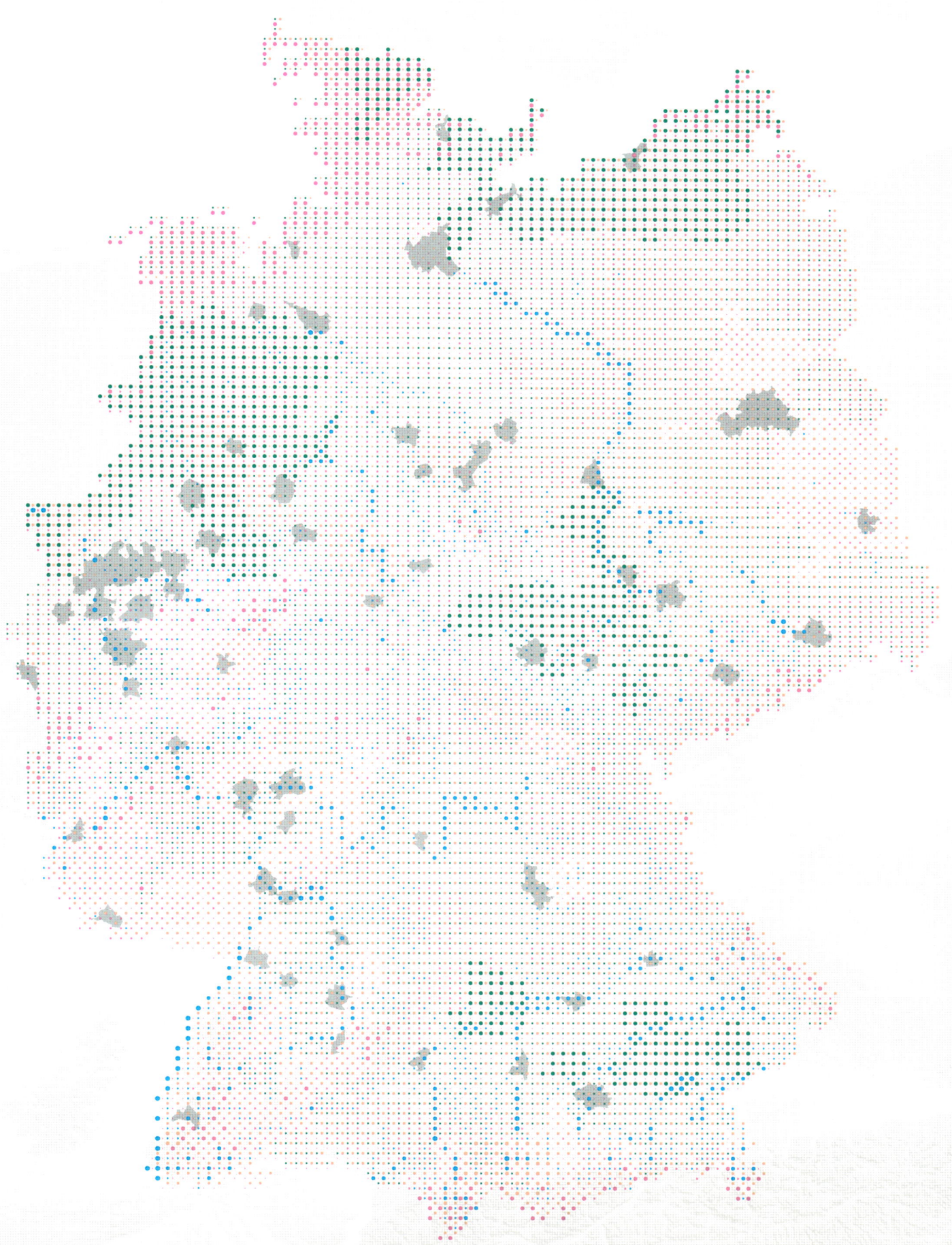

100 km

Biomass Energy

**Biomass energy
potential**

**Biomass energy
status quo**

In GJ per hectare

·		to	5
·	5	to	15
●	15	plus	

· Biomass

How will land conflicts in the cultivation of biomass for energy purposes be resolved?	● 233
Will the production of biomass energy lead to new monocultures?	● 208
Will the creation of a unified energy industry in rural regions be necessary?	● 42

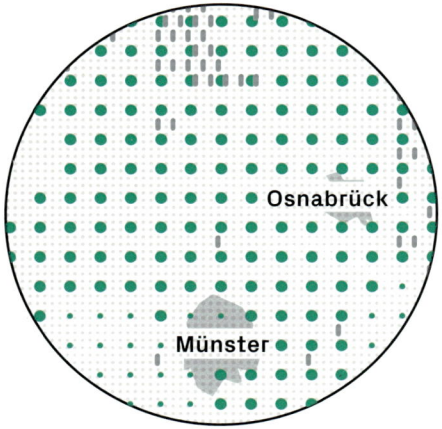

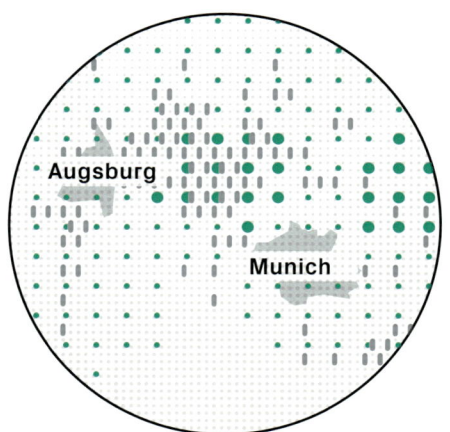

200% / ⌀100 km

100 km

Hydroelectric Energy

Hydroelectric energy potential

Hydro power, in kW/km

Hydroelectric energy status quo

· Low
· Medium
• High

╱ Water

Will the conversion of energy-producing regions entail new possibilities for hydroelectric power?

● 208

How will hydroelectric potential develop as a result of climate change?

How will the energy infrastructure change if water becomes an export commodity?

● 100

Saarle-Orla-Kreis
● 129

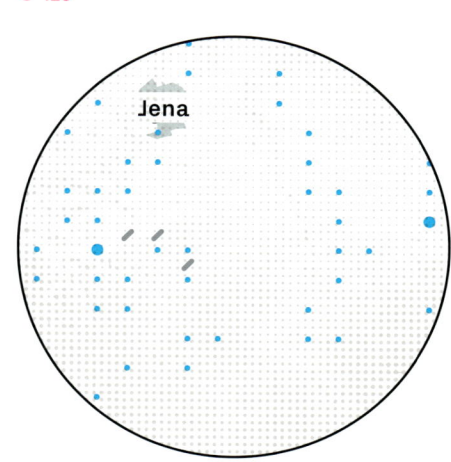

200% / ⌀100 km

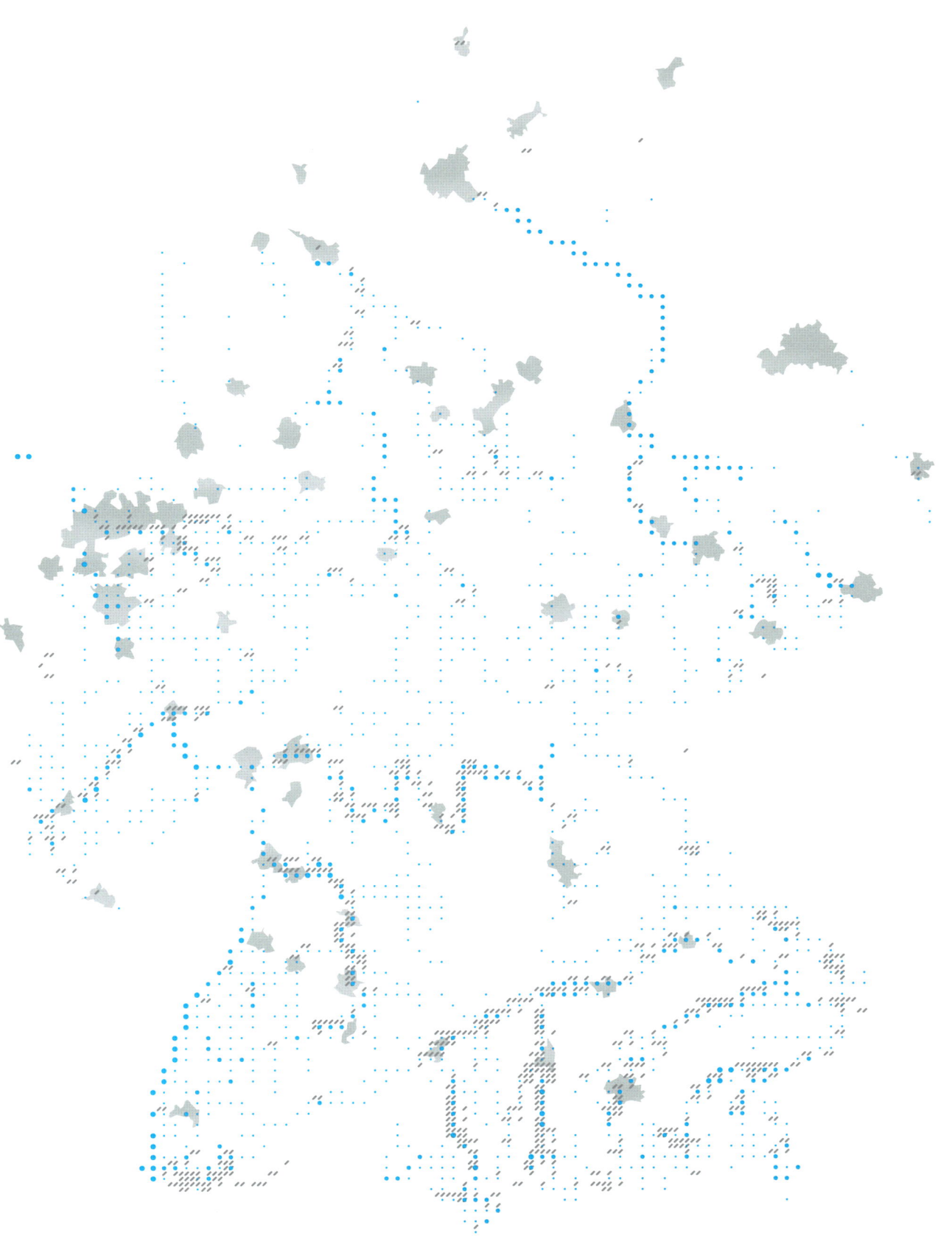

100 km

Wind Energy

Wind energy
potential

Wind energy
status quo

In percent of reference gain, 2005

·   to   60   -   Wind
·   60   to   100
· 100   plus

Will the future of wind energy be dominated by local
worries and fears?

● 42
208

Given the advances in solar energy technology, is it right
to develop wind energy?

● 19

Will wind energy in the future be supplied primarily by
offshore wind parks?

● 205

Ostfriesland

Saarle-Orla-Kreis
● 129

Jena

200% / ⌀100 km

100 km

Solar Energy

Solar energy potential

In kWh/m²

Solar energy status quo

	to	900
900	to	950
950	to	1,000
1,000	to	1,150

Solar

Will solar energy alone be able to cover all our future energy requirements?   ● 205

Will solar energy continue to be subject to a north-south divide?

What effect will photovoltaic farms have on the countryside?   ● 208

Saarle-Orla-Kreis
● 129

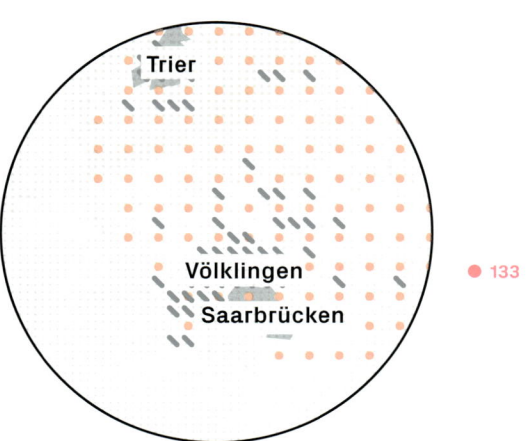

Trier

Völklingen
Saarbrücken

● 133

Jena

200% / ⌀ 100 km

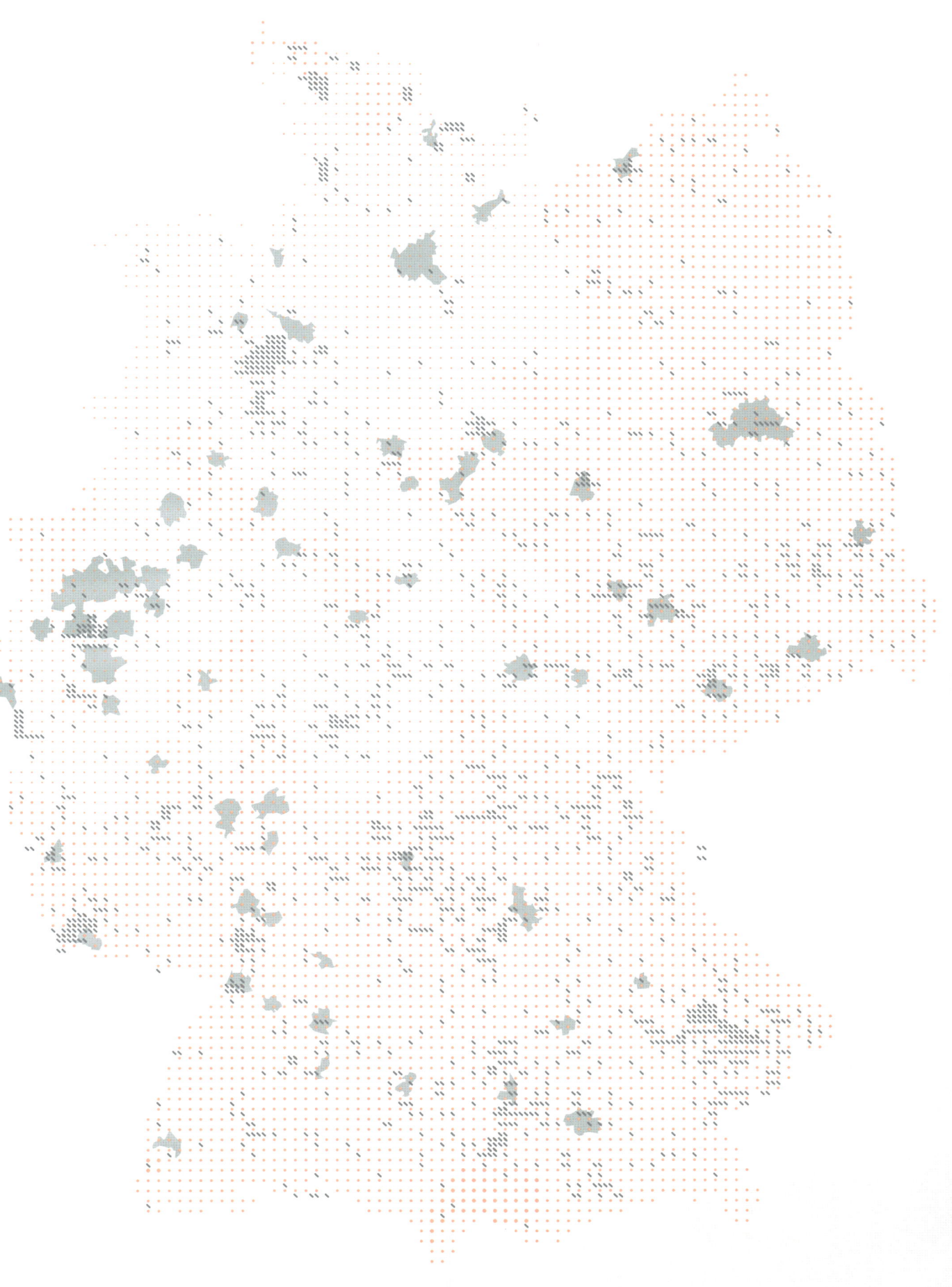

100 km

Empty Apartments and Net Migration

Empty apartments

In residential buildings 2011,
in percent

	to	2
2	to	4
4	to	6
6	to	8
8	to	10
10	plus	

Net migration

Per 1,000 population, 2012

	to	1.3
1.3	to	2.5
2.5	to	3.8
3.8	to	5.4
5.4	to	10

How will cities and regions develop under conditions of in-migration?

● 18
20

Will the regions with the highest ratio of empty apartments and houses experience the heaviest in-migration?

● 18
25

Will prospering regions with scarce living space continue to be the prime destinations for in-migrants?

● 103

Saarle-Orla-Kreis
● 129

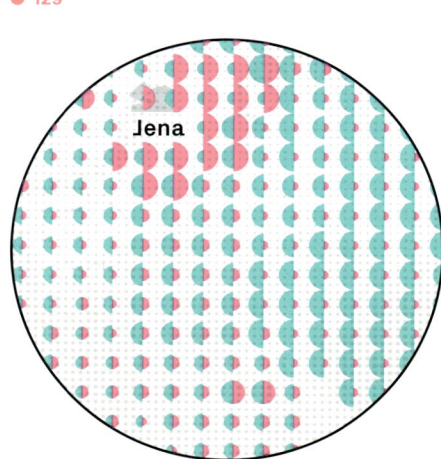

Trier

● 133

Völklingen

Saarbrücken

Jena

200% / ⌀ 100 km

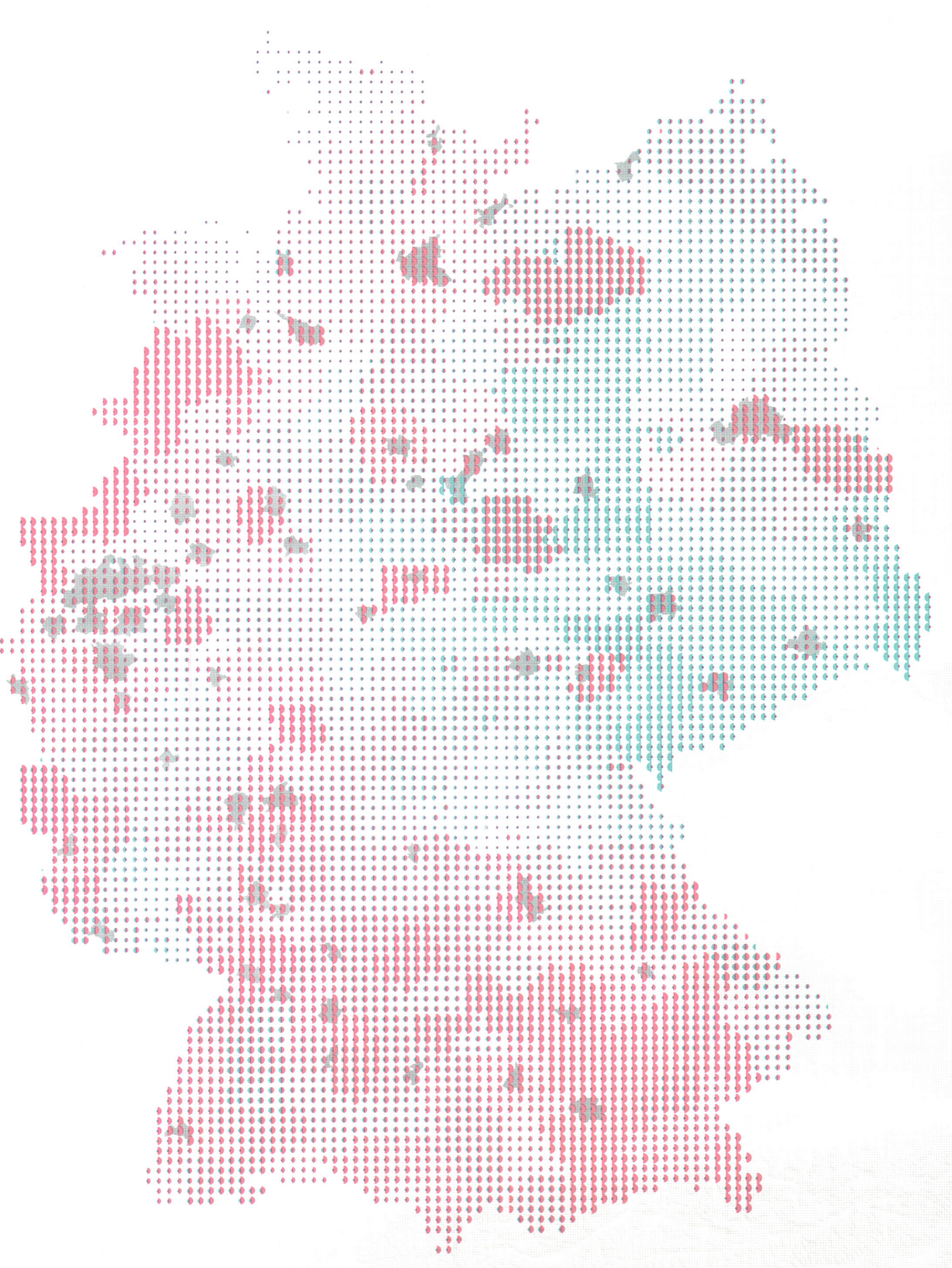

100 km

Hospital Accessibility and Population Density

Population density

Population per one km² grid, 2012

	to	100
100	to	200
200	to	500
500	to	1,000
1,000	plus	

Hospital accessibility

Car distance to nearest hospital for primary medical care, in minutes, 2008

20	plus	
15	to	20
10	to	15
5	to	10
	to	5

Will health care in rural regions continue to be trimmed down?

● 22
99

Will alternative forms of health care become necessary in sparsely populated areas, supported for instance by new information and communication technologies?

● 37

Can cross-border projects provide for better health care?

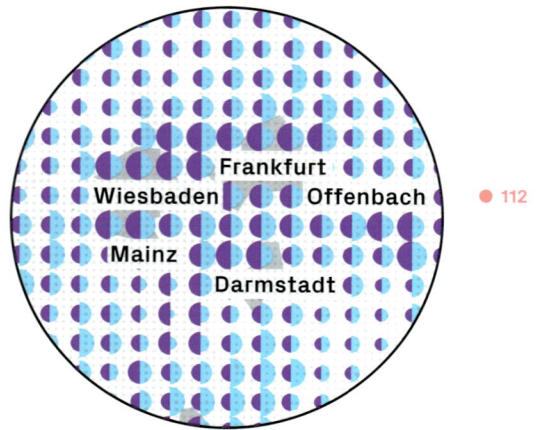

● 112

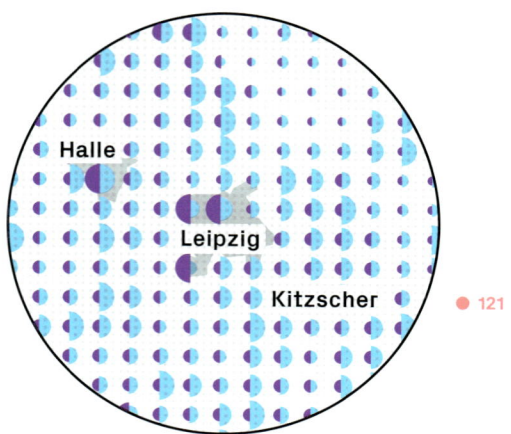

● 121

200% / ⌀ 100 km

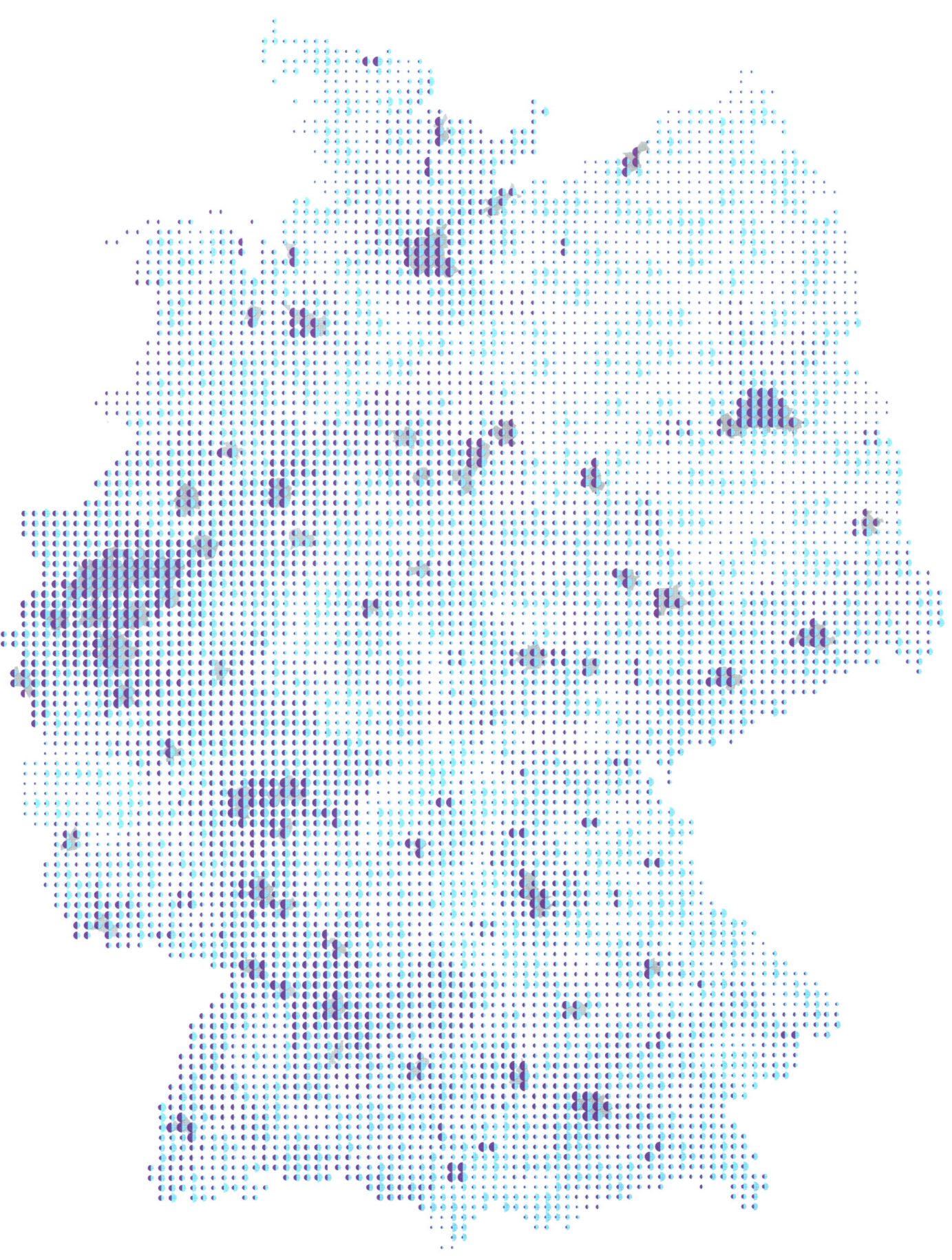

100 km

Secondary-Sector Employment

Population density

Population per one km² grid, 2012

Secondary-sector employment

Employed in secondary-sector (WZ 2008) per 100 employed, 2012

to 100	to 25
100 to 200	25 to 30
200 to 500	30 to 35
500 to 1,000	35 to 40
1,000 plus	40 plus

Will the deindustrialization of cities and metropolitan regions continue? ● 23

Will structural changes toward a digitized society completely transform the secondary-sector? ● 22
254

What effects will these changes have on peripheral regions? Where might new incentives for growth originate? ● 260

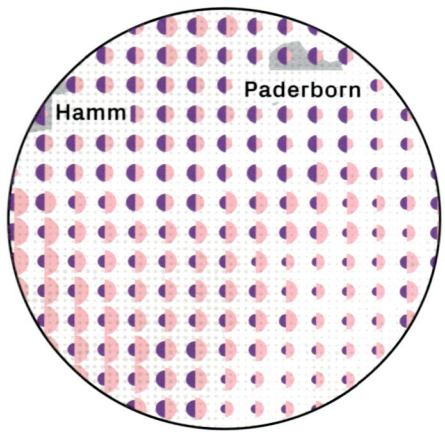

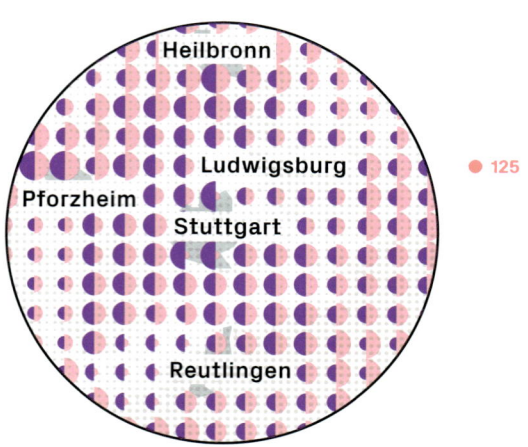

● 125

200% / ⌀100 km

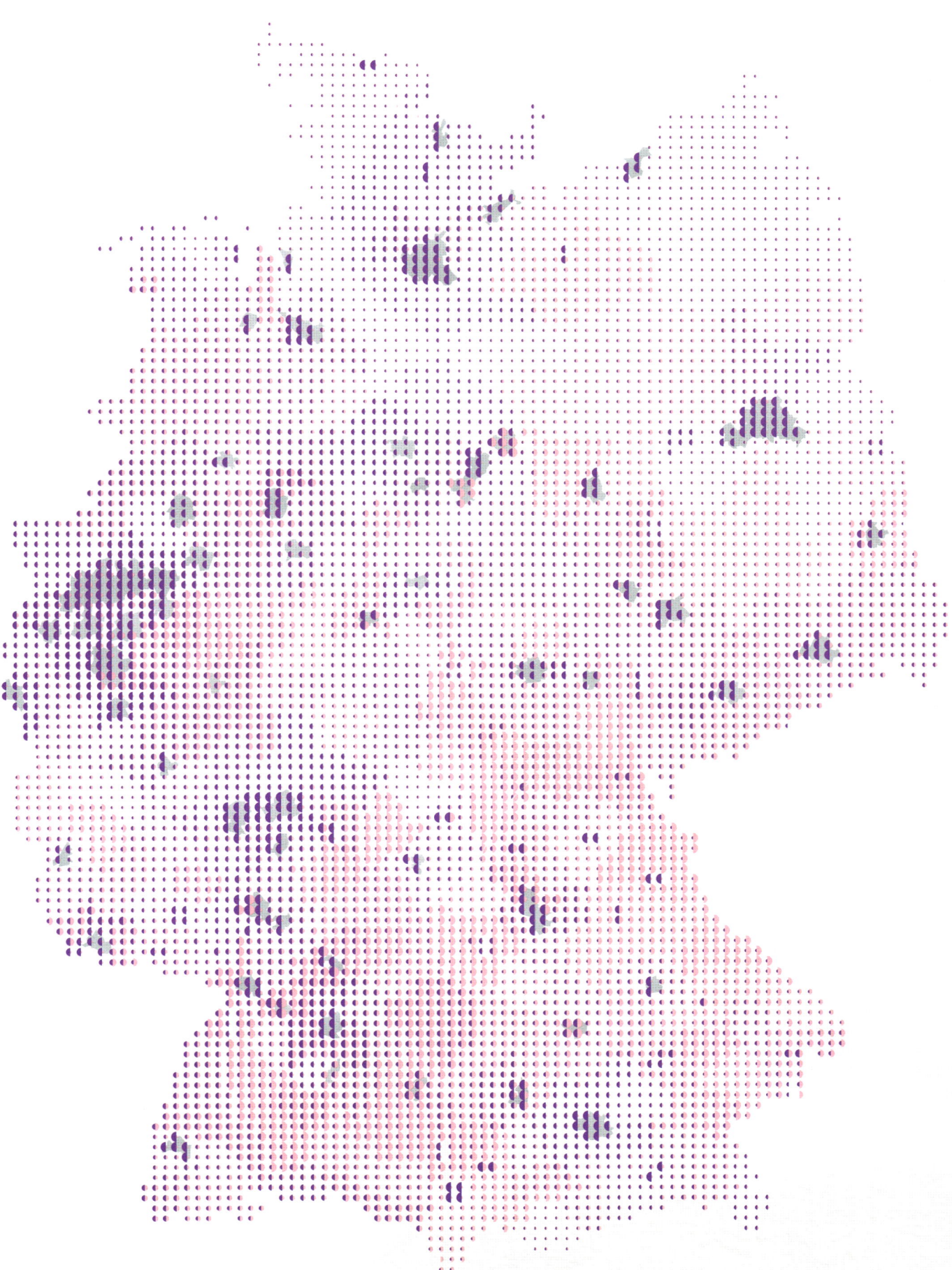

100 km

Community Debts and Real Estate Prices

Community debts

In euros per inhabitant, 2012

	to	500
500	to	1,000
1,000	to	1,500
1,500	to	2,500
2,500	plus	

City states

House purchase prices

Average purchase prices for used, vacant single- and two-family houses, in 1,000s of euros, 2012

	to	150
150	to	250
250	to	350
350	plus	

How can the social housing markets and the capitalized real estate markets be harmonized?

- 18
  41
  234

Is solidarity compensation necessary for impoverished cities and communities?

- 17
  100

Does the real estate market present any long-term option for reducing municipal debts?

- 37
  232

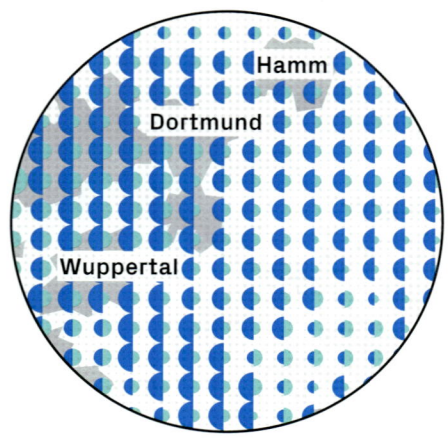

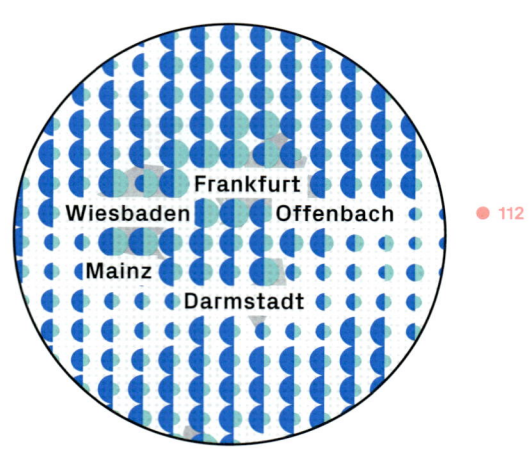

- 112

200% / ⌀100 km

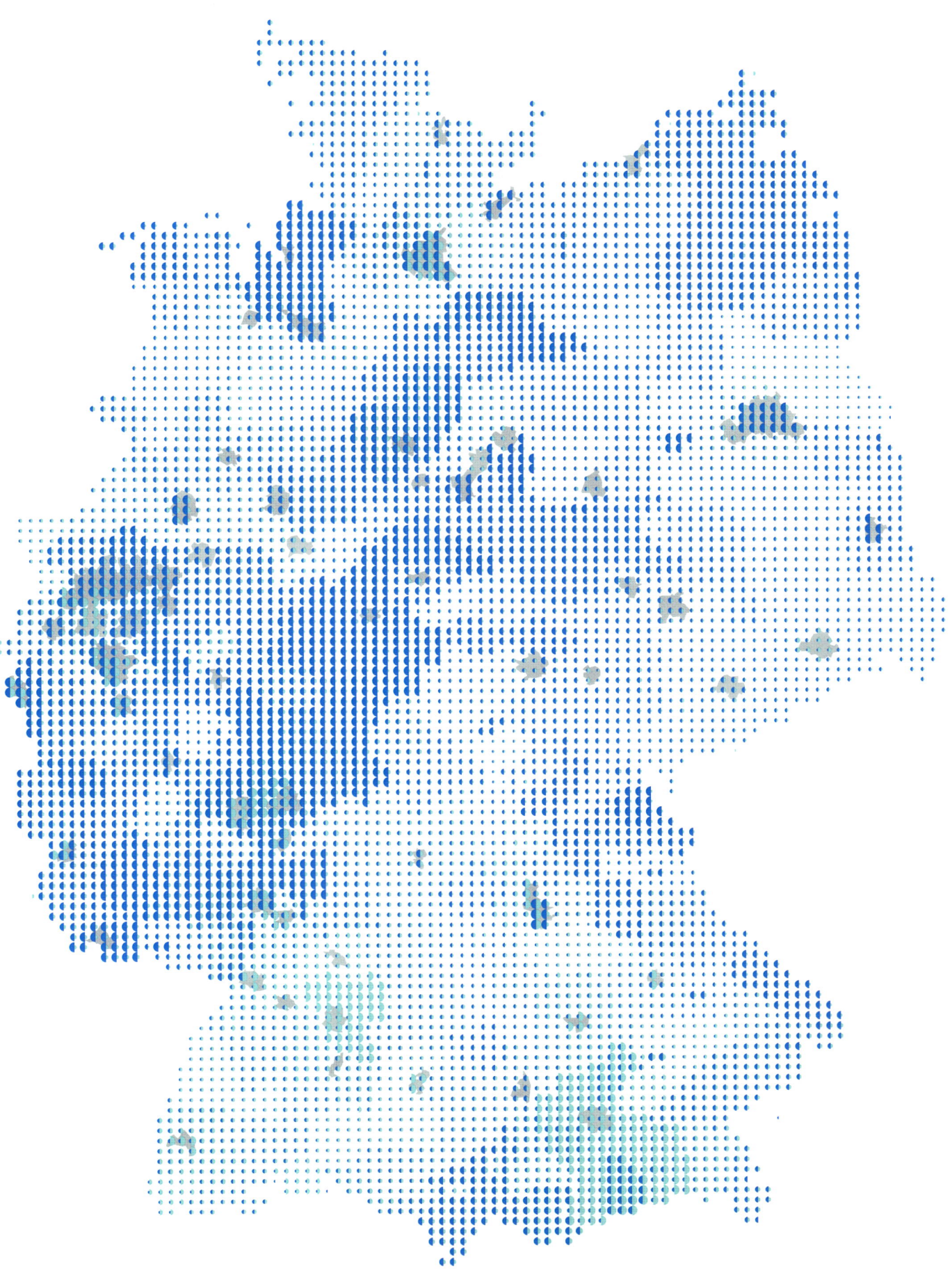

100 km

Car Ownership and Population Density

Car ownership

Cars per 1,000 population, 2012

	to	500
500	to	540
540	to	580
580	to	620
620	plus	

Population density

Population per one km² grid, 2012

	to	100
100	to	200
200	to	500
500	to	1,000
1,000	plus	

Will car infrastructures become obsolete or will their value increase as a result of driverless mobility? ● 32

How will cities deal with space gains resulting from driverless mobility? ● 40 / 211 / 262

What planning paradigm will cities and regions decide on to ensure sustainable mobility? ● 33 / 236

How will the motorization ratio in rural areas compare with that in cities, for instance through the development of new mobility services? ● 34 / 236

Hamburg Metropolitan Region
● 117

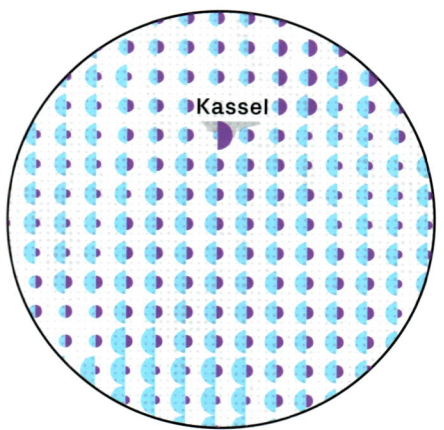

200% / ⌀100 km

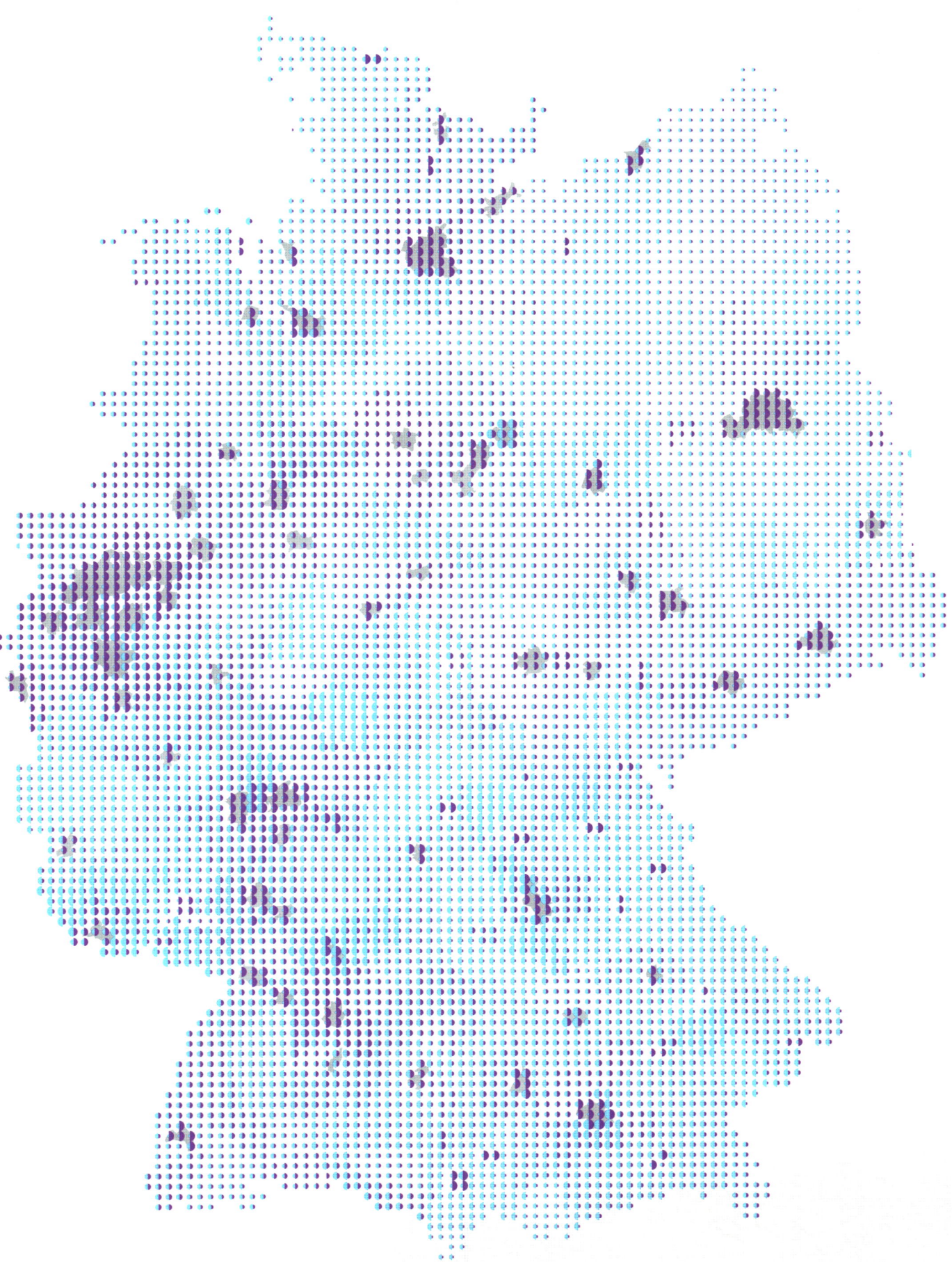

100 km

Commuting Distances and Purchasing Power

Commuting distances

Average commuting distances of all socially insured employees in a location, in km, 2013

	to	14
14	to	18
18	to	22
22	to	26
26	to	30
30	to	34
34	plus	

Purchasing power

Euros per inhabitant, 2012

	to	17,500
17,500	to	18,500
18,500	to	19,500
19,500	to	20,500
20,500	to	21,500
21,500	to	22,500
22,500	to	23,500
23,500	to	24,500
24,500	plus	

How will the ratio of purchasing power to distance develop? Will only the wealthy be able to afford to live in the cities in the future?

● 22

Will personal mobility status continue to determine the demand for living space in suburbia?

● 34
40

Will the "compact city" be followed by the "compact region"?

● 19
39
236

Hamburg Metropolitan Region
● 117

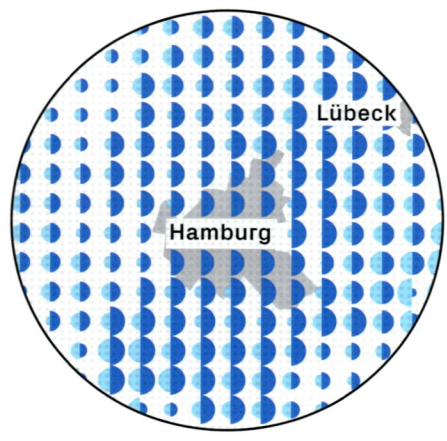

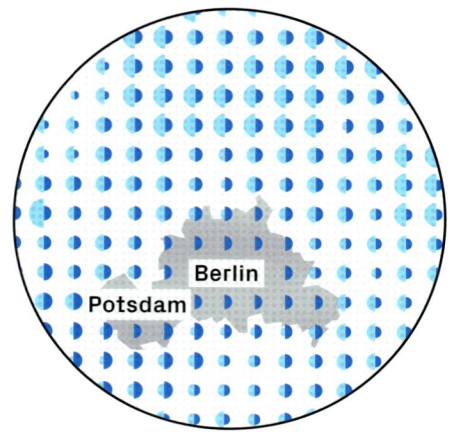

200% / ⌀100 km

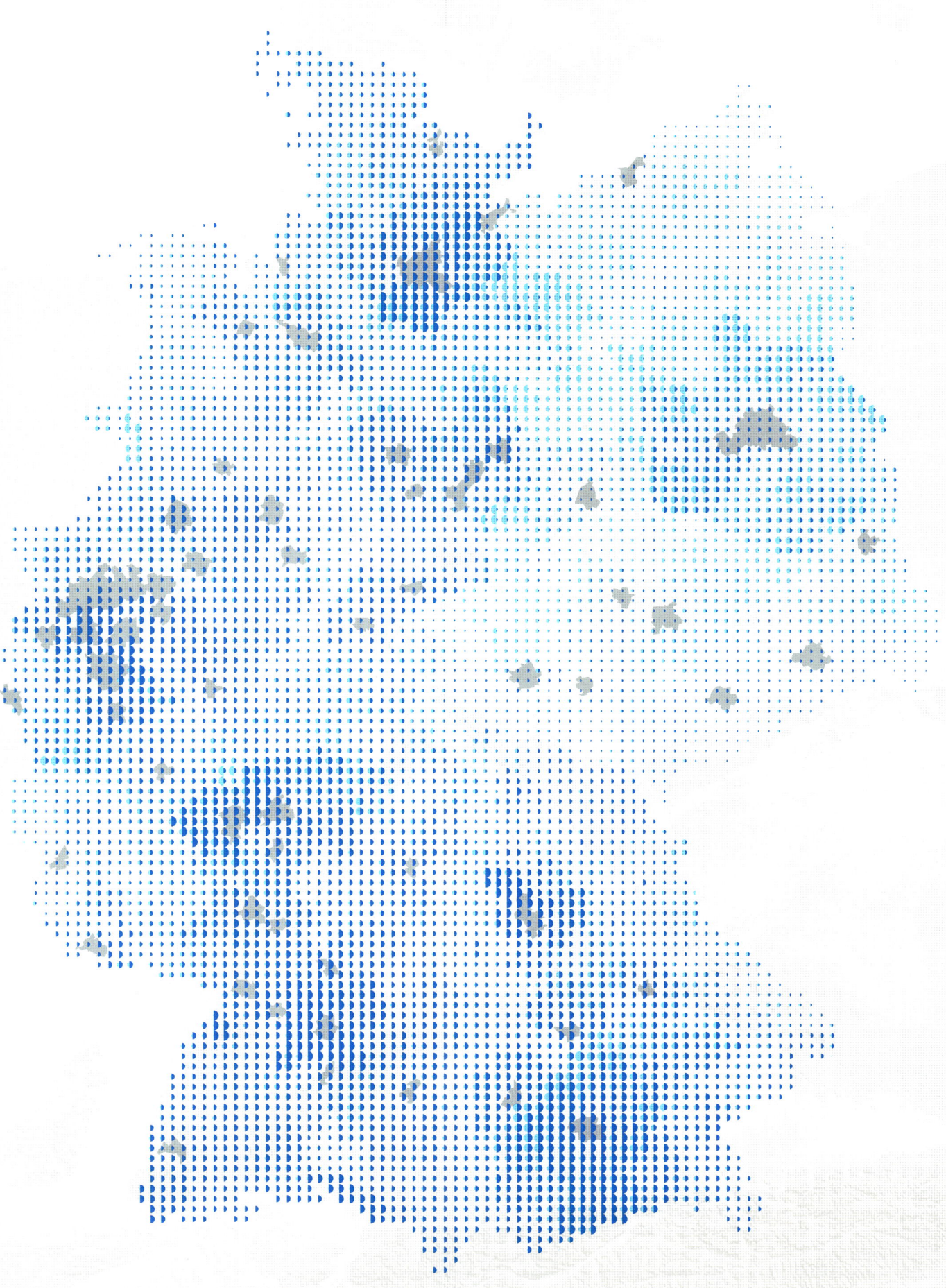

100 km

Voter Participation and Hartz IV

Voter participation

Voter participation in Bundestag elections 2013, in percent

·		to	60
‹	60	to	65
‹	65	to	70
‹	70	to	75
‹	75	plus	

Hartz IV

Quota of employable and non-employable receiving money from Social Insurance Code II (SGB II) per 100 population under 65 years, 2012

·		to	4
	4	to	8
›	8	to	12
›	12	to	16
›	16	plus	

How will political participation be expressed in forms other than voting?   ● 21   31

How will the opinions of all relevant social groups be included in urban and regional planning?   ● 28   44

How will it be possible to raise voter participation for underprivileged groups?   ● 15   17

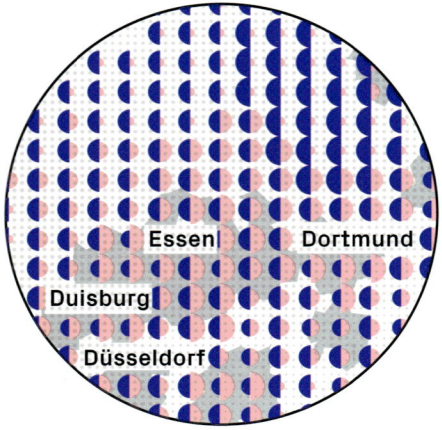

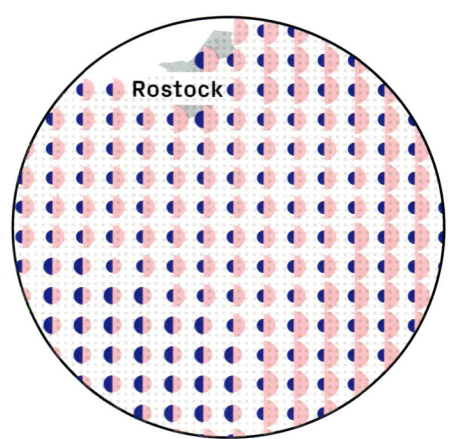

200% / ⌀100 km

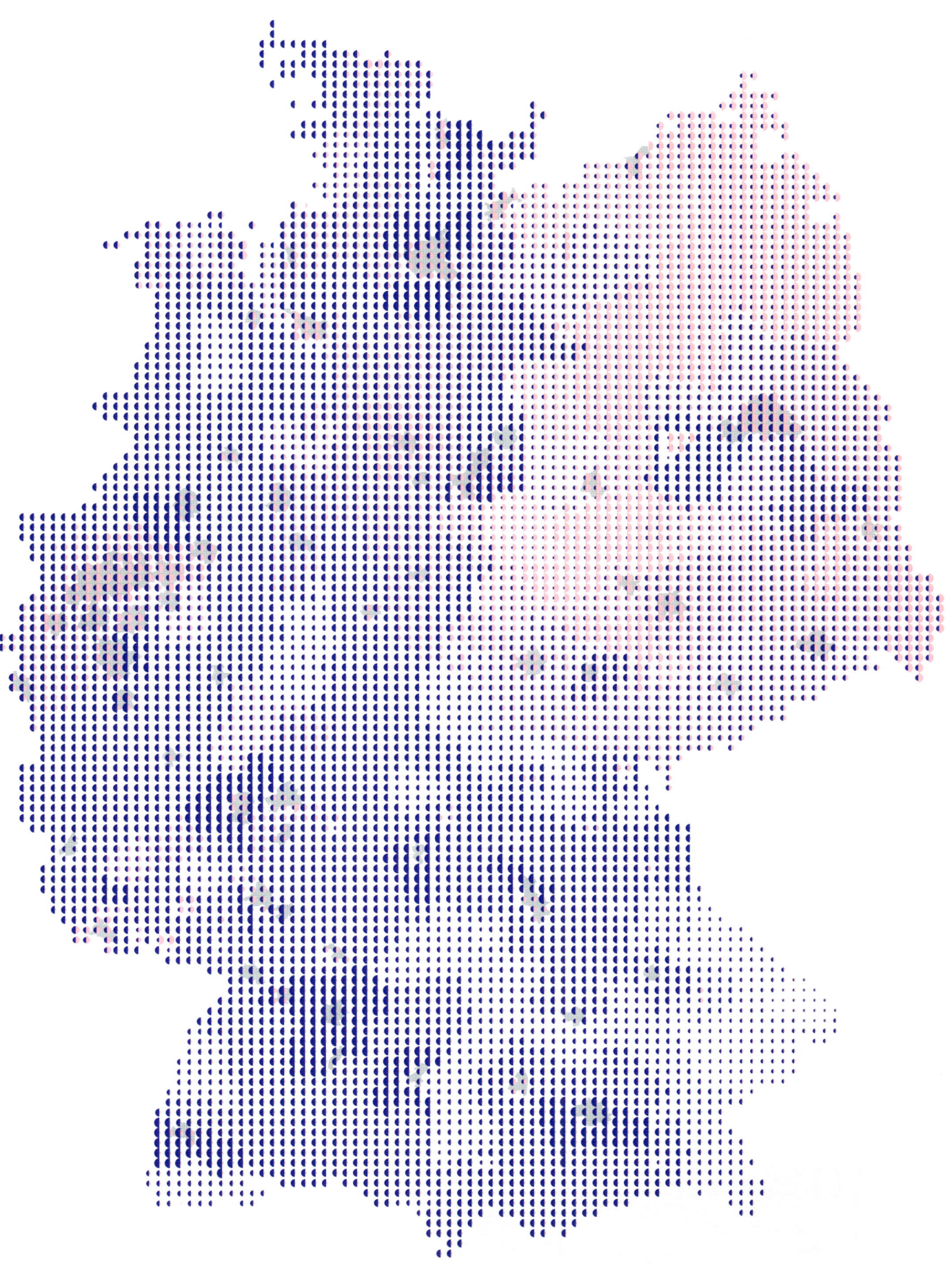

100 km

Births and Graduates with Academic Degrees

General birth statistics

Live births per 1,000 population, 2011

Graduates with academic degrees

Proportion of graduates with academic degrees, in percent

	to	6
6	to	7
7	to	8
8	to	9
9	to	10
10	plus	

	to	9.4
9.4	to	11.2
11.2	to	13
13	to	16.8
16.8	plus	

Will academic education households have the highest birthrate in the future?   ● 24

Is increasing average birth-giving age an achievement of postmodern societies?   ● 231

Will children be born only in cities in the future?   ● 31

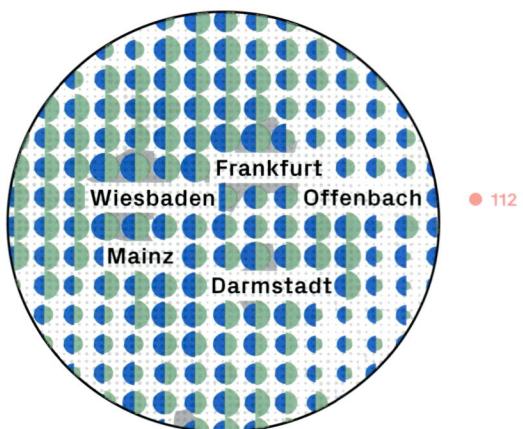

● 112

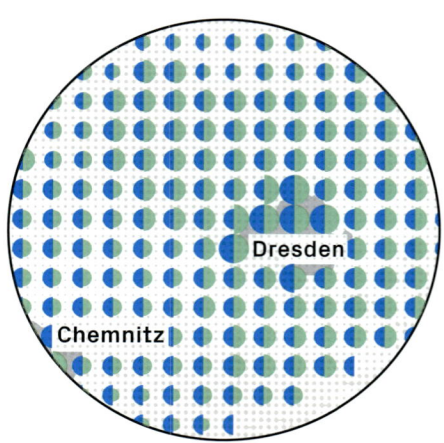

200% / ⌀ 100 km

100 km

Female Graduates with Academic Degrees and Fathers Taking Parental Leave

Paternity pay

Fathers who received paternity pay, per child born, in percent, 2012

	to	20
20	to	26
26	to	32
32	to	38
38	plus	

Female graduates with academic degrees

Proportion of female graduates with academic degrees, in percent, 2014

	to	6.3
6.3	to	7.7
7.7	to	9.6
9.6	to	12.2
12.2	plus	

What role models exist in cities and regions? ● 15
231

How different are the role models and what does this entail for family and home planning? ● 231

Will the new role models lead to women participating more in the working world? ● 24

Hamburg Metropolitan Region
● 117

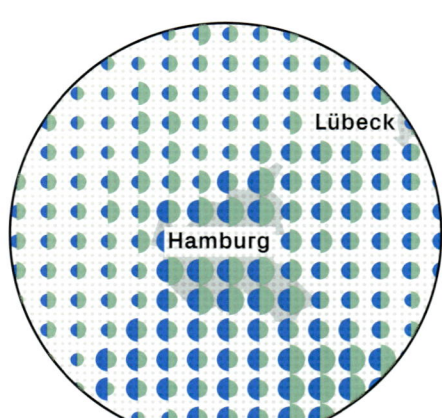

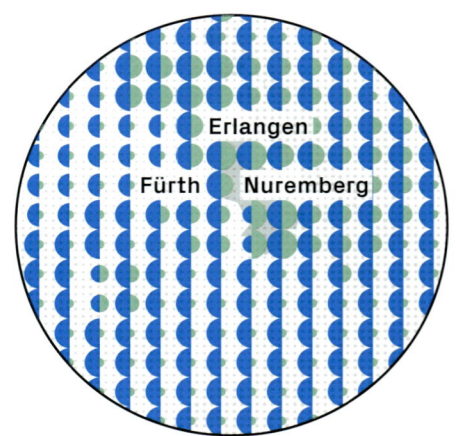

200% / ⌀100 km

100 km

Population with Migratory Background and Rents

Population with migratory background

Ratio of population with migratory background, in percent, 2011

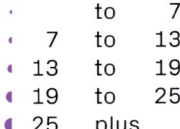

	to	7
7	to	13
13	to	19
19	to	25
25	plus	

Rents for apartments

New rental and re-rental prices excl. running costs, in euro/m², 2014

	to	4.5
4.5	to	5
5	to	5.5
5.5	to	6
6	to	7
7	to	8
8	to	9
9	plus	

Which are the "arrival cities" among the cities and regions?   ● 19

How can cities and regions function as a social diving board without a communal housing market?   ● 18
20
41
232

Will the level of rents in eastern Germany approximate to those in western Germany as a result of high in-migration?

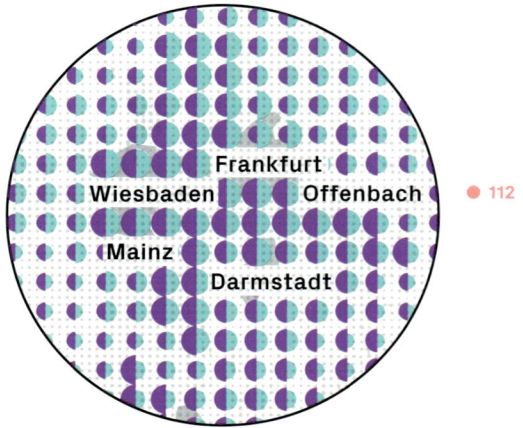

● 112

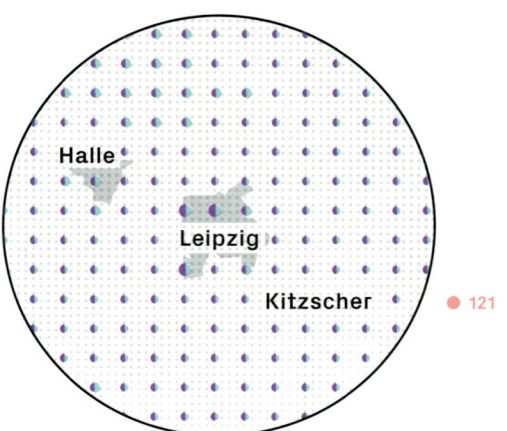

● 121

200% / ⌀ 100 km

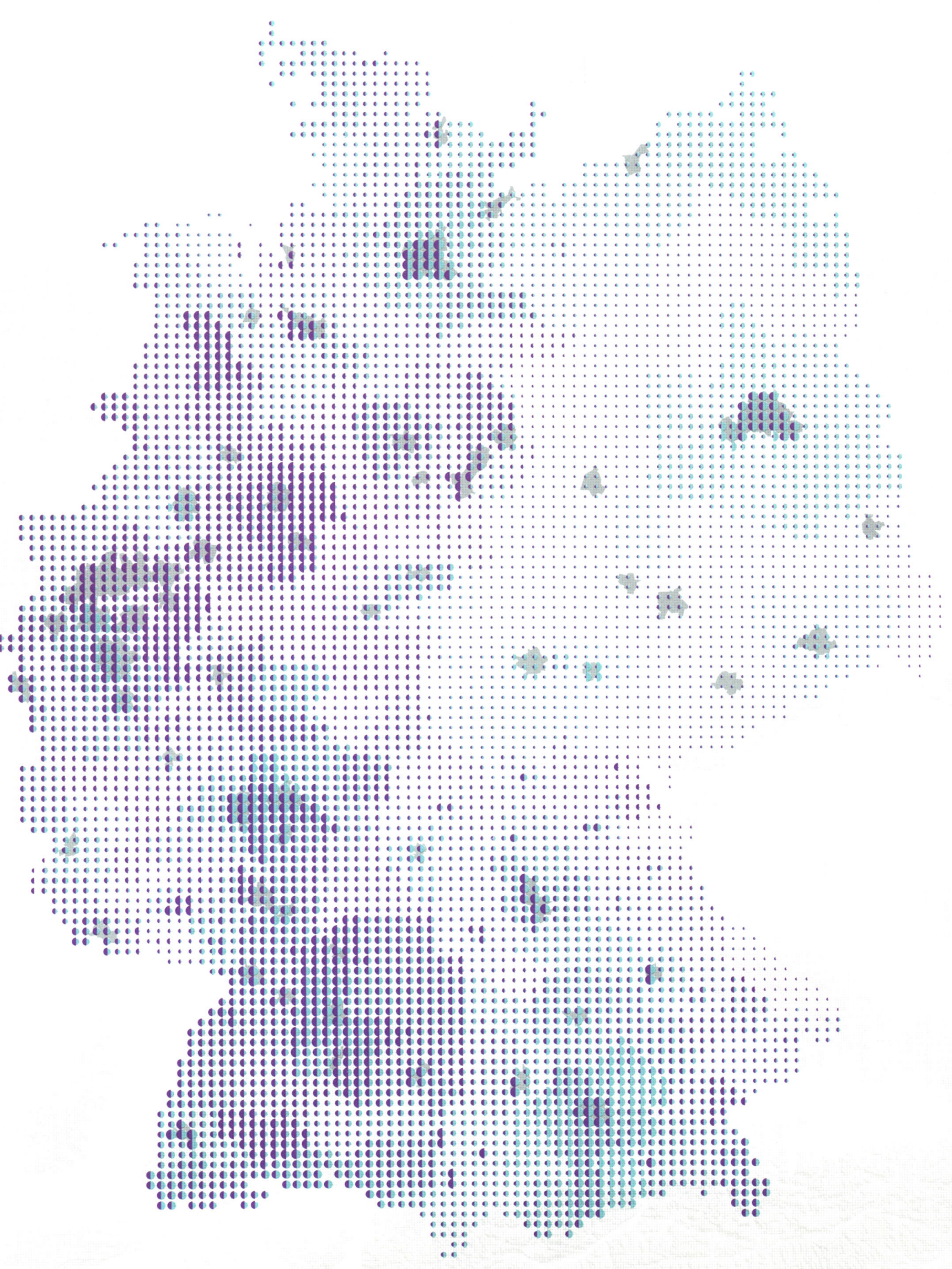

100 km

Youth Joblessness and
Employment of Older Persons

Youth joblessness

Jobless rate of 15- to 24-year-olds

**Employment
of older persons**

Persons 55 years and older,
employees liable to social
insurance, per 100 population, 2012

		Youth joblessness				Employment of older persons
	to	4.6			to	15
4.6	to	6.1		15	to	16
6.1	to	7.2		16	to	17
7.2	to	9.2		17	to	18
9.2	plus			18	plus	
No data						

In which regions will it be most difficult to find work in the
future?

● 19
27

How will the structural transformation to a digital society
change the geographic distribution of jobs in Germany?

● 26
259

Who may, must, or can work where?

● 15
22
24

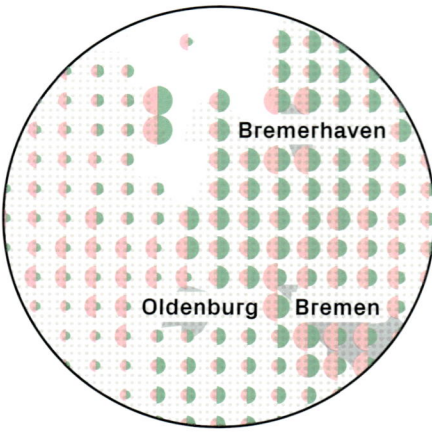

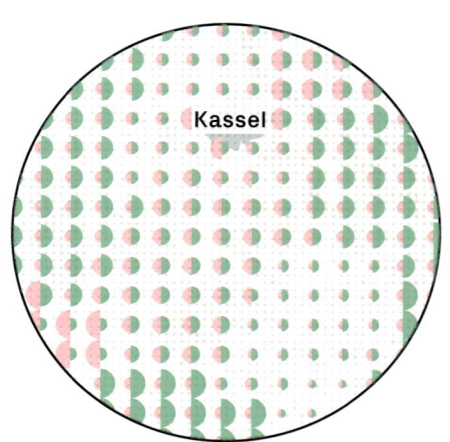

200%/ø100km

100 km

Young and Old People

Population ages 6 to 18

Ratio of 6- to 18-year-olds in population, in percent, 2012

	to	10
10	to	11
11	to	12
12	to	13
13	plus	

Pension-age household

Households whose head is 60 or older, per 100 households, 2010

	to	30
30	to	33
33	to	36
36	to	39
39	plus	

Where will different generations continue to live together? • 229

Will western Germany remain young and eastern Germany old? • 32
231

Will the high-birthrate generations, the baby boomers, give rise to a new geographic distribution when they reach retirement age? • 19
30

Fichtelgebirge

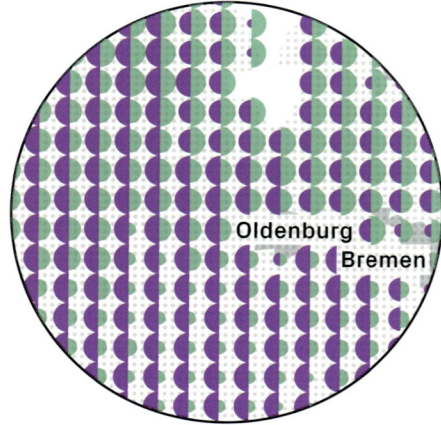

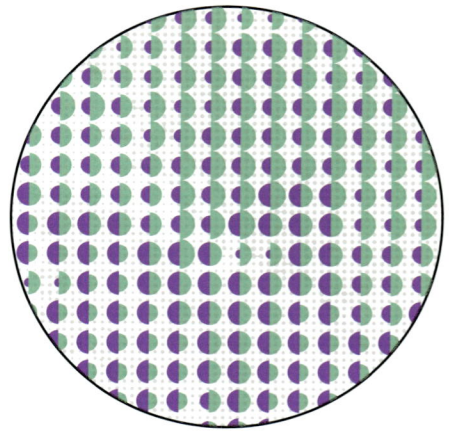

200 % / ⌀ 100 km

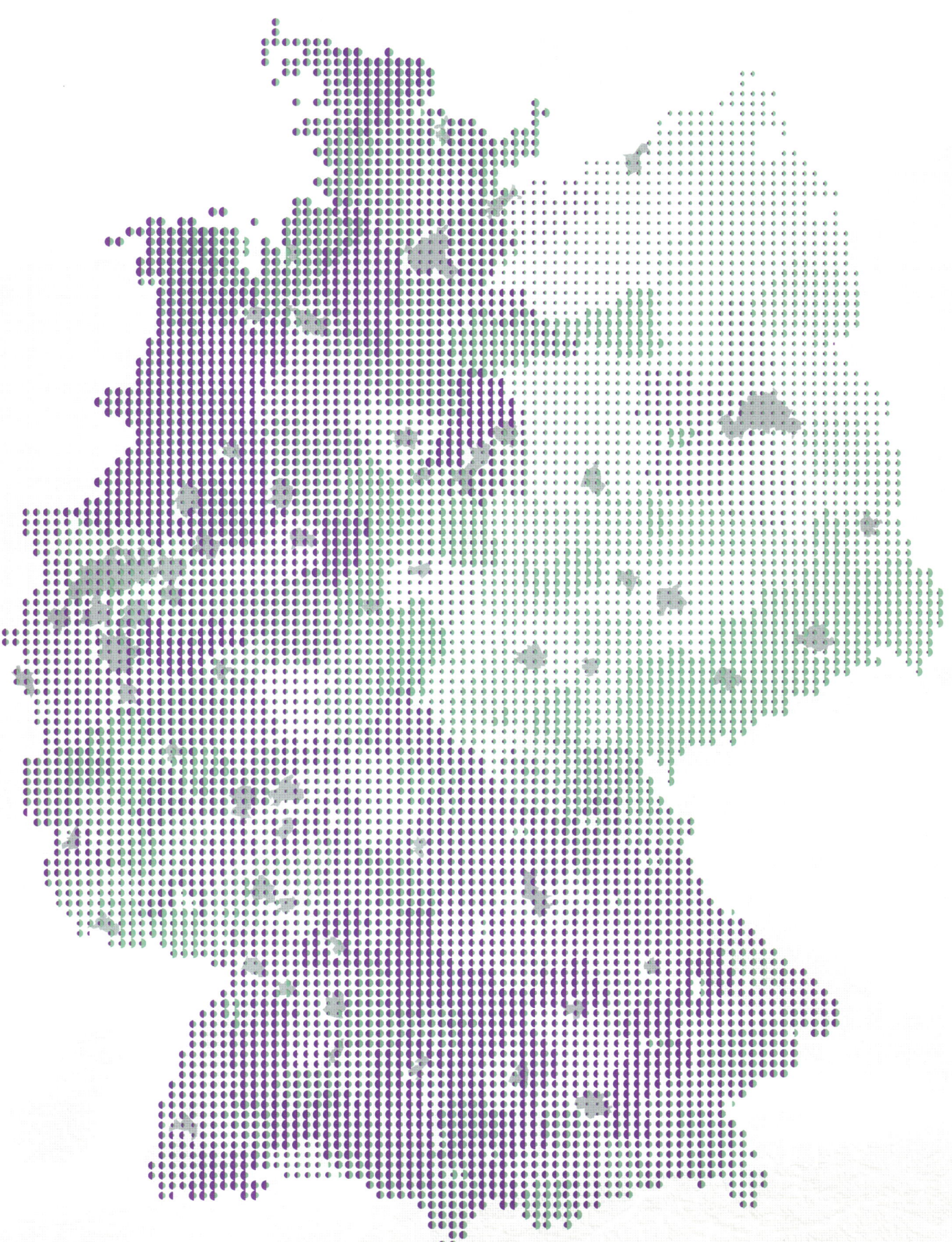

100 km

Community Debts and Hartz IV

Community debts

In euros per inhabitant, 2012

	to	500
500	to	1,000
1,000	to	1,500
1,500	to	2,500
2,500	plus	

City states

Hartz IV

Quota of employable and non-employable receiving money from Social Insurance Code II (SGB II) per 100 population under 65 years, 2012

	to	4
4	to	8
8	to	12
12	to	16
16	plus	

How will left-behind, debt-burdened cities and communities continue to secure social integration?

● 20
229

How will planners react to the social challenges in densely populated areas?

● 24
44
264

Can cities afford sufficient financial investments in the future, especially in education, infrastructure, and social cohesion?

● 17
26
230

Saale-Orla-Kreis
● 129

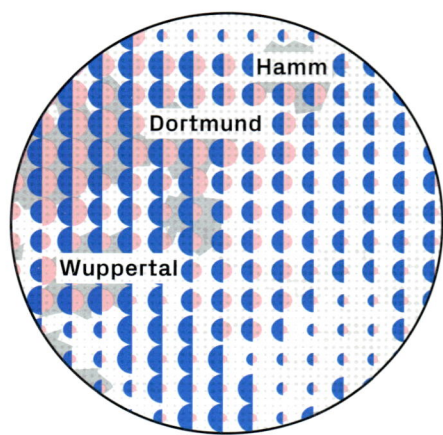

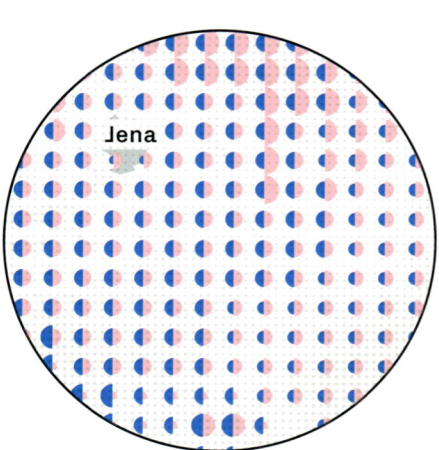

200% / ⌀100 km

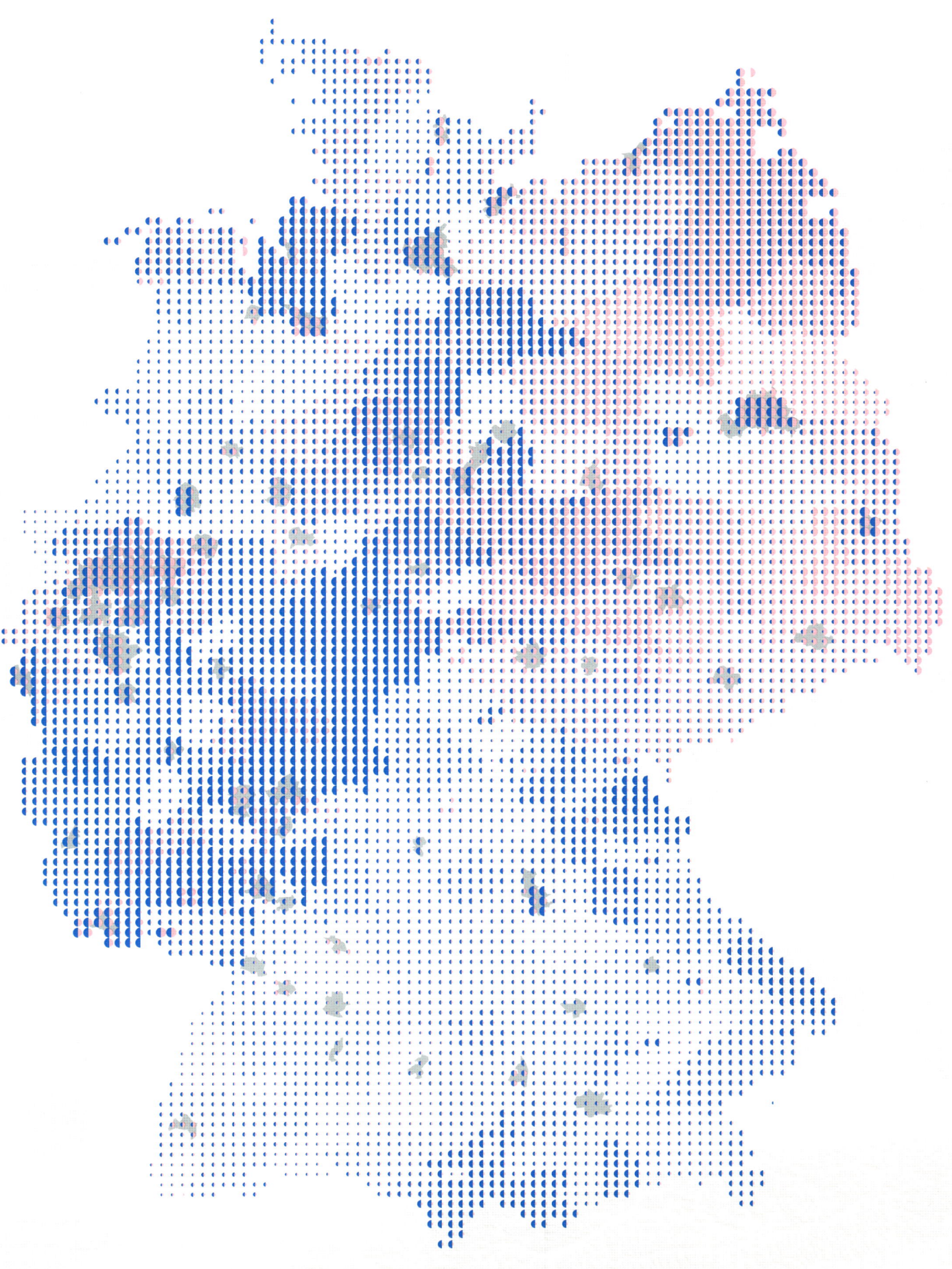

100 km

Specu-
lations

How might Germany change between now and the year
2050? The speculations presented here are the product of
the Zukunftswerkstätten/Workshops conducted with
interdisciplinary participants. On the basis of the preceding
analysis, they run through three widely diverging paths of
development up to the year 2050. The possible spatial and
geographic effects of the three scenarios are then localized
and applied to six specific cities or regions.

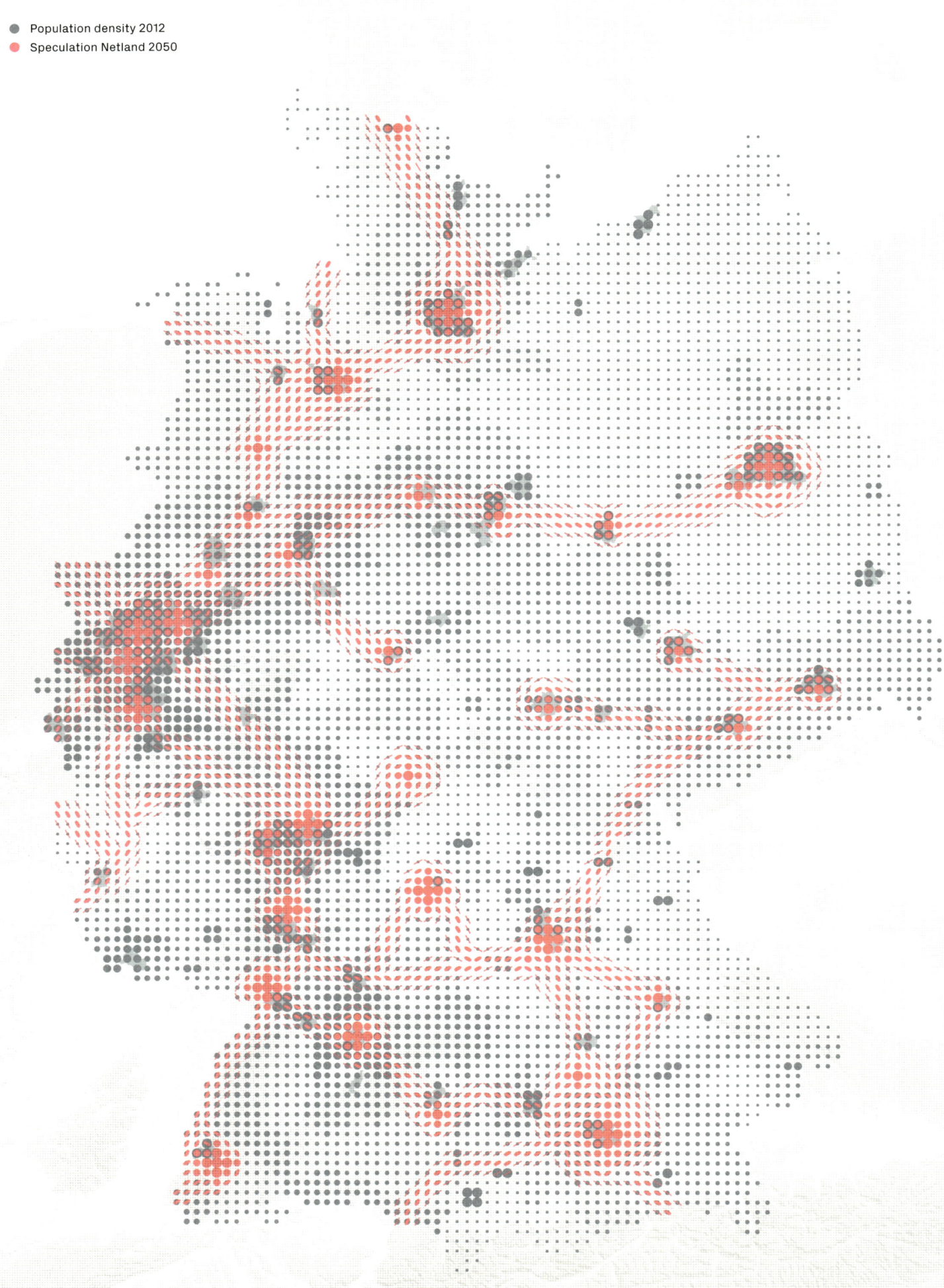

Population density 2012
Speculation Netland 2050

100 km

Netland

Germany today, in the year 2050, is a nation that exports energy, raw materials, foodstuffs, and water. With the revenue from these resources the country can ensure the bulk of its population, which has shrunk to sixty-five million and is overaged, a secure life. A small number of large enterprises that control the transport and energy infrastructure networks have promoted the construction of new workplaces, residences, and dormitory estates between the big cities, and with them a new superstructure within which practically the entire population lives. The superstructure connects major and medium-size cities, and, alongside the energy and water supplies, it controls communication, trade, and transport. Private and goods transport is effected exclusively by driverless transport capsules. Rural regions and small towns not connected to the superstructure have been transformed into solar and windpark energy-landscapes, replaced by water-intensive agriculture and fish farms, flooded as energy reservoirs, or they have been abandoned. There are exceptions though: in recent years increasing numbers of the few young and their children have formed minimal communities outside of the superstructure and its support-clusters to experiment with various models of opting out.

● 52

● 262

● 209

● 232

In Germany today a small number of large enterprises determine how and where the population lives and works, simply because it is they who administer, channel, and extend the transport and energy infrastructure networks. Given the worldwide shortage of resources and, consequently, their huge economic importance, political control of local energy and raw materials production has been centralized. An experiment was once conducted. A system of pipes was set up and an ant population placed in it at maximum distance from the only food source, to investigate their swarm intelligence in finding, communicating with each other, coordinating, and transporting food. But instead of developing complex patterns of movement as expected, the ants migrated en masse to the food source. The entire population sat motionless in the nutriment and seemed happy. The situation in Germany today is comparable. The causes lie in the recent past. Crises of political leadership in Europe, fundamental global-economic insecurity, and sky-rocketing energy costs have led to massive internal migration while immigration has pretty much come to a halt. Despite global crises, nationalistic sentiment combined with a rhetoric of deterrence repels foreign immigrants, and borders are heavily secured to protect resources. Within Germany, the rural and small-town populations have moved into the spaces on the infrastructural axes between the larger cities to form the basis of what is today's superstructure.

The welfare-state public services withdrew from the sparsely populated areas even more rapidly than their populations did. Over the years this has forced those remaining to likewise migrate, some destitute, to cities and in-between cities, leaving behind their now worthless real estate in an infrastructural nowhere. The big energy and resource providers created reception areas for these migrants—narrow quarters from which the new arrivals, like refugees in years gone

72 ●

76 ●

by, passively witnessed the swift restructuring of the country. Today's dense infrastructural network where high-income strata and the socially disengaged coexist with almost no contact, though linked by the superstructure, is a result of this developmental dynamic. Within this sociocultural fragmentation a variety of networks has developed. The higher-income strata, whose wealth derives almost exclusively from holdings in energy and raw materials enterprises, profit both from the density and the networks. Rapid, intelligent transport, energy, and communication structures facilitate intensive interchange and movement within Germany and beyond its borders. The driverless transport capsules have been put at the public's disposal by the big corporations for whom they are primarily a decentralized way to temporarily store energy, taking advantage of power surpluses when they occur.

New forms of work and living have emerged, especially in the areas between regional alliances like the Heidelberg-Karlsruhe science corridor, specializing in the development of energy storage and transport infrastructures, or the Munich-Augsburg economic corridor, with a monopoly over almost the entire production of driverless vehicles. These infrastructure-oriented developments are also developing in emerging value-creation zones such as the Leipzig-Dresden raw materials corridor, devoted to the managing of anthropogenic waste sites and the local mining of precious raw materials—rare earths, but also lignite—that has recently been resumed. In weaker infrastructural corridors such as Hannover-Kassel, Berlin-Leipzig, and Saarbrücken-Mannheim, islands of poverty have developed—a kind of parallel society providing for itself with small-scale, local food cultivation, erecting its dwellings in uninhabited niches in the superstructure, and tapping the energy and water supplies.

Given the worldwide shortage of resources, local energy and raw-materials production is of central economic and political importance. Water energy reservoirs and the infrastructural results of the early twenty-first-century campaign for the population of eighty million to transform energy production and storage—known in its time as the "energy revolution"—have put Germany in the comfortable position of being an energy-autarchic net exporter of sustainably produced electricity. Although the dismantling of the old energy system severely strained tax revenue at times and made energy a luxury good for many, the transitional years of austerity are now paying off for the vastly reduced population. The driving force behind this development was the big energy corporations and electricity providers who exercise oligarchic control over today's energy markets. To cope with additional power volumes in recent years, the energy corporations have been operating big energy-storage water reservoirs in deserted and peripheral parts of the country. This includes the once densely populous Ruhr region. Created by extensive flooding of the Emscher, this lakeland is now one of Europe's largest and most important reservoirs, though it meant flooding the entire northerly part of the Ruhr area and compulsorily relocating the area's remaining inhabitants.

Because Germany, compared with other parts of the world, has been only slightly affected by unchecked climate change—though the summer months have become perceptibly hotter and there has been no significant snowfall in Germany for years—as a nation rich in rain and groundwater, it can export water, a raw material that has become increasingly valuable on a global scale. Only Germany completed the transition to renewables in time, while other countries have practically depleted their fossil resources, and the two-degree limit has nearly been exceeded. The conversion of an old oil pipeline linking Germany and the Middle East, which has been badly hit by the climatic disruptions, generates additional revenue. Moreover, various types of food production have profited from the plentiful supply of water. Hence, while the world's oceans are being increasingly drastically overfished, Germany has become an important fish-farming area. In agriculture, water-intensive cultivation of vegetables such as tomatoes and cucumbers has enabled formerly heavily subsidized produce to become competitive again on the world market.

In addition to this efficiency-driven combination of urban superstructure and rural production regions, there are still residual areas where experiments in alternative living are under way. Here and there, in depopulated districts, dropout communities are struggling to establish themselves outside the superstructure and its energy and economic networks. Villages can be purchased at a nominal price in many places for the founding of autarchic communities of like-minded individuals. At the start of the century, only a few people dropped out to establish organic villages in Brandenburg and Mecklenburg-Vorpommern. Now increasing numbers of—particularly young—people are opting for de-networked modes of existence between fish farming, agriculture, and man-made lakes in areas untouched by the superstructure.

● 232

255 ●

● 203

● 64

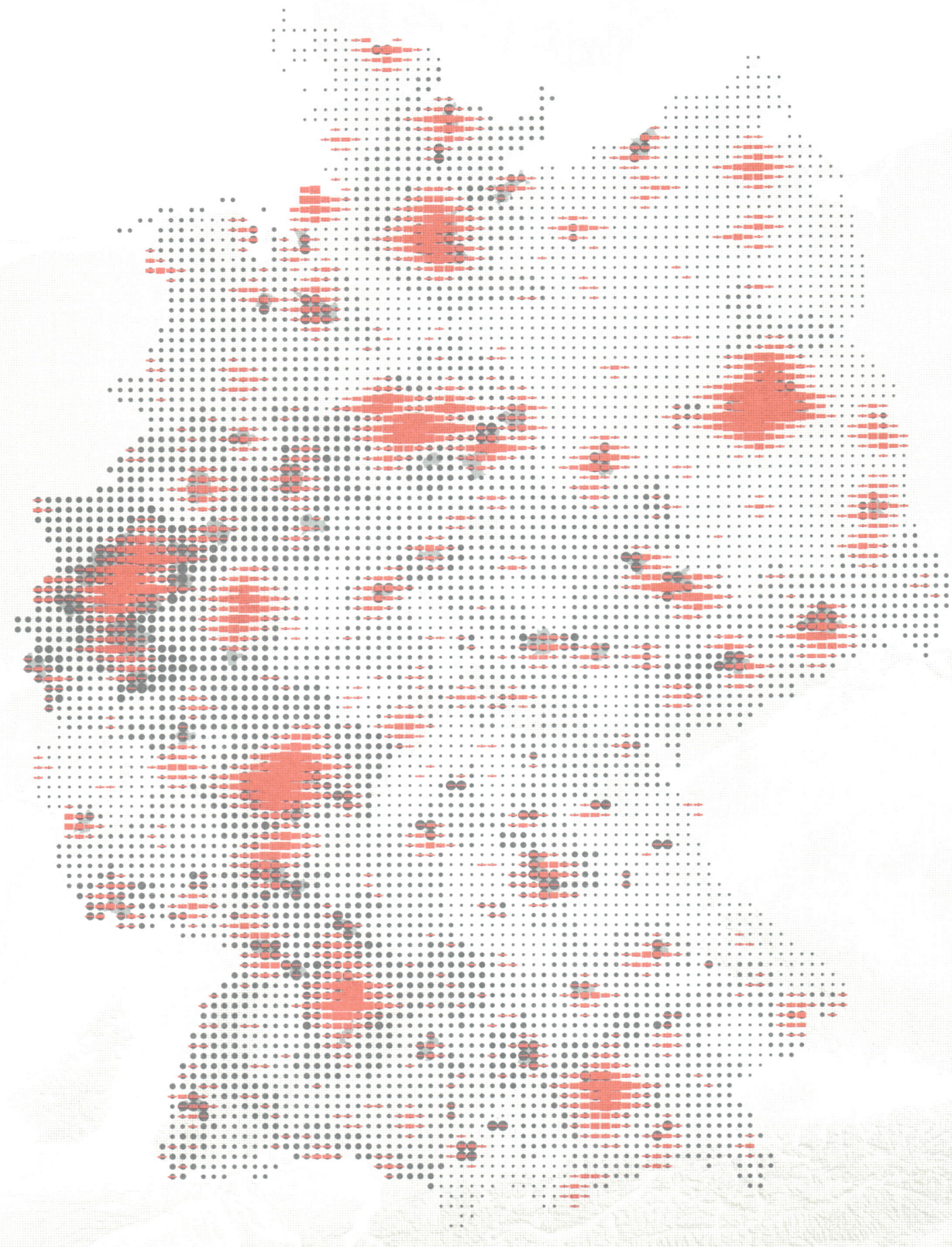

Population density 2012
Speculation Integralland 2050

100 km

Integralland

Germany today, in the year 2050, is a communitarian, organic country of immigration offering the bulk of its population access to top-quality educational options in a stable democracy characterized by civic commitment. The country's federal structure has been trimmed to five administrative units—north, east, central, west, and south Germany—that have become regionally specialized: east Germany is the site of international institutions and educational facilities primarily oriented toward eastern Europe and Asia; central Germany is a high-tech production location; west Germany is a stronghold of environmental technology in high international demand; south Germany is a knowledge-based service economy; and north Germany is a progressively organic agricultural and energy region. Almost the entire population of sixty-five million lives in cities. Thanks to economic-sector management planning and migration restrictions in densely populated metropolitan regions, as well as positive attitudes to foreigners, migration has not centered on a few big cities but has promoted the spread of smaller cities across Germany. The cities of Germany today are compact and have attractive urban centers and local flair. Urban sprawl has been largely checked: peripheral commuter estates are edged by organic belts and nature zones; green buffer and local recreation areas border on depopulated landscapes now used as farms for the production of renewable energy and foodstuffs. Attacks on urban participation centers and minor acts of sabotage against energy facilities are on the increase of late. And occasional protesters are sometimes seen in urban parks being discreetly led away by the police.

● 29

● 22

Germany still seems to be high on the list of potential destinations for qualified, well-funded, internationally sought-after migrants. More people are arriving each year. Are things in other countries really so bad for them? Or are prospects in Germany just too attractive? Or is Germany a collecting point for global decelerators—those who are no longer interested in big cities and anonymity? For whatever reason, a vibrant culture of participation aimed at reinforcing community has evolved, supported among other things by the population's general high level of education. Solidarity centers on a joint set of values around the question: How do we want to, or must we, live together in highly populated urban space? The explicitly urban ideals of education and communication provide a basic social consensus and are the backbone of the community. While the prevailing culture of welcome looks on new arrivals and migrants as assets for society and strives to integrate them as efficiently as possible, foreign lifestyles and ideals meet with no real understanding—assimilation, rather than integration, is the goal.

Germany's economic success is founded on knowledge-intensive service industries, modern skilled crafts and trades, and on broad sections of the middle class

● 70

230 ●

● 237

in state-aided and state-organized clusters of excellence at universities and production sites in nearly all cities. Under an agenda of enhanced living quality, the five administrative units have developed models to promote developmental capability between the units and their cities: east Germany is the site of international institutions and educational facilities primarily oriented toward eastern Europe and Asia; central Germany is a successful high-tech production location; west Germany is a developer of internationally sought-after environmental technology; south Germany is a knowledge-based service economy; and north Germany is an organic agricultural and energy region. Through goal-directed investment in education, particularly where educational and hence economic opportunities were formerly below par, citizens have acquired a capacity for active social participation. This has proved possible because local characteristics have been demanded and promoted at social, economic, and political levels. Established, valued German quality concepts, such as the country's middle-class orientation and social mobility, are recuperating again today: regional foci of the new values—often reflected in the conversion and transformation of religious and otherwise once representative buildings—are springing up all over the country, from self-organized educational facilities and local energy-supply concepts to cross-generational residential projects and socio-ecological entrepreneurship.

Advances in energy efficiency, in recycling management and renewable energies—resulting from the research and activities of interregional cooperations between north Germany and south Jutland, for instance, between south Germany and Tirol, west Germany and Gelderland—have given rise to a pragmatic approach to resources. The growing readiness to cooperate and develop tighter networks, generally and in detail, between states and cities, cities and surroundings, is leading to the realization of trans-European models of cooperation—for instance for the storage and distribution of green energy. The intensive exchange of energy between cities and surrounding regions has made the latter integral components in local resource-consumption cycles; their small populations profit not only from highly popular local organic agriculture, but also from jobs created by windparks and solar farms. Neighborhoods and the local have emerged as the key developmental aspect in Germany. Nearness is not only a feature of the country's residential and living areas but of its economic regions as well. Long-term planning and decision-making determine the recycling-economy mentality that society favors. Primarily socially useful projects that create lasting social stability are being promoted in urban development. Small trades and utility providers come together in all these areas. Big shopping centers with extensive parking facilities have yielded to the revitalization of decentralized, local retail trade. The connecting elements today are not cars and streets but networks, communication, and interrelations among business, city, and people.

Clearly-formulated models of urban development inform specific areas of value, business clusters, and cultures of planning and building, living and dwelling. Parallel to large-scale immigration, Germany is experiencing a wave of re-regionalization—a return to the local. Cities are promoting historical awareness with the concept of "life quality" at its core. The new-old models are Göttingen, Münster, Tübingen, Heidelberg. Leipzig and Jena are once again drawing on local traditions and have gained enormously in flair as a result; Düsseldorf, early on, was one of the first cities to reinvent itself as a "zero carbon city" and has become a pioneer in economic and ecological structural change. With broad-based sustainability strategies, Aachen, Dresden, and Freiburg have established themselves as attractive cities for technophile green milieus. Bonn, on the other hand, has pursued a policy of downsizing, deflecting regional expansion onto Sauerland, Bergisches Land, and Westerwald. The innovative Ruhr area shows that industrial landscapes can be effectively urban and rural at the same time. The city of Kassel has carved itself new niches: in addition to documenta 21, due to take place in 2052, there are urban farms specializing in apple cultivation, server farms, and international climate refugee reservations. Free neighborhood networks have developed in city districts, organizing their own autonomous citizen parliaments. People refer to themselves as hailing not from Cologne but from Kalk, not from Hamburg but from Blankenese; dynamic, harmonious relations are cultivated between neighboring districts, communities, and cities. Isolated resistance to such developments is met with—protests that cities are being turned into villages. The metropolitan, urban idea, it is said, is being expelled from Germany. These protesters are not wholly wrong—anyone looking for free, unorganized space, big-city anonymity, or counterculture will have a hard time finding them in Germany today.

212 ●

● 251

206 ●

238 ●

● 52
255

● Population density 2012
■ Speculation Wattland 2050

100 km

Wattland

Germany in the year 2050 is a service economy and knowledge society with high energy requirements. A second—digital—environment has extended across the land and determines the actions of its sixty-five million inhabitants. Knowledge is global and freely available in databases; algorithms are power; large industries are on the decline and are being replaced by decentralized, arbitrarily adjustable automatic modes of production. The primarily digital educational options and a state-organized health system encourage constant immigration to Germany, especially from the global crisis areas of the earth. Society's core driving force is no longer the euro but the watt—energy, a permanently scarce good. Hence the watt economy dictates geographical developments: a large part of the country's population has migrated to the heavily populated metropolises to benefit from the energy-optimized conditions of homes and workplaces. Only the watt-wealthy can afford to leave the densely populated cities and withdraw to energy-autonomous rural enclaves. They leave the cities to the lower and middle classes, the new arrivals, and to the global experimenters passing through who want to earn a few quick watts.

● 263

● 254

● 204

Germany is a country with a small number of densely populated metropolitan regions: Berlin, Hamburg, the Ruhr area, Frankfurt, Cologne, and Munich are the centers of the service economy and knowledge society. The influx of inhabitants to the cities has not only occurred from rural areas but also from the unstable countries of the world, because Germany can promise new arrivals a properly functioning health system, favorable climatic conditions, and a high-quality educational system of world renown. Even if a full-blown culture of welcome is lacking, a society along international lines has developed, where the fittest prevail and succeed from generation to generation. Ethnic and language barriers no longer play a role. The few concentrated metropolitan regions are the result of practical energy constraints: energy is so expensive that there has been no alternative but to focus more strongly on energy efficiency, recycling economics, and profitability. Decentralized energy production and the extension of power-transmission infrastructures are important political areas of development, because fossil energy sources are finally being depleted and renewables have been unable to replace them completely.

Consequently, new energy-optimized living space, urban agricultural technology, energy-efficient transport systems, and intra-city energy production facilities are springing up in the metropolitan regions.

The new upper class—educated, networked, and withdrawn—consists of a digital elite whose wealth is measurable in terms of their bank balance in watts. A large part of this class lives in areas that are both geographically and socially isolated, where many produce the energy required for their efficient lifestyle themselves, gainfully feeding surpluses into the state energy systems. A small number live on the edges of the metropolitan regions. These few have succeeded in preserving their material wealth in cities such as Ingolstadt, or the peripheral greenbelts of Stuttgart and Munich, despite the radical transformations occurring in the wake of the energy shortage. In recent decades, they have settled, becoming digitally networked in primarily nonurban open spaces. These programmers of their own lives no longer need face-to-face communication. Some people say there is a danger of an energy-defined feudal structure, where quantity of watts guarantees power and influence, progressively eroding democratic

251 ●

256 ●

culture. The political system is increasingly organized via virtual voting processes; participation in reaching decisions, however, is watt-intensive, so that a person's political influence can be read from their watt account: no watt, no vote.

● 259

The digitization and technologization of daily life encourage a trend toward singularization and erosion of community. The lack of direct personal interaction leads to individual isolation, and there are fears of a loss of social cohesion in the metropolitan regions in the long term. But although communication and work have been virtualized to a high degree, most people are still dependent on the physically dense cities and their urban infrastructure. Cities have become the sole viable habitat for watt-poor life, unless one wants to drop out of society altogether. Given this situation, particularly in the sphere of transport, watt-efficient concepts of joint and individual utilization—from tandem bikes and rowboats to lightweight solar cars—have become more attractive and define today's supraregional transport system. Urban mobility is largely accomplished on foot or by bike. The popularity of residential areas and neighborhoods is proportionate to their density of population and hence energy efficiency.

● 260

● 213

The high cost of raw materials due to their unfavorable energy balance has led to mass production being almost completely abandoned. Consumers are simultaneously producers now, manufacturing the products they require with the aid of freely accessible blueprints and decentralized 3-D printing systems optimized with regard to watt-consumption and materials. These two technological achievements, combined with a liberal business ethic, have put Germany at the top of the worldwide health-system ranking: medical technicians can replicate body parts at low watt-cost. A year ago, an aggregate of tiny laboratories announced decisive breakthroughs in the production of organic structures, making it possible to grow energy-optimized housing elements in water-rich areas. Foods that are expensive on the world market because of their high energy balance are produced locally at urban peripheries.

Local Speculations

● Population density 2012

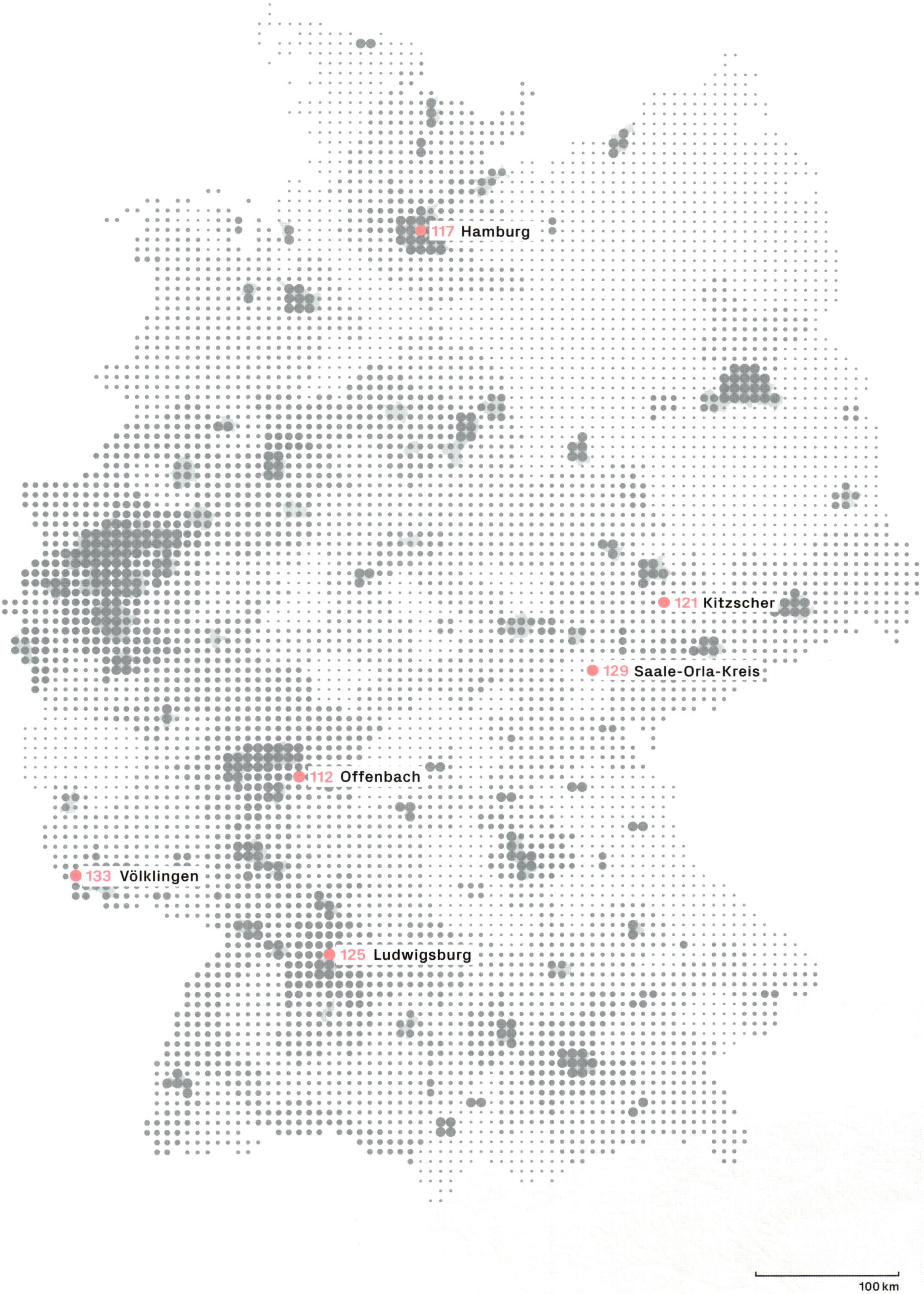

● 117 Hamburg

● 121 Kitzscher

● 129 Saale-Orla-Kreis

● 112 Offenbach

● 133 Völklingen

● 125 Ludwigsburg

100 km

Local Speculations Offenbach

Status quo

Area
44.9 km²

Population
119,203

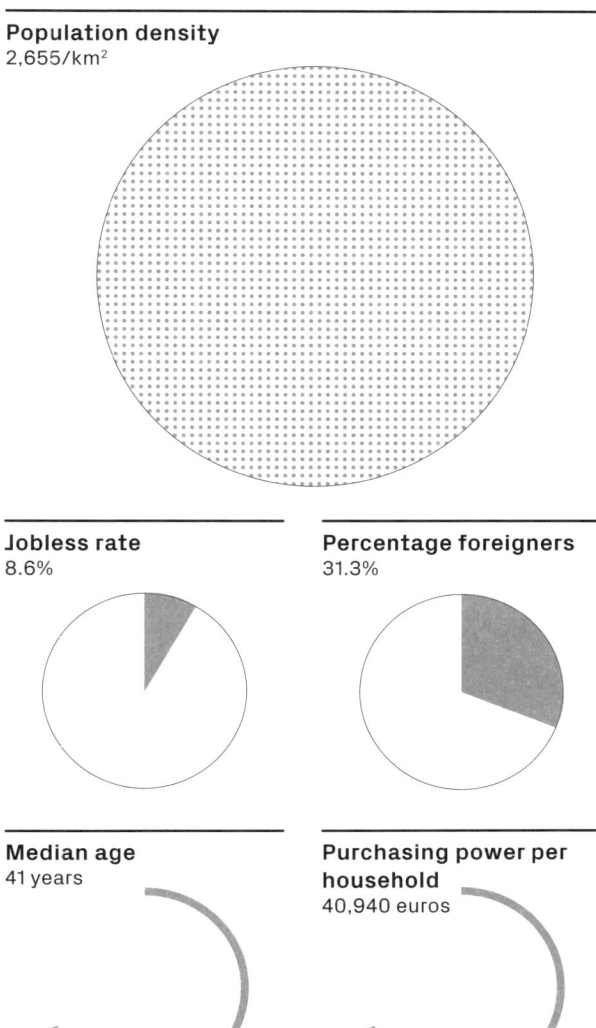

Population density
2,655/km²

Jobless rate
8.6%

Percentage foreigners
31.3%

Median age
41 years

Purchasing power per household
40,940 euros

Figure-ground map Offenbach

The urban municipality of Offenbach borders on Frankfurt/Main to the southeast; it has a population of 120,000 (2011) and is the fifth largest city in Hesse. Offenbach, Frankfurt/Main, Wiesbaden, Mainz, and Darmstadt constitute a metropolitan region. The city of Offenbach benefits from its favorable geographical situation within this structure, lying south and east of the Main, directly opposite a number of Frankfurt city districts. Frankfurt/Main airport, the third largest European passenger airport and largest freight handler by volume, is nearby. Both the Frankfurt highway interchange and Frankfurt rail station are among the busiest in Germany.

Offenbach has a long history of leather production. Today, with around 3,000 companies, it is one of the major design centers in Germany. In the context of the Rhine-Main region, its concentration of creative-sector employees liable to social insurance is above-average. The relevant firms deal in architecture, typography, film/animation, graphics/web design, industrial and automobile design. The Hochschule für Gestaltung Offenbach is the institutional linchpin for this business cluster. Despite the dense spread of these businesses, population growth has been negative since the mid-1990s.

Offenbach is a seismograph for urban social developments in the fields of integration and in-migration. The challenges accompanying this role are great because, partly as a result of its central location, the city is a stopping-off point for large numbers of migrants looking for work. Particularly in the inner-city districts of Offenbach, the high pressure on living space is reflected in extremely short tenancy periods. At around 36 percent (2014), the proportion of foreign inhabitants is above average. The proportion of inhabitants with a background of migration is higher still:

58 percent (2014). Offenbach is thus the first German city to have a majority population with a migratory background. This sofar unique shift in the Federal Republic of Germany makes Offenbach a major reference point in the developing debate on integration and inclusion.

Netland

Offenbach has established itself as a city relief zone in the immediate catchment area of Frankfurt/Main's major airport in the Rhine-Main urban agglomeration. The airport is a thriving hub of international logistics and passenger traffic. The population has remained constant, bolstered by continuing in-migration. Administratively a part of Frankfurt, Offenbach is a central superstructure gathering and transit point for foreigners. Novel transit-dwellings and workplaces make the city an attractive location for the network operators' highly mobile labor force. In work and project spaces provided by the big corporations, workers passing through within the superstructure come together briefly in flexible miniature modules. Offenbach, in its capacity as "transit city," has succeeded in expanding its educational options. Immigrants in transit prepare for their future work assignments with the big energy and resource corporations in crash courses at training centers before being directed to different workplaces in the network. But effective integration of the foreign migrants is also posing unforeseen problems for Offenbach: relocated to new living and work environments in the Offenbach network by the big corporations, immigrants from the region's rural areas are experiencing difficulties orienting themselves in Offenbach's multicultural, open society.

● 18

Integralland

Long an insider tip among Frankfurt's creative professionals, Offenbach has continued to develop into an attractive location for the region's economically established middle class. For years now, it has ● 230 enjoyed a brisk influx of inhabitants from Germany's five administrative areas as well as international immigrants, and has established itself as an attractive place to live with its varied cultural (particularly culinary) offerings and a lively club and music scene. Businesses and hotels have settled here, making Offenbach a vibrant and dynamic transit city where people from all over the world gather for joint projects, congresses, and conferences. The city is not visually beautiful; yet it is inspiring to live in because, parallel to its economic growth, a high degree of international

cultural diversity is developing, which is reflected in the built environment. Offenbach, like Rotterdam, is famed for this far beyond its boundaries. With its experimental architectural structures ranging from temporary pavilions, converted parking garages, residential cooperatives with collective kitchens and common rooms to container high-rises, multi-story collective gardens, and interdenominational places of worship, it is obviously a city of new living and dwelling spaces. Several years ago it was designated an experimental area for creating forms of transit-city housing as short-term accommodation for the hordes of transnational migrants passing through. In the meantime, it has proved a good location for surprisingly up-to-date, not to say long-term, habitation, living, and working. Many who intended to stay only a short while have put down roots and are living out their different ideas of family, particularly in various forms of multigenerational cohabitation. Once viewed as problematic, the cultural diversity that the city has long represented has paved the way for a new urban society. Life in Offenbach today is not only cross-generational but also cross-cultural.

Wattland

Offenbach today is Germany's most prominent arrival city, a model for the efficient integration of new arrivals throughout the country. For years now, its favorable position within the Rhine-Main urban agglomeration has brought the city a massive population influx because high mobility is possible here at comparatively low watt-expense. The privatized transport system is jointly operated by an association of regional employers and is chiefly used for the efficient transport of workers and goods. The city's population is one of Germany's

densest, to the benefit of its inhabitants—per capita energy consumption falls in proportion to diminishing per capita living space. Hence, Offenbach becomes more energy efficient with each new inhabitant and—watt be praised—more and more affordable.

Concern for the social stability of Offenbach ran high when one of the region's big employers, Frankfurt airport, had to be shut down. High energy costs had rendered the entire air industry, goods traffic in particular, uneconomical. While the Rhine-Main region has still not come to terms with the collapse of the air traffic and logistics trade, Offenbach, in spite, or perhaps precisely because, of its more peripheral social and economic endowments in the shadow of Frankfurt, quickly managed to reorganize its local economic structures. Not only the city's geographical situation proved favorable here but above all its socially and culturally heterogeneous population's ability to adapt swiftly to the new realities. Offenbach's economy

● 227

● 230

● 211

today is based on staff-intensive, low-energy, service-sector businesses, where people are taking over activities that could only be performed by machines at high watt-expense. The city pursues a policy of transparency, making all possible information about its inhabitants available on its servers so that businesses can feed in and efficiently allocate work assignments on the basis of inhabitants' availability, location, skills, and health. However, these positive economic developments do not rule out polarization and segregation within the city: with its many old and new inhabitants from all over the globe, Offenbach is a regular site of disputes concerning the use of scarce accommodation space and especially of its now almost nonexistent public space. The city has set up a digital platform that not only regulates the allocation of living space upon registration and puts in-migrants on a digital file—it also decides where, when, how, and who can celebrate, picnic, demonstrate, or take a walk. Without prior application and permission, even for just sitting on a park bench, activities in public space are strictly forbidden.

● 263

● 234

Local Speculations
Hamburg Metropolitan Region

Status quo

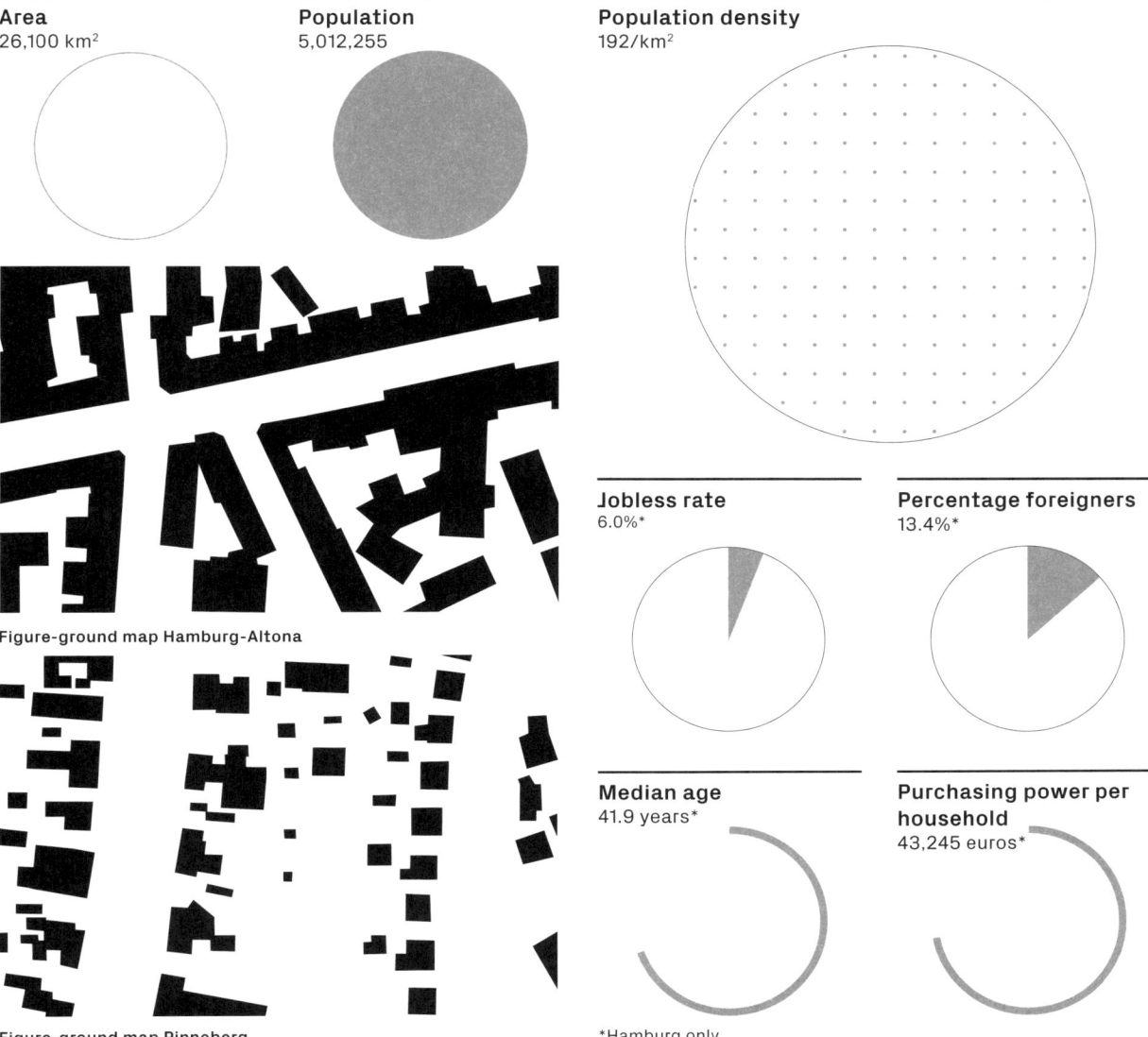

Area
26,100 km²

Population
5,012,255

Population density
192/km²

Figure-ground map Hamburg-Altona

Jobless rate
6.0%*

Percentage foreigners
13.4%*

Figure-ground map Pinneberg

Median age
41.9 years*

Purchasing power per household
43,245 euros*

*Hamburg only

The Hamburg Metropolitan Region is a political construct, a voluntary cooperation of the Free and Hanseatic City of Hamburg and the participating areas of the Federal States of Lower Saxony, Schleswig-Holstein, and Mecklenburg-West Pomerania. The Metropolitan Region is unique in the Federal Republic, being a city-state region situated on the territory of four Federal States. It covers an area of more than 26,102 square kilometers and supports a population of approximately five million (2013).

Economically, politically, and administratively the city-state of Hamburg exerts a shaping influence on this regional structure, both internally as well as beyond the borders of the region. The structures of the Metropolitan Region consist in a complex interplay of decentralization and adaptability, diversity and complementarity. As is evident from inbound commuting patterns, Hamburg eclipses the economic significance of the region.

Current foci of activity in the Metropolitan Region are settlement development, local recreation and leisure, nature and landscape. These have been supplemented in recent years by topics such as cluster development, business, employment market, science, and research. The Metropolitan Region's primary future concern will be to develop its role as a deliberative and executive platform for regionally significant issues. This includes areas such as traffic and transport or the promotion of regional business and the employment market. The future role of the port of Hamburg is uncertain because competition from ports in Rotterdam, Wilhelmshaven, and developing eastern Mediterranean harbors is on the increase. Effective regional cooperation has so far been seriously impaired by administrative limitations—as for instance in competing claims for housing and industrial development, or in the strategic development of an offshore terminal for Hamburg.

Netland

The metropolitan region of Hamburg has become highly networked, not so much socially, however, as in terms of preexisting and new transport and traffic

infrastructures. The region is primarily defined by the links in its infrastructural corridors, and has become a linear city spread out along these networks. The population is concentrated along the main streets and the driverless transport capsules' stations. These heavily trafficked transit corridors have now outstripped Hamburg's Fuhlsbüttel airport. Anyone who wants to fly abroad, whether in Europe or internationally, catches the quick link to Amsterdam, Frankfurt/Main, or Copenhagen airports. Bremen, Lübeck, Lüneburg, and Elmshorn have continued developing into suburbs of Hamburg in this far-flung agglomeration. While they have strong links to the economic and cultural center, they are themselves little more than pleasant dormitories. The metropolitan region of Hamburg's economic basis has changed vastly. No longer are the port, the media, and trade of prime importance, but rather the finance industry (banks, insurance companies), innovation centers, and science parks.

The threats posed by rising sea level and increasingly extreme tidal amplitudes have induced Hamburg to build a tidal power station near Glückstadt. Not only has this reduced the danger of flooding, but it has also enabled high-quality living and working space to develop along the Elbe. The Elbe itself has become a heavily trafficked speedboat route. As the population is largely confined to Hamburg's surroundings and hinterlands, the empty spaces along the A1 freeway have been filled with wind turbine parks. Together with the tidal power station and the newly built center for recycling and upcycling in the sprawling former port area, these are an important energy-producing basis

for the metropolitan region. Large port areas are also used for processing and upgrading products and resources.

Integralland

The population of the metropolitan region of Hamburg has increased. This growth is due to the upgrading of towns and communities through the establishment of new science and cultural facilities with state intervention. From the present-day perspective, the principle of a center-oriented, inner-based logic of growth, to which the city of Hamburg long adhered, can be said to have failed. The city could no longer maintain its position of independence but had to espouse cooperation with the region. The result is a panorama of cooperative ventures—strategic alliances in the spheres of housing, business, transport, and culture—between city and surrounding communities. Hamburg and its suburbs are organized on the "grapevine principle": everyone tries to specialize in businesses or commercial sectors that promise future viability. The powerful growth throughout the region could only be contained with the aid of decentralized growth cores directed by the "Metropolitan Region Planning Committee." Development of the port of Hamburg was a further major factor boosting the trend to decentralization. Transformation of the port, and the economy connected with it, led to Hamburg's opening up to the region. The port today, a high-tech smart port employing a minimum of human labor, has been moved out into the region. The logistics industry profits enormously from this high-efficiency inland distributor.

251 ●

262 ●

● 255

Wattland

A large proportion of those living in Hamburg today have migrated here in recent decades from all over the world. While the first waves of immigration posed massive infrastructural problems for the city administration, the Hanseatic city's virtual, Internet presence has brought further migration under at least some control. Prospective newcomers must register on a platform and be checked: "made transparent." Each candidate must spend a few days in the city's virtual world to apply for an apartment and a provisional work profile in Hamburg's service and science economy. Having acquired a Hamburg permit, the candidate is free to move to the city; a chip implant feeds his continuously updated profile into the city's digital infrastructure and logs him in to the health and education systems. In addition to the (on energy grounds) necessary re-densification of living space, Hamburg's interest in a continuous, well-regulated influx of population is driven by its open-source education system, whose quality increases with each new citizen—newcomers 210 ● put all their know-how and qualifications at the disposal of the digital Hanseatic University, which not only instructs 150 million students worldwide but also runs small research labs in the metropolitan region. These labs develop and research efficiency strategies for producing, storing, and utilizing energy and for integrating all utility products into a maximum energy-saving recycling and production system.

Hamburg's heart—its port—has changed. Whereas merchandise from all over the globe was imported and shipped here in the past, today it is mainly a site where energy-intensive commodities are produced and integrated into the region's local goods and recycling cycles. Despite vociferous protest from Hamburg's citizens, large areas of the port were filled in to create space urgently needed for production, research, and housing. A production scene that has become economically important for Hamburg has established itself on 255 ● the grounds of a former shipping company. Here, popular production scripts and innovative, energy-saving hybrid materials for printed products are produced. At one of the port's last, still-functioning terminals, Germany's biggest 3-D printer producer has set up assembly lines for big equipment used primarily for producing the smaller printer models. From here the firm's product (one of the few that still justify the expense of such energy-intensive logistics) is shipped ● 258 to all parts of the globe. On the water-rich soils of other

parts of the port, organic structures (now five stories high) have been planted. These growing edifices are already overoccupied: their roofs boast tent cities and informal solar collector and rainwater-treatment facilities, indicating both the need and the will to live together energy efficiently in a minimum of space. Because of the high running costs of elevators, pumps, and heating systems, high-rise living is an exception reserved to Hamburg's rich or, as in the case of the Elbphilharmonie, informal settlements of digital refugees, set on evading Hamburg's virtual surveillance, who strive to remain watt-independent with autonomous food cultivation and energy production.

● 260

Local Speculations
Kitzscher

Status quo

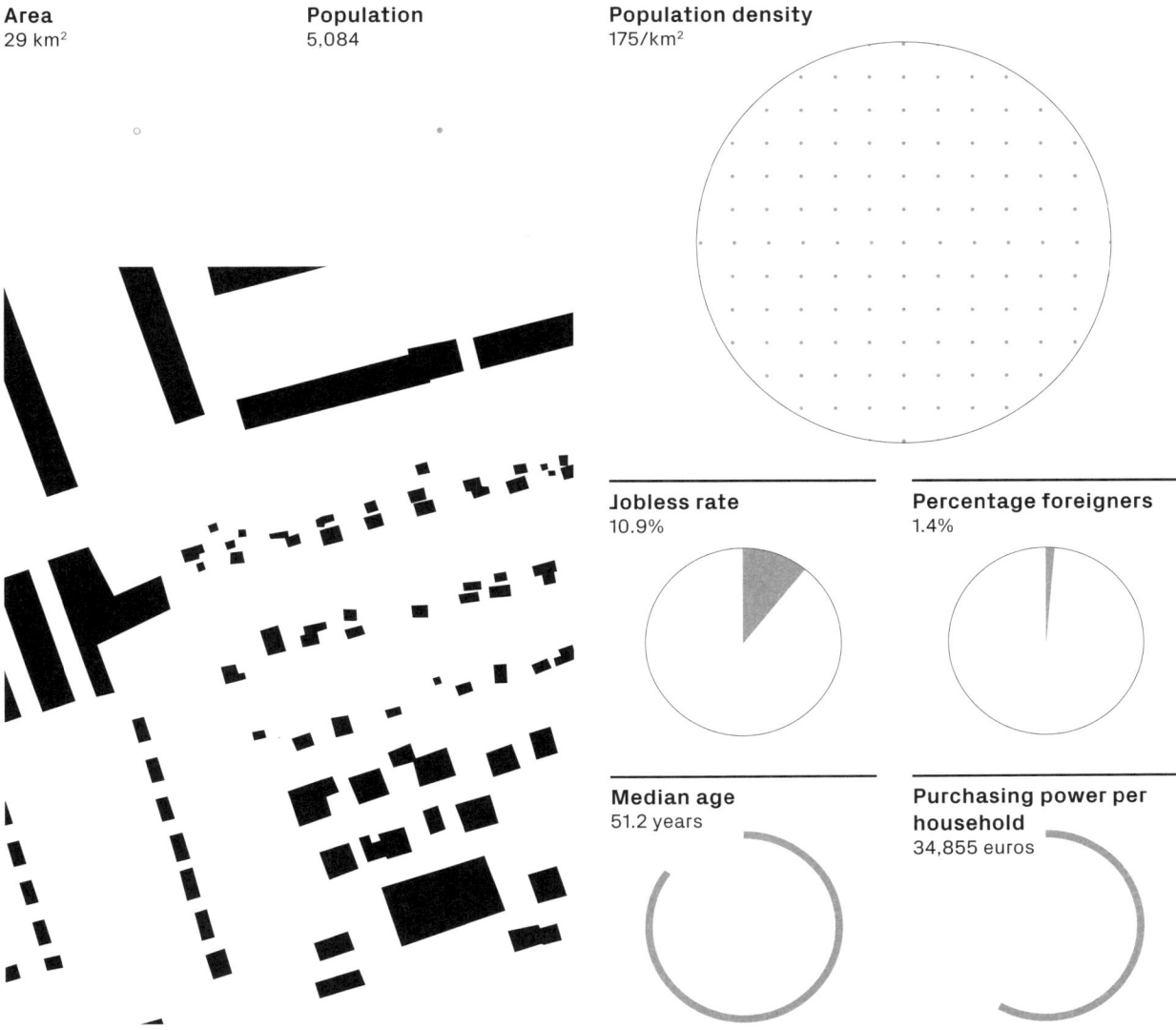

Area	**Population**	**Population density**
29 km²	5,084	175/km²

Jobless rate
10.9%

Percentage foreigners
1.4%

Median age
51.2 years

Purchasing power per household
34,855 euros

Figure-ground map Kitzscher

Kitzscher is situated in the Leipzig lowland bight and is connected to Leipzig twenty-five kilometers to the north by the B95. Access to local public transport is provided by the district town of Borna seven kilometers southwest. External factors have powerfully influenced the growth and development of Kitzscher. In the course of military armament preceding World War II, surface mines were opened and a processing plant constructed in Espenhain, the then biggest in Germany, and in the 1940s hundreds of workers were settled in the town. Boosted yet again by the expansion of the German Democratic Republic's lignite-based energy industry, what had once been a farming village with forty properties turned, over the years, into a major mining town of more than seven thousand inhabitants. The drastic increase in demand for housing was met by a works settlement. However, the construction method employed—multistory, segmented, concrete

prefabs—precluded the area's being opened up satisfactorily to urban development. The uninterrupted expansion of the site since the 1960s has led to its population increasing more than fivefold. Nonetheless, despite this growth period in Kitzscher, the town chose not to set up its own administrative offices, high schools, cultural and leisure facilities, preferring to fall back on existing infrastructures in nearby Borna.

Economic developments brought about by German reunification led to a radical cutback in lignite mining and processing in west Saxony. Job losses contributed toward a population decline the effects of which the town is still contending with today. With its five thousand plus inhabitants, Kitzscher is a good example of an economically one-sided and, in the meantime, economically weak post-mining region with high average population age, rapid demographic change, and age-selective exodus of the young.

While the population of Leipzig is increasing again, those of the majority of its surrounding communities are on the decline, though there are significant differences between urban agglomerations and rural areas. The populations of some of the former, such as Markkleeberg, approximately twenty kilometers distant, have succeeded in increasing to this day, while Kitzscher has had to cope with high losses. As a result of the low birth rate, the 6- to 18-year-old age group has decreased markedly. The biggest discrepancy between the populations of Leipzig and its surrounding communities, however, is in the 18- to 35-year-old age group. The reasons are to be sought not only in educational migration but in the superior attractiveness and career opportunities that Leipzig has to offer young families. In outlying communities such as Kitzscher, viable living and job prospects for young people are few and far between.

Netland

Kitzscher is situated a short distance outside the Leipzig-Dresden raw materials corridor. Too near the axis to operate independently, and yet not close enough to profit from the new networks in the region, the town has been absorbed by the service landscape of the Leipzig urban agglomeration. As a producer and processor of energy and foodstuffs, Kitzscher is part of the supply network that has evolved on the periphery of Leipzig. Unlike the idyllic lacustrine regions in the vicinity, the town offers neither natural nor recreational spaces that are worth preserving, and many areas of the surrounding countryside are now used for the generation of sustainable energy by wind and solar power. Small-scale, water-intensive farming operates on the high-quality soils of the town's open spaces. The population of Kitzscher has continued to decline. Because industries here are highly automated, not many people are needed to serve and maintain the hybrid food processing, organic farming, and energy production. Kitzscher's wealth of water has promoted the development of industrial fish farming. In addition, over the years, server farms have been put in the fishponds, helping to meet the country's need for mass storage in the sphere of communications technology. Fish breeding and server farms have entered an energy symbiosis—in winter the servers warm the ponds that cool the servers in summer, facilitating efficient fish production all year round. The membranous surfaces covering the fishponds are used to support photovoltaic facilities.

● 203

Integralland

233 ●

Small-scale, piecemeal organization is a regular feature of Kitzscher. Its plentiful allotment gardens are a reflection of the autonomously organized dropout

community that has grown up here. The town not only has room for experimentation in architecture and space-usage but also in alternative lifestyles. Rather than having been cut back, its buildings have been adjusted to changed conditions with the active aid of its inhabitants, new and old. Old precast concrete structures now house multistory house apartments, loft apartments, and studios. Vegetable gardens or wild park landscapes are now found on rooftops and in abandoned empty spaces. Kitzscher is a prime example of the communal promotion of private initiative sites launched by the state, which has opened up developmental perspectives even in disadvantaged situations. Thanks to the thriving city of Leipzig's provision and maintenance of transport and energy infrastructures, as well as social infrastructures for medical and educational care, Kitzscher manages to survive. In return, the yields from large-scale industrialized farms and extensive solar parks in the immediate vicinity of Kitzscher, which in many places have meanwhile become unpopular, are passed on to Leipzig free of charge.

Wattland

With the growth of the Halle-Leipzig urban agglomeration, and particularly since air travel has become unaffordable for many people, the lacustrine countryside south of Leipzig has established itself as an attractive tourist destination. Many of the local inhabitants spend their vacation here each year. The recreation area is reached at low watt-expense in shared minibuses; camping, hiking, swimming, or just digital time-out can be watt-inexpensively enjoyed—the digital infrastructure being underdeveloped, the energy cost for linking up with the virtual spheres is

proportionately high. Individual vacationers have more space at the lakes than in the neighboring city where each single watt has to be fought for. However, this "more space" has been declining in recent years. Many of the lakeside properties have been fenced in and are no longer accessible to townspeople looking for relaxation. At such properties, the wealthy are preparing to take their leave of the city. High-performance

● 229

● 260

123

solar collectors and wind turbines provide the luxury of energy autonomy, satellite dishes an abiding link to the digital world, and fields, enclosures, and fountains a self-sufficiency that is efficient and watt-inexpensive—all investments that pay off in the watt-economy almost instantaneously for those who can afford them.

Kitzscher lies forsaken, in a nowhere between Halle-Leipzig and the lakeside enclaves of the rich, and from nowhere reachable at low watt-expense. The disused lignite mines have been reopened. Powerful, fully automated excavators chew their way efficiently through the seams. A number of Kitzscher's former residential areas have already had to make way for the coal pits.

Local Speculations
Ludwigsburg

Status quo

Area
43.3 km²

Population
89,639

Population density
2,070/km²

Jobless rate
4.2%

Percentage foreigners
19.2%

Median age
42.1 years

Purchasing power per household
48,116 euros

Figure-ground map Ludwigsburg

Ludwigsburg is situated some twelve kilometers north of downtown Stuttgart. It is the largest city of the administrative district named for it and the tenth largest in Baden-Württemberg. Ludwigsburg benefits from the road and rail networks of greater Stuttgart. Ludwigsburg station is one of the busiest in the federal state of Baden-Württemberg. In addition, there is a transfer terminal for freight traffic close by. Downtown Stuttgart can be reached within only a few minutes on the rapid transit system (S-Bahn). The A81 links the city to the interstate network, and the—partly six-lane—B27 (Stuttgart–Heilbronn) traverses the city area. Around seventy thousand vehicles are counted daily on this section alone, which is in line with the city's heavily car-traffic oriented character. Consequently, there are large parking lots throughout the inner city and in the immediate vicinity of the Baroque buildings that date back to the foundation of the city.

Two powerful fields of force have defined Ludwigsburg's rise and decline over the centuries: the Württemberg court and the military. As the onetime biggest garrison town in southwest Germany, Ludwigsburg still bears the nickname "Swabian Potsdam." Over sixty hectares of military property were rededicated for civil purposes after the American forces had withdrawn. The conversion of barracks into cultural sites, residential estates, service centers, and trade areas successfully transformed the city. In the wake of this, a further parallel to Potsdam (Babelsberg) occurred in Ludwigsburg: the city has now become a major film and media location in the region.

The city's economic base consists of a large number of family firms. Many of the medium-size companies in the region are world leaders in their product range. More patents are filed in the Stuttgart region than anywhere else in Germany. Commuting ratios indicate the interrelations that exist between parts of the region. It can be observed how increasing numbers of people who work in Stuttgart are moving to Ludwigsburg, which is (still) less expensive and offers similarly high quality living and housing. In order to preserve this high quality in the years ahead the city is increasingly focusing on protecting its periphery, for instance through the restoration of the River Neckar.

The municipality of Ludwigsburg is pretty much debt-free. For several years now the city's government has concentrated its energies on social sustainability and participative urban development that is actively concerned to include the 40 percent of Ludwigsburg inhabitants with a background of migration.

Netland

Developments in recent decades have led, first and foremost, to the Swabian car industry and its distributors merging in production networks that specialize in driverless transport units and temporary energy storage. Ludwigsburg today is inhabited by the employees of the big energy corporations and by the new mobility-service companies' engineers and managers. The total population of the city has remained pretty much unchanged. Especially in regional competition for the young and high-income earners, Ludwigsburg has proved itself a small-size, manageable alternative

with all the advantages that transregional networking brings. Development of the suburbs-to-town-center transport facilities, begun early on by the city, has not only improved the city's regional standing as a business location, but has helped promote communications outside the city, with the result that the energy corporations' workers commute long distances to their workplaces in comfort. These achievements also benefit the more distant surroundings that, thanks to a number of Ludwigsburg companies specializing in the efficient use of local resources and sustainable renewable energy production, have become important energy producers. This gives the city a certain independence from the big corporations and their supply infrastructures, although they are the region's main employers. These economic developments have also changed the face of Ludwigsburg. The transport network's connecting stations are spread throughout the city. Traffic zones have adapted to the new conditions: while there has been compact development around the city center, large areas of road space have been rededicated. Ludwigsburg used to be characterized by a superfluity of streets, garages, parking lots, and of course cars—these spaces are now green areas, parks, or educational, residential, and meeting facilities, (à la AMP/ Mobility). Pedestrians and cyclists, rather than cars, dominate the urban traffic scene. Local goods traffic is managed during the night by means of the network's transport modules, which in the daytime are used by commuters.

● 36

262 ●

227 ●

Integralland

Ludwigsburg is faced with the challenge of growth, overcrowding, and housing issues. More and more people are moving to the city to benefit from its economic strength, its cultural offerings, and the high quality of life of its provincial milieu. It is a magnet for qualified foreign employees who work in its small and medium-size local businesses. The proportion of foreigners and inhabitants with a background of migration has continued to rise. To keep population density in residential areas within tolerable limits, growth has been lateral. Here and there, open space has been enclosed and developed, and population density has been cautiously raised by adding stories to existing buildings, but only where this harmonizes with Ludwigsburg's character as a town. Today, Ludwigsburg combines up-to-date living and working with small-town charm, while at the same time offering generously cut apartments that are especially

attractive to families as well as creative professionals and their offices. Transformations in local private traffic have been a significant factor in spatial expansion. Means of transport are available as needed. Shared vehicles—electric cars, hybrid minibuses, pedelecs—consume fewer resources than transport in the past. Simultaneously, public transport has spread sideways: streetcars link Ludwigsburg to the surrounding region; extensive areas are covered by controlled driverless passenger transport systems. Regional cooperations between Ludwigsburg and surrounding communities are of great importance because the only way of coping with the pressure of migration is to coordinate the planning of living and leisure space.

Wattland

Ludwigsburg's aggressive marketing strategy—launched by the city on the model of the living and working culture of Silicon Valley in order to profile itself as a location for digital research, teaching, and living—has borne fruit. The city managed to break its dependence on manufacturing just in time to be able to emerge as a stopping place for digital nomads when the global migration movements hit Germany. Not just Baden-Württemberg's former leading industry—the car business—but all the other energy-intensive and energy-consuming businesses in the watt-economy have been unable to continue in their previous forms. Ludwigsburg's timely preparation for the watt age has established it as a research lab and excellence center for digital modes of life. A digital elite lives here today, together with the workers in the service sectors who look after this elite. Ludwigsburg's digital platform organizes and regulates, pilots and alters itself with the active aid of its networked citizens. A continuous flood of innovations optimizes local forms of energy production and use; the nutrient-rich soils of the Neckar region have become research grounds for genetically optimized food cultivation; the inhabitants themselves are eloquent testers of new forms of knowledge development and health care.

Ludwigsburg looks much the same today as it used to, yet it has changed entirely. The city's virtual image is a complex of information and digital traces that its inhabitants, all permanently online, leave behind them wherever they go, because for years now communication in Ludwigsburg has taken place almost exclusively online. With its public squares, cafés, restaurants, stores, and fitness studios, its streets full of joggers and people out walking, the city bustles with life; yet Ludwigsburg today is above all the livable backdrop for the real, digital life that the residents live through glasses and screens while pursuing essential activities such as eating and physical training in the city. Almost no one in Ludwigsburg talks about the watt because everyone has enough of them for the little bit of energy required for his or her digital existence.

254 ●

257 ●

235 ●

Local Speculations
Saale-Orla-Kreis

Status quo

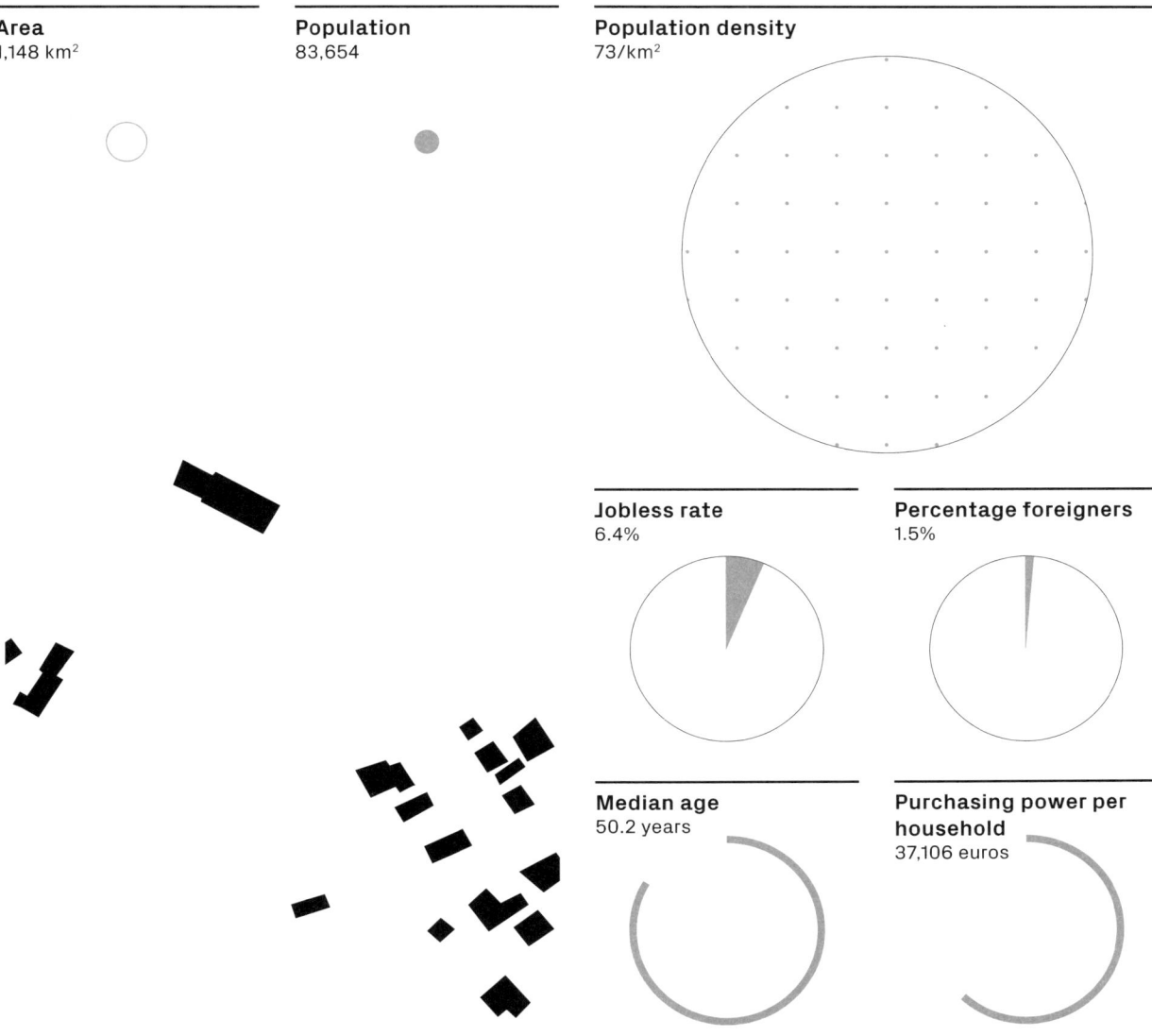

Area
1,148 km²

Population
83,654

Population density
73/km²

Jobless rate
6.4%

Percentage foreigners
1.5%

Median age
50.2 years

Purchasing power per household
37,106 euros

Figure-ground map Saale-Orla-Kreis

The Saale-Orla-Kreis has an area of 1,148 square kilometers. It is situated primarily in the Thuringian Schiefergebirge and where this gives way to the Thuringian woodland region and the Vogtland. More than 80 percent of the district lies above 400 meters. The region, therefore, has a distinctly low mountain range character. In 2014, the largest towns were Pössneck (pop. 12,072), Neustadt an der Orla (pop. 8,164), and Schleiz (pop. 8,477).

Road traffic centers on the B9 (Berlin–Nuremberg) which crosses Saale-Orla-Kreis from north to south. The district's historical railroad network has been drastically cut back, in particular since German reunification. Only 77 of an original 158 kilometers are frequented by passenger trains, and currently Saale-Orla-Kreis offers no long-distance urban connections (Jena, Saalfeld, and Lichtenfels are the closest intercity express stations).

The Saale-Orla-Kreis has no waterways suitable for industrial purposes. Nevertheless, its water resources are its great strength—apart from providing drinking water, its dams play a central role in energy production. The course of the upper Saale is interrupted by five dams along a length of more than eighty kilometers. Dating to the 1930s, this dam system is the second largest aggregate of hydroelectric power stations in Germany. One of the five dams in the system, the Bleiloch, is Germany's largest dam, giving rise to the country's biggest barrier lake. The pumped-storage station at Goldisthal, with a capacity of 1,060 megawatts, is the largest hydroelectric power plant in Germany. The importance of wind turbines, biomass, and photovoltaic plants has also grown continually in recent years. Given the diversity of its potential, nature in the Saale-Orla-Kreis has increasingly come in conflict with its energy-productive exploitation with wind turbines, for instance, being installed in wooded areas.

Although the district's natural resources offer ideal conditions for tourism, the current economic structure of the Saale-Orla-Kreis is characterized by a relatively high density of industry (over ninety industrial jobs per one thousand inhabitants). The jobless rate of 7 percent is below the Thuringian average (7.8 percent).

As in many rural regions, demographic change has also hit the Saale-Orla-Kreis, leaving it with an overaged and depleted population. From 1990 to 2010, the population declined by around 16 percent. In particular the exodus of young people, and the resultant lack of skilled labor, has posed a great challenge to the economy of the region. Aside from these problem areas, social commitment has developed strongly in the Saale-Orla-Kreis. This is reflected in its flourishing associations and in multigenerational housing projects.

Netland

The population of the Saale-Orla-Kreis has now dropped by 50 percent. The remaining inhabitants continue to live in decentralized structures and are involved in various forms of energy production, the Saale-Orla-Kreis having now focused on energy production based on water power and other regenerative energies. The Saale-Orla district's natural geographic properties are the region's chief resource in sustainably ensuring its continued existence. Energy, and areas of natural raw materials, wind, plants, and forest, represent a big transregional potential. Lakes are used to store energy, thus generating additional revenue. Big corporations still run major projects such as the hydro-dam; biogas energy production, however, is firmly in the hands of communities and their farmers. Energy from biomass and wind is fed into the national power network. Further, wind is

used for the efficient and cheap hydrolytic production of gas, which is then stored locally. This form of energy storage depends on close links to the network. Private transport in the corridor has been taken over by driverless minibus companies in order to ensure that as little as possible of the precious export commodity gas is used. It is from here that the infrastructure is installed and developed; at the same time, energy is delivered via a gas infrastructure to the town chains. All in all, the region features a highly compartmentalized network of energy production and storage. Businesses range from small, independent firms to energy oligarchs; the energy is then respectively destined for self-sufficiency or export. Forests continue to be exploited for building materials but need also to be preserved as sources of renewable raw materials and for use in the chemical industry.

205 ●

Integralland

A productive triad consisting of food production, energy production, and tourism has evolved in the Saale-Orla-Kreis. Climate change has proved a positive developmental factor in the region. At the Plothen Lakes there are weekend farms where "weekend comrades" pursue communal organic food production. As the name suggests, these comrades come out to the country at the weekends only; during the week they live in the surrounding towns and cities, their farms being tended by agricultural workers. The farms and lakes together constitute big energy-food cooperatives, in which the inhabitants of the Saale-Orla-Kreis are able to buy shares. Water and wind energy are sustainably produced and fed into the regional supply network. However, efficient development of the energy supply is slow because interventions need to be harmonized with preserving the attractions of the countryside—the region has benefited vastly from

203 ●

233 ●

● 255

208 ●

the growing regional ecological tourism trend of recent years. Hiking trails have been upgraded. New "raised routes" have been laid out through the tree-tops. Tourists and hikers experience untouched nature as they spend the night in little tree houses on the wooded slopes. Organic farms have summer and winter programs for families. Kayak tours, white-water rafting, and cross-country ski runs complete the all-year-round local recreational activities.

Wattland

The Saale-Orla-Kreis is naturally rich in energy because of its plentiful supply of regenerative sources—forest, water, wind—and has profited from the currency reform and the general rise in energy prices that came in its wake. The Bleiloch Valley dam provides the region with a big reservoir used for temporary energy storage. Practically everyone living in the Saale-Orla-Kreis

209 ●

rks in the energy sector, which has organized itself into the Saale-Orla energy network with its headquarters in Bad Lobenstein. Under the auspices of this network the productive relation of energy supply and landscape conservation is researched at the technical university in Pössneck. To stabilize the population and create incentives for further influx, the district administration rewards direct participation in energy production and storage with privileged access to reduced watt-units, doubly favoring the local inhabitants: not only is more energy available for their private use, but their watts are cheaper than in other parts of Germany with equal spending power—with the result that some neighborhoods can even afford their own electric car for excursions and shopping trips. Widespread watt-wealth has had a positive effect on communal leeway and hence on local infrastructures and services. The Saale-Orla energy network in recent years has offered a platform to a range of actors working on diversifying the district's value creation structures—because in the long term the Saale-Orla-Kreis is keen to establish an additional source of revenue alongside energy production and storage. Thus, in Schleiz, new professional training courses are offered for Germany's energy efficient, decentralized, and digitized education and health systems. New forms of education and health security are already being tested on energy network workers. The goal is to establish the Saale-Orla-Kreis as an education center for digital learning and healing for Germany as a whole.

● 209

Local Speculations
Völklingen

Status quo

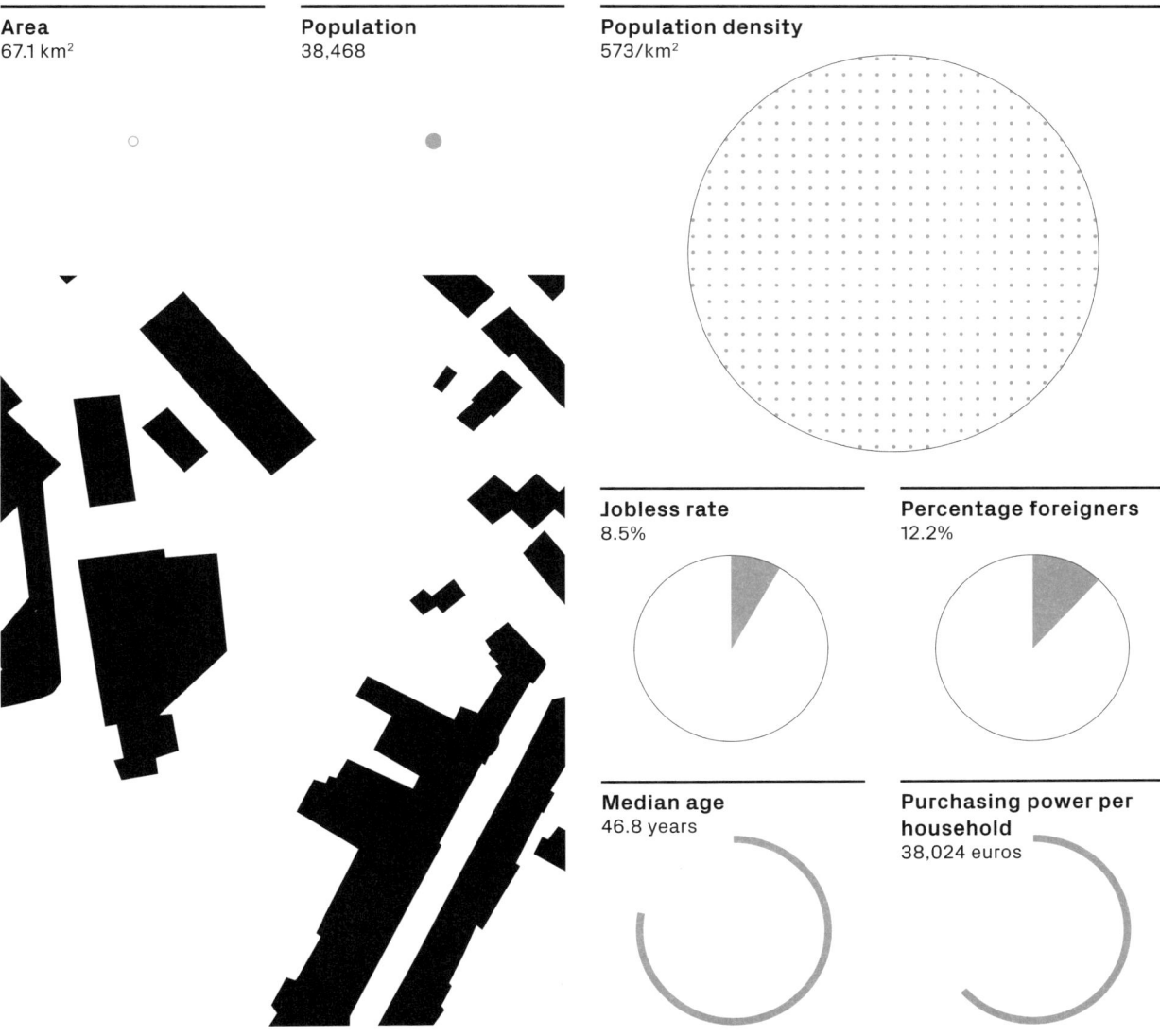

Area
67.1 km²

Population
38,468

Population density
573/km²

Jobless rate
8.5%

Percentage foreigners
12.2%

Median age
46.8 years

Purchasing power per household
38,024 euros

Figure-ground map Völklingen

Völklingen is a medium-size town situated directly on the river Saar close to the French border. It is well integrated in the regional rail network—Saarbrücken is only a few minutes distant, offering intercity express and intercity connections as well as the TGV to France. Its harbor, a relic of the heyday of industrialization, with its newly refurbished quay is now little more than a tourist attraction.

Völklingen's identity has been largely shaped by its coal and iron-mining and steel-producing past. The first iron melting hut, in Geislautern (today a district of Völklingen), dates to 1572. Carl Röchling founded the ironworks known as the Völklinger Hütte in 1881 and in 1883 the first blast furnace came into operation there. The plant grew rapidly, especially after World War II, and came to dominate the town's economic and infrastructural development. The importance of the mining and steel-producing industries began to wane in the

1970s and the numbers employed declined; the population has been falling since the 1990s. The town's current problems, no less than its former success, are intimately bound up with the ironworks. The ironworks diminished the attractiveness of the town center in particular. The proximity of the Völklinger Hütte to downtown Völklingen, as the structure of retail trade and the housing supply indicates, powerfully influenced the town's development. The loss of more than twelve thousand steel industry jobs is particularly evident in the frequency of empty houses and properties.

Today, the grounds of the former ironworks are divided between the Saarstahl AG and the Völklinger Hütte Museum and World Cultural Heritage Site. Around 15 percent of Völklingen's employed still earn their living by mining or in the energy sector. With 3,700 workers, the Saarstahl AG continues to be the town's biggest employer. In 2010, one of the world's largest hammer forges went into operation. The project, involving an investment of 450 million euros, created several hundred jobs and one of the most modern production sites of its kind. In 1994, the Völklinger Hütte was the first industrial monument to be declared a World Cultural Heritage Site by Unesco. While around four hundred thousand people visited the Völklinger Hütte World Cultural Heritage Site in 2011, the town of Völklingen has still not succeeded in harnessing tourism on a broader scale. The institutional disconnect between town center and the Völklinger Hütte site is enshrined in the town's architecture: the view of the city from the World Cultural Heritage Site is blocked by the Globus shopping mall.

Coping with the structural and economic changes of the post-mining-and-steel-production era continues to be a major task for Völklingen where the jobless rate remains above average in the Saarland. Above all young people are turning their backs on the city, because it offers them little in the way of future prospects.

Netland

The proximity of France and the important waterway of the Saar are still significant factors shaping Völklingen. The infrastructure of the Saar valley, with which Völklingen is connected, has been progressively developed by the big energy corporations. The town has shrunk drastically; only along the Saar have the populations of the surrounding villages remained stable. And yet Völklingen has managed to recover from this shrinkage: recognizing the city's potential as an energy-producing location, the big energy and resource corporations have lent it particular support. It is one of the medium-size industrial and high-tech locations within the network that benefits especially from its proximity to France and Luxembourg. The border region has developed positively as a result of the merging of European energy infrastructures, particularly in relation to France. Here are staff and services that receive and maintain goods and energy exported from Germany, ensuring their smooth delivery to France and southern Europe. Because of these developments, Völklingen industry is now sustainable and fully fit for the future: the power produced by a pumped storage hydroelectric plant and photovoltaics is fed into the energy network to produce revenue. Steel refining at the Völklingen steelworks has become profitable again as a result of the increased demand for material in equipping and extending the energy network. In order for the steel industry to become competitive again on a long-term basis, options are being canvassed to make the works self-sufficient by exploiting local renewable energies. Moreover, credit for the successful resuscitation of the town's fish farming economy through specialization in tuna—blue and red tuna from Völklingen are now on the menus of several gourmet restaurants around the world—goes to a Japanese cook.

60 ●

Integralland

Although geographically Völklingen is a linear city in the Saarbrücken-Völklingen-Dillingen regional patchwork, the town has become isolated and development has been retrogressive. The inhabitants of Völklingen are increasingly oriented toward France; not a few commute over the border. Through efficient use of the limited means available, attempts have been made in recent years to guide the town's development in a positive direction. With small-scale, qualitative redensification, and intelligent conversion and upgrading of green areas and undeveloped spaces, the community is intent on creating a new type of town where parks, bike paths, and footways link up unconnected, attractive areas. In line with this strategy, a large part of downtown has been abandoned—the town center is deserted. The town center's core market function is without any basis in this new Völklingen of urban islands in nature. Overall, there are strong regional

connections, and in the conduct of their daily lives the inhabitants interrelate with their immediate neighborhoods and neighboring regions; the residential areas are intact and communally organized. The Völklingen steelworks World Cultural Heritage site has undergone no further development and is slowly disappearing in the green of the rampantly growing wild vegetation.

Wattland

Ever since steel-producing Völklingen was definitively forced to its knees by African competition, things have not looked good for the once proud industrial town. Since industry left, the town treasury is empty, the chance of linking up to the digital world lost. Hence, Völklingen has not profited from the wave of German migration in recent decades—digitally the town did not exist. Only along the Saar, toward Saarbrücken and France, has the population remained constant, thanks to unstinting campaigning by the Saarland's small digital elite—but not Völklingen. What already loomed at the start of the century has meanwhile become reality: the town center lies in waste; investments never materialized; even the virtual world has black holes. Now that everyone lives online and tries to self-produce the necessities of daily life at home, the importance of the Globus shopping mall that once shaped the town has diminished. It is now a hypermarket for low-energy recycling products, an inexpensive alternative to the energy-intensive, individualized, decentralized consumer culture. Society's energy-poor from downtown Völklingen purchase the bare necessities of life here. Homeowners in Völklingen withdraw into their own four walls—having one's own plot of land is a kind of anchor or enclave for people in times of expensive mobility. Seated in front of big screens, they try to forget what's happening outside their front door. However, many are dependent on short, frequent, energy-intensive trips over the border to France for the necessary articles of daily life. Because energy there is so much cheaper—the neighbor nation still clings to its nuclear power stations—the people of Völklingen commute to top up their watt-accounts. Transport costs having continued to rise, small boats and ships are frequently used on the Saar, floating downstream to France at no expense to tank up on watts. These watt-commuters even put up with the more arduous, upstream return journey that often uses up a good part of the watts they have just tanked.

That the town has not completely given in is due to the initiative of an inhabitant of Völklingen. His SOS to the global digital community has already opened up some development prospects. A team of drones, controlled from Nevada, is investigating the possibilities

52

251

of deep and near-surface geothermal energy production in the former mine shafts. First tests have proved positive and may impel the town to develop in the next few years. The SOS was also heard by a Völklingen pharmaceutical company. Taking advantage of the relaxed regulatory framework of the innovative initiative for medical technology in Germany, it has now opened small research laboratories with a view to serially producing kidneys and lungs for the world market. The town's low digital visibility is a location bonus for the current prototype research. Aided by the project developers at London's Battersea Power Station, the Völklingen steelworks World Cultural Heritage site has also been further opened up to tourism. The steelworks is now a huge museum ground where visitors can discover what the world looked like when energy was still affordable. So far, however, the hoped-for floods of tourists have not shown up. The journey is too expensive for the masses. An investor is still being sought to create, run, and finance the watt-intensive project of a virtual tour through this "Cathedral of Industrialization."

● 260

Reflec-
tions

Can the future be planned? Three reflections bring together critical ideas exploring options for future-directed thought and action in the present. Matthijs Bouw's *Baukulturkasten* serves as a communicative tool for geographically locating and discussing scenarios. Erik Swyngedouw and Armen Avanessian question the premises underlying what can be planned and the politics that inform these premises.

Baukulturkasten

Matthijs Bouw

A Speculative Model Kit

Making future scenarios is a tricky business. In the end, however, the idea behind our research was not to be right about the future. The idea was to have a discussion about what needs to be and can be done in the near term in order to shape a certain future *Baukultur*. If one studies the Dutch tradition of using scenarios in spatial planning, one sees a remarkable shift in the definition of the drivers behind the scenarios. In the late 1980s, in a manifestation called "Nederland Nu als Ontwerp" (which came complete with a big book and an exhibition in the Beurs van Berlage), the drivers were ideological, based on different political outlooks. There was a "dynamic" scenario, a "critical" (in the Frankfurt School sense) scenario, a "careful" scenario, and a "relaxed" one.

In the 1990s, however, the late Dirk Frieling, the planner behind "Nederland Nu als Ontwerp" and the brain behind much of the large-scale planning in the Netherlands, realized that planning on an ideological basis was quite problematic. First, with the Dutch need to build coalitions in government, which changed every four years, any direction would to a large extent cancel the other out. National planning simply had too long a life span. And secondly, the gradual introduction of a more and more liberal and privatized economy meant that the instruments for planning would be largely out of the hands of the State.

In the aughts, when I became involved with much of the national planning, we therefore changed both the drivers and the application of the scenarios. The scenarios we produced for the "Structure Vision Randstad 2040" were meant to demonstrate the effects of different models for governance, and to provide insight into the big planning issues for the Randstad (the western part of Holland). Rather than offering a choice between futures, the scenarios were meant to make possible a discussion about the so-called "robust elements"; the scenarios were built such that all the main issues of Dutch planning were articulated distinctly in each scenario. And with regard to the drivers, we started to look at labor, housing, and mobility markets and networks on a more abstract, or systemic, level. We based the agenda of each one on the OECD evaluation of the Netherlands, which called for more transparent and integrated markets, with more critical mass. On that basis, we formulated three different strategies of how to achieve that: the "spider" (in which network planning followed the bifurcated logic of the Global City), the "ladder" (a more integrated, redundant network), and the "archipelago" (minimal state involvement with the network).

As can be expected with such a method, the eventual "Structure Vision Randstad 2040" described much more a process than a project. It limited itself to describing the most basic major changes in Dutch planning: it redirected planning from one based on

networks to one based on quality of place; it abolished the egalitarian approach to distinct cities; and it put the water management question high on the agenda, and as such rethought the notion of the Green Heart. In addition, it limited the role of the national government, making way for local government, companies, NGOs, and citizens.

My collaboration on the "Baukulturatlas Deutschland 2030/2050" research project aimed less at transferring Dutch planning practices to the German context, more at offering my knowledge to help spark a novel political discussion of planning processes with scenarios as the basis. Any such discussion starts with questions such as "Who does?" "Who gets to do?" "Who makes?"—in short, which actors get to use what instruments to help shape our environment. In that sense, our discussions have been inherently political.

When asked to come up with our own interpretation of the process and what we had learned in the course of our participation, we realized that it might be better to go one step back, focus less on certain technological outcomes, but to design a more open visual method that could help facilitate further discussions on the transformative spatial aspects of speculation. Our little model kit, the *Baukulturkasten*, therefore consists of elements with which different environments can be configured, visualized, and talked about. It is made up of elements that shape our lived-in environments and that can be assembled in different configurations into cities, villages, and landscapes and their interdependencies.

In order to demonstrate the use of these elements we developed the speculations and their real-time spatial consequences from specific stakeholder perspectives. Each perspective operates with a different set of political forces shaping the respective spatial dynamics in favor of each stakeholder. In "Decentralized" the environment is shaped by the individual; in "Community-Driven" new forms of the collective are explored on different scales; and in "Exclusive" the stakeholders in charge are abstract entities like big corporations and powerful governments. Although we are well aware of the interdependencies between these stakeholders, we wanted to visualize each perspective's opportunities and threats by making explicit how these forces would react on Germany differently, when shaped by decentralized forces, by communities, or the exclusive few.

While many of the following visualizations have a resemblance to the speculative narratives of future Germany in this publication, the purpose of our model kit is to free the speculations for a use in the discussion about the forces that shape the future of our environment and how these need to be considered now. For example, in the workshops' discussions there were different opinions about the availability of energy: some suggested it would be scarce, some said it would be abundant. With the *Baukulturkasten*, both these can be made visual. Simultaneously, by being more abstract, the visualizations displayed here can be compared easier and recombined into new possibilities. After all, many types of forces compete in shaping our territory.

The *Baukulturkasten* is made up of elements that shape our lived-in environments and that can be assembled in different configurations into cities, villages, and landscapes— a SimCity-like engine to speculate about and illustrate different environments. The elements combine on different scales and under different organizational perspectives to give insight into the principles and forces that are shaping our *Baukultur* nowadays and in the future.

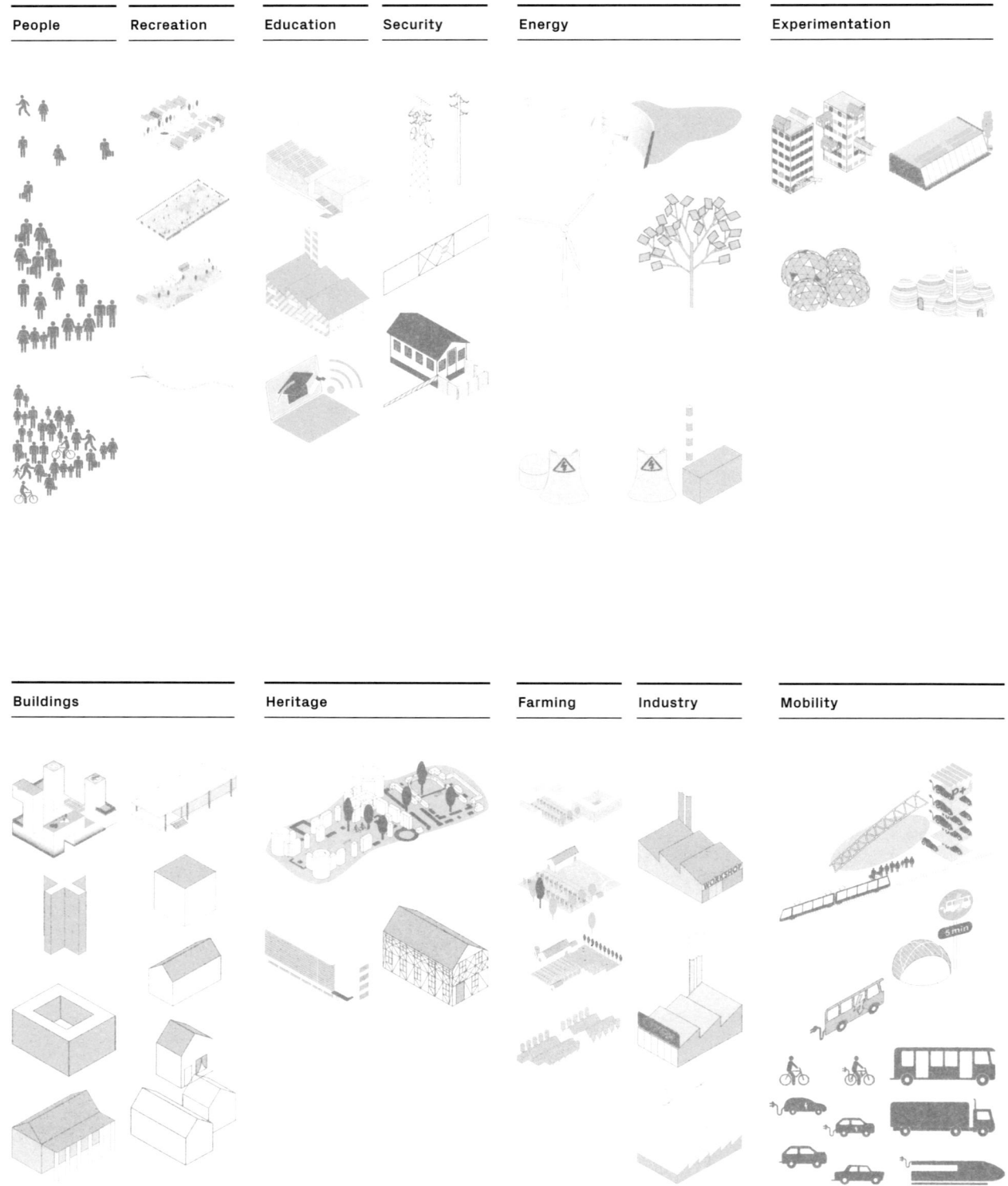

People Recreation Education Security Energy Experimentation

Buildings Heritage Farming Industry Mobility

Each environment is laid out on a base layer. The ground plate is divided into a grid. The scale of the grid shows the scale at which certain forces are shaping things. In "Decentralized" these forces are rather atomized, because individuals and small groups shape the environments, leading to cities and landscapes that consist of small units. In "Community-Driven" the environments will be shaped by larger groups, hence making it necessary to switch to a wider grid. In "Exclusive," actors must be interpreted on an even larger scale and their actions thus are provided with a much larger scale and grid.

A City

A typical city will be developed on a per plot basis. This creates many different environments: small plots (with some empty) and, on the other plots, a very diverse buildup. A new building may be next to a vacant old one. A house may be adjoining a small company. On each plot, the owners might express themselves individually. Because neither buildings nor public spaces are organized through larger institutions or organizations, parks are small and haphazard, mostly the result of individual efforts on neglected spaces. The public spaces are rather unbuilt open spaces than nice squares; the parks are more like overgrown fields than designed recreation areas. They are made in a very practical way, to serve as playgrounds for children, or to grow vegetables.

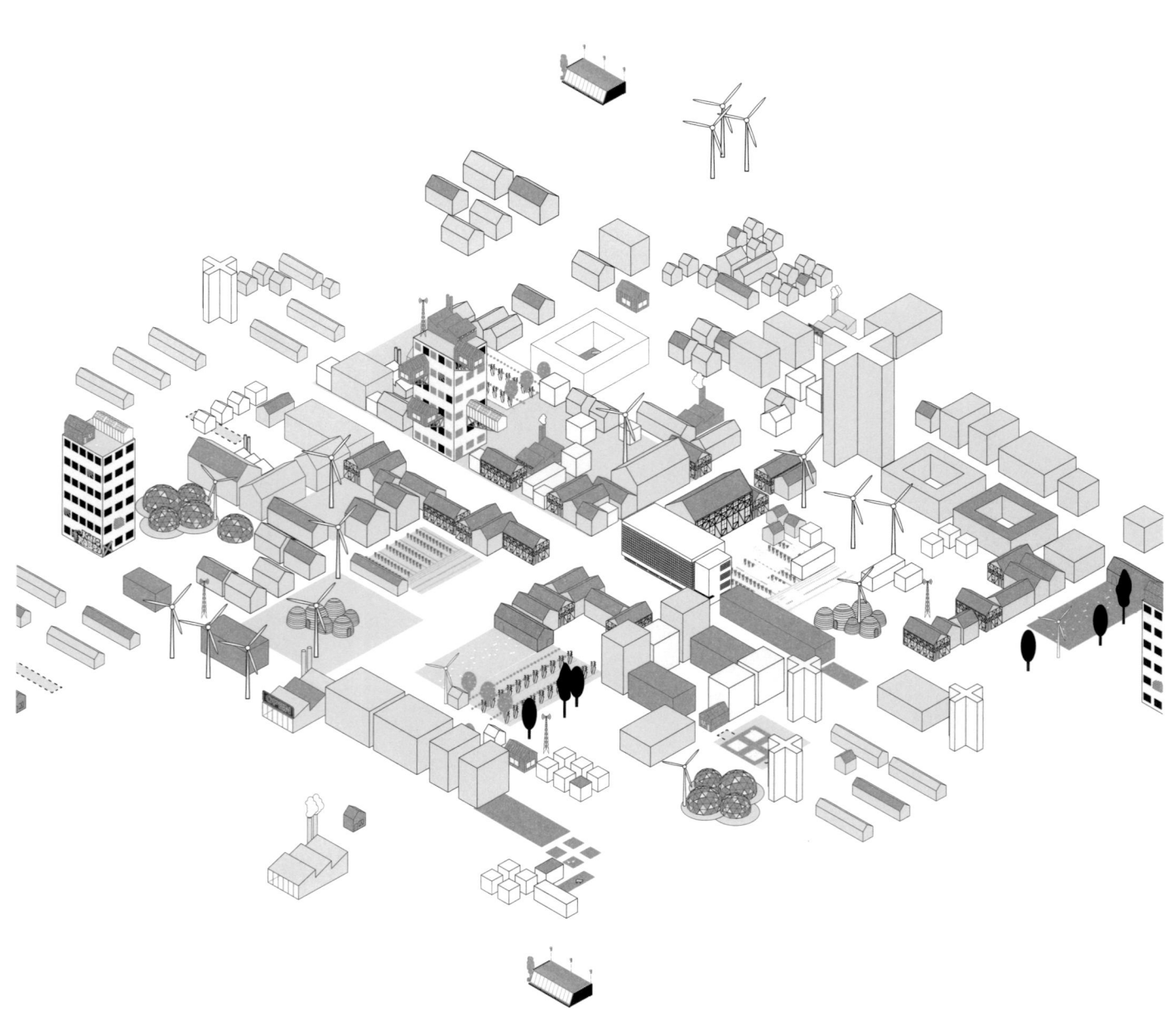

Experimentation/D.I.Y.

One can see a culture that fosters experimentation. Not bound by many restrictions or directives from authorities, the people will tinker with their houses, their workshops, and their machines. The city will be "hackable." Practicality and a sense of fun reign. This zoom-in shows experimental buildings that thrive in this planning scale: "Bucky domes," earthships, and parasites on existing buildings.

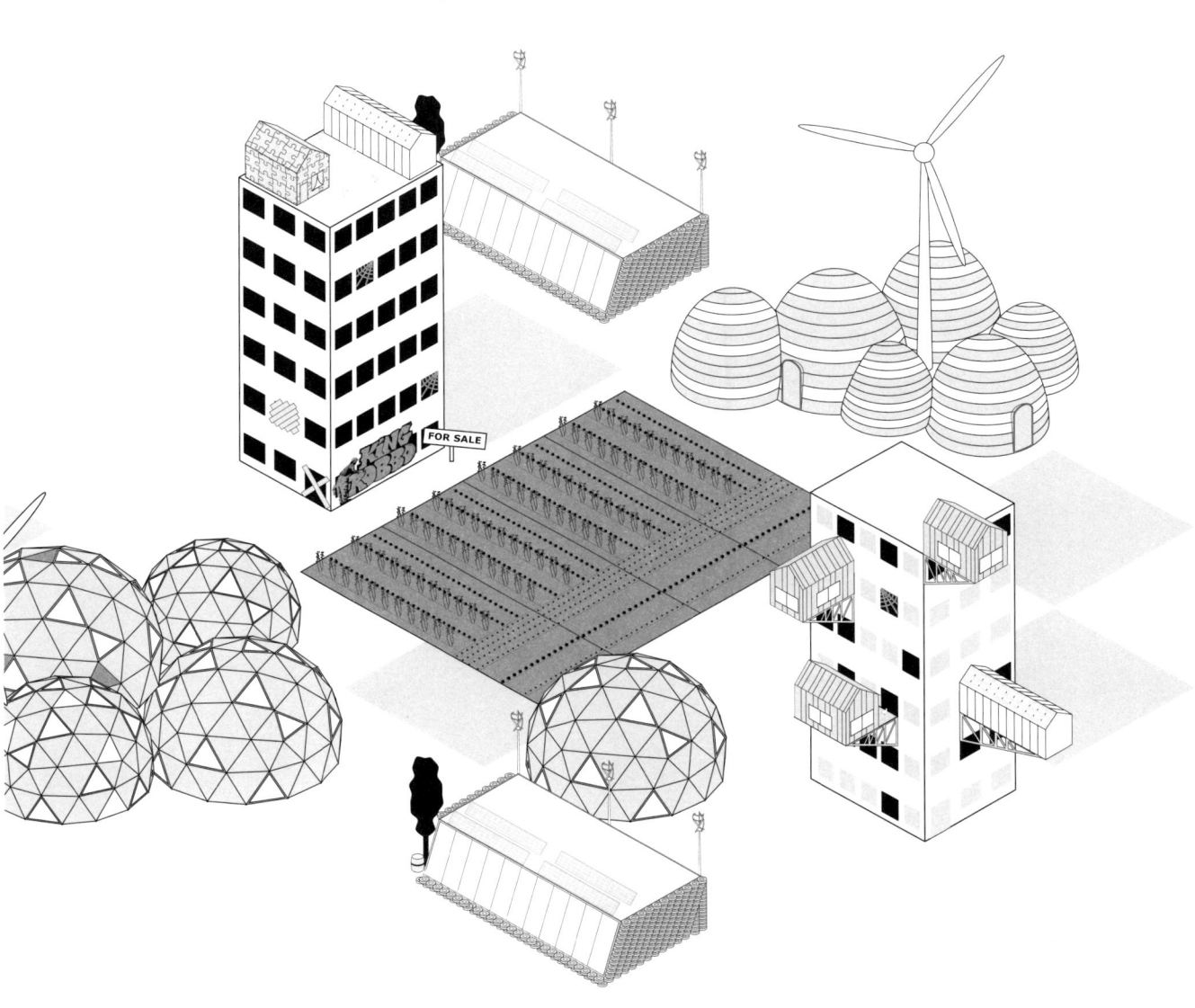

A Landscape

In rural areas, this smaller scale can also be found. Farms are kept small, are often organic, and tend to consist of a mixed-use—both livestock and arable farming. In all likelihood, the production of energy will also take place locally. Non-farm houses and settlements will show a great variety of uses. Here we see a small farm with both crops and animals. The farm produces its own energy with biogas from plant and animal waste, aided by wind turbines and solar panels. Near the farm, a village is revived through knowledge workers who moved there, transforming former agrarian infrastructure into small production spaces.

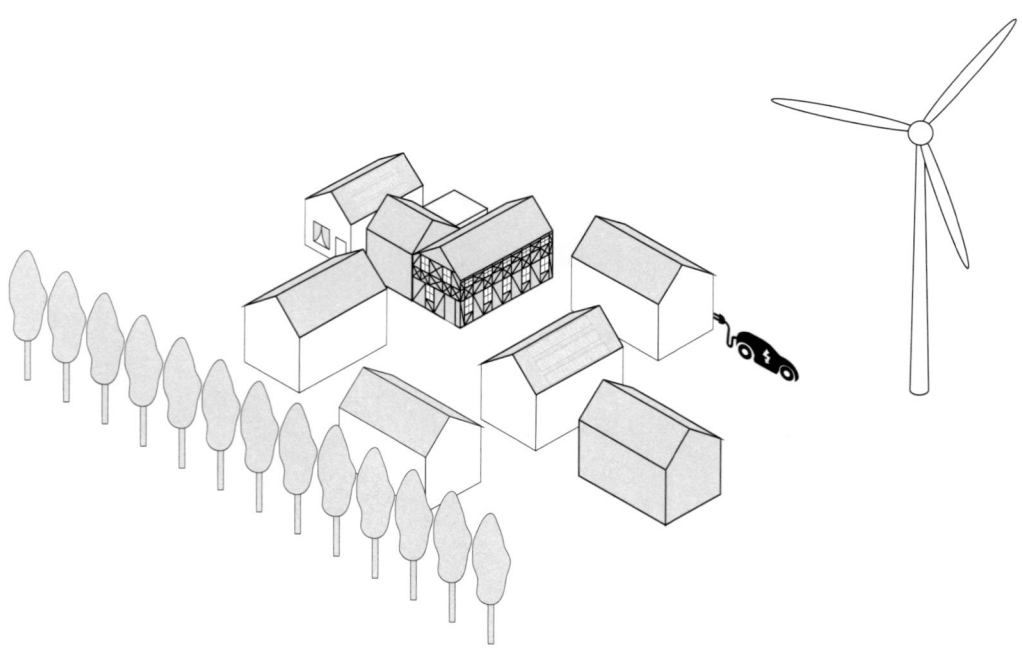

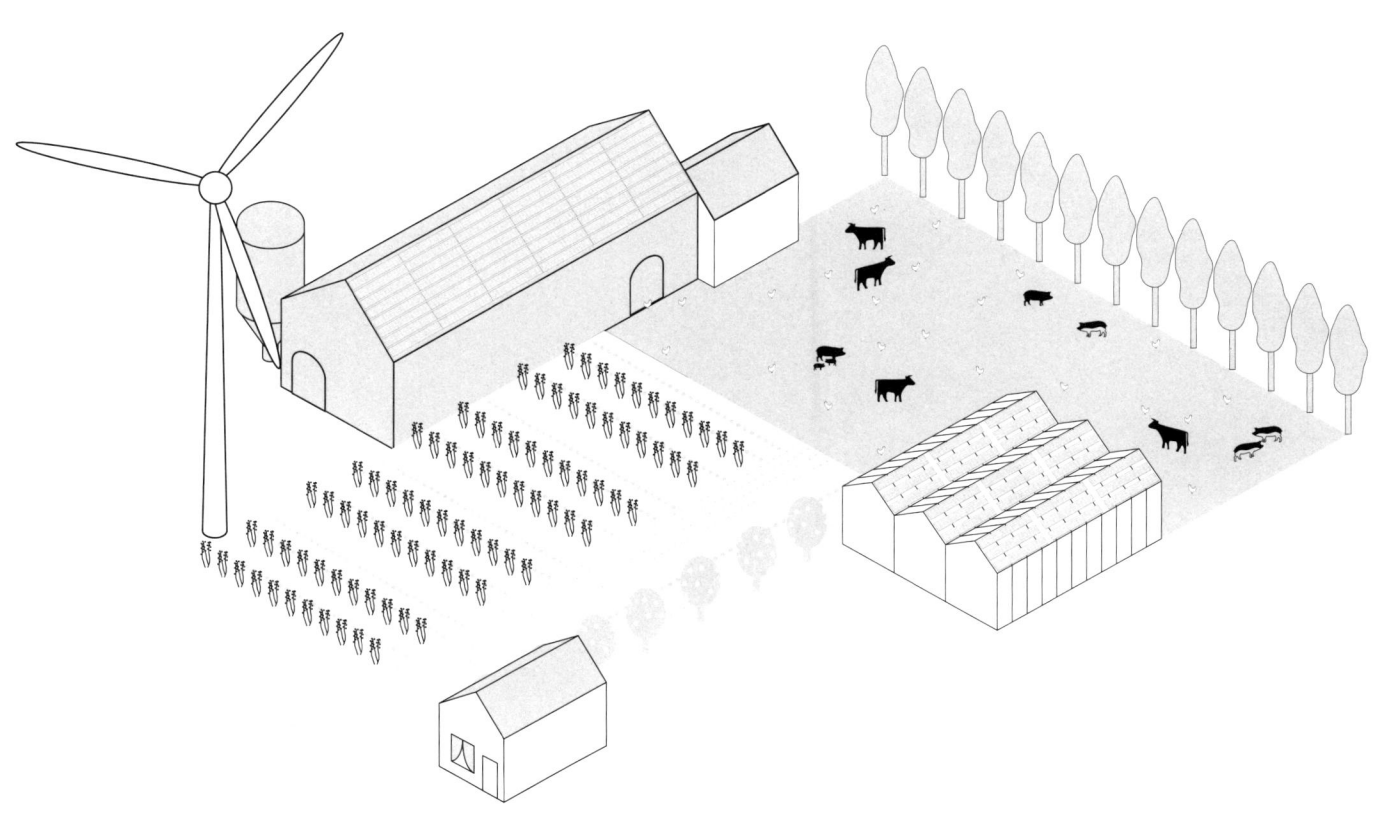

Decentralized

Influence of Digital Technology

Settlements, rural areas, small and big cities are evenly distributed with little hierarchy or concentration. Here, the distribution over the country is visualized: the relationships between big cities, towns, and rural areas. There is not much top-down planning; developments happen through millions of individual decisions. Aided by the possibilities of digital media, they follow the path of least resistance. Individuals will develop there where it is easy. This leads to a relatively equal distribution of developments across the country. Many cities and settlements keep their original size, sometimes at lower densities, sometimes at higher densities, through a more efficient sharing of resources.

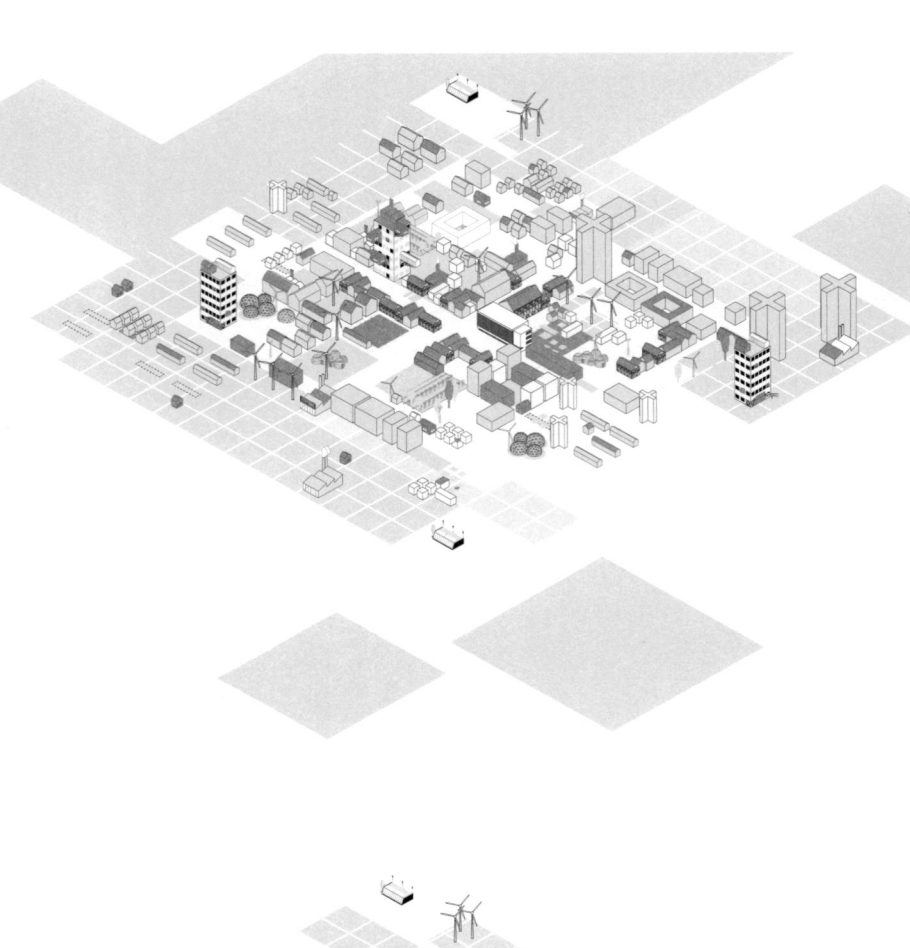

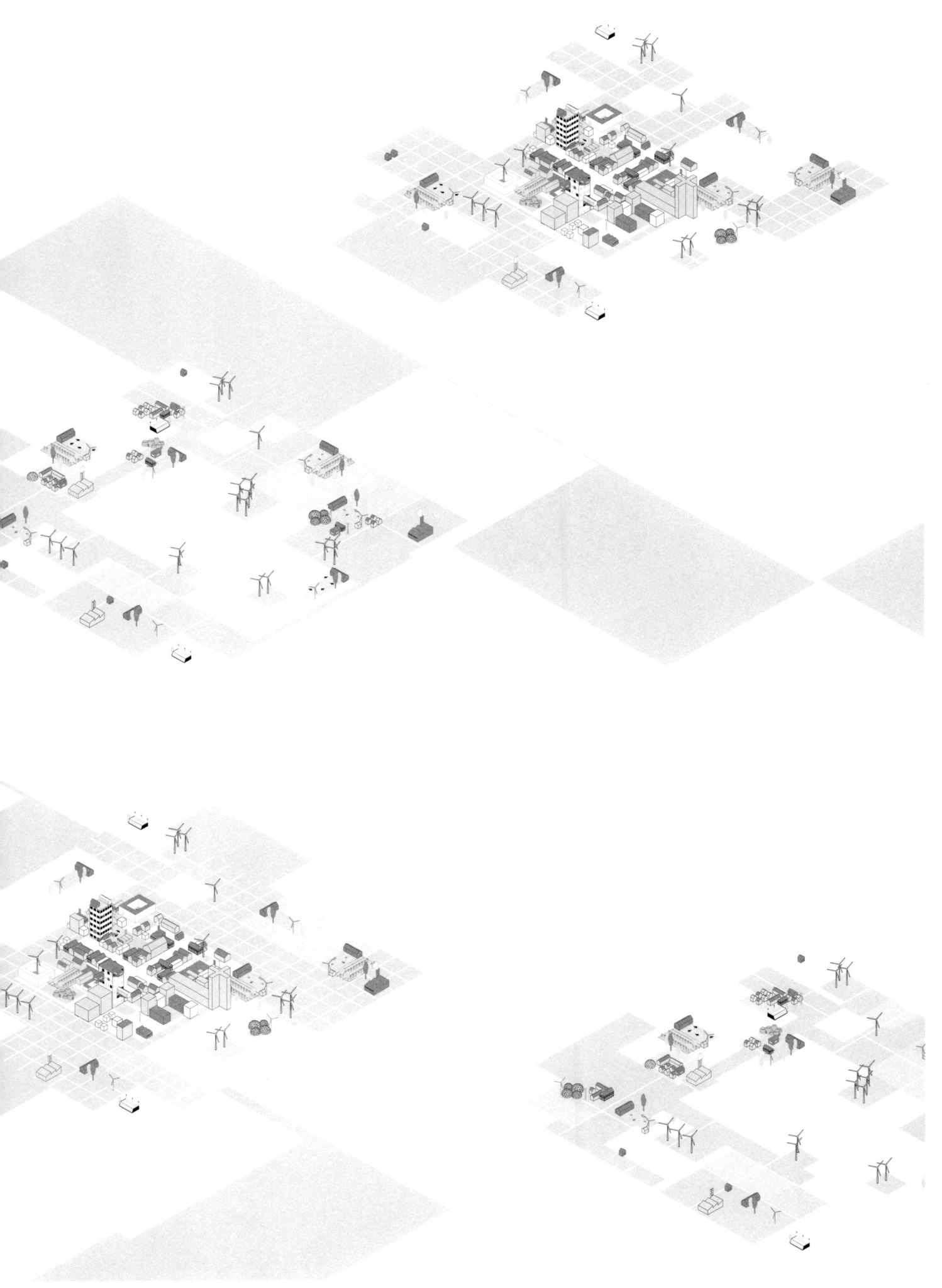

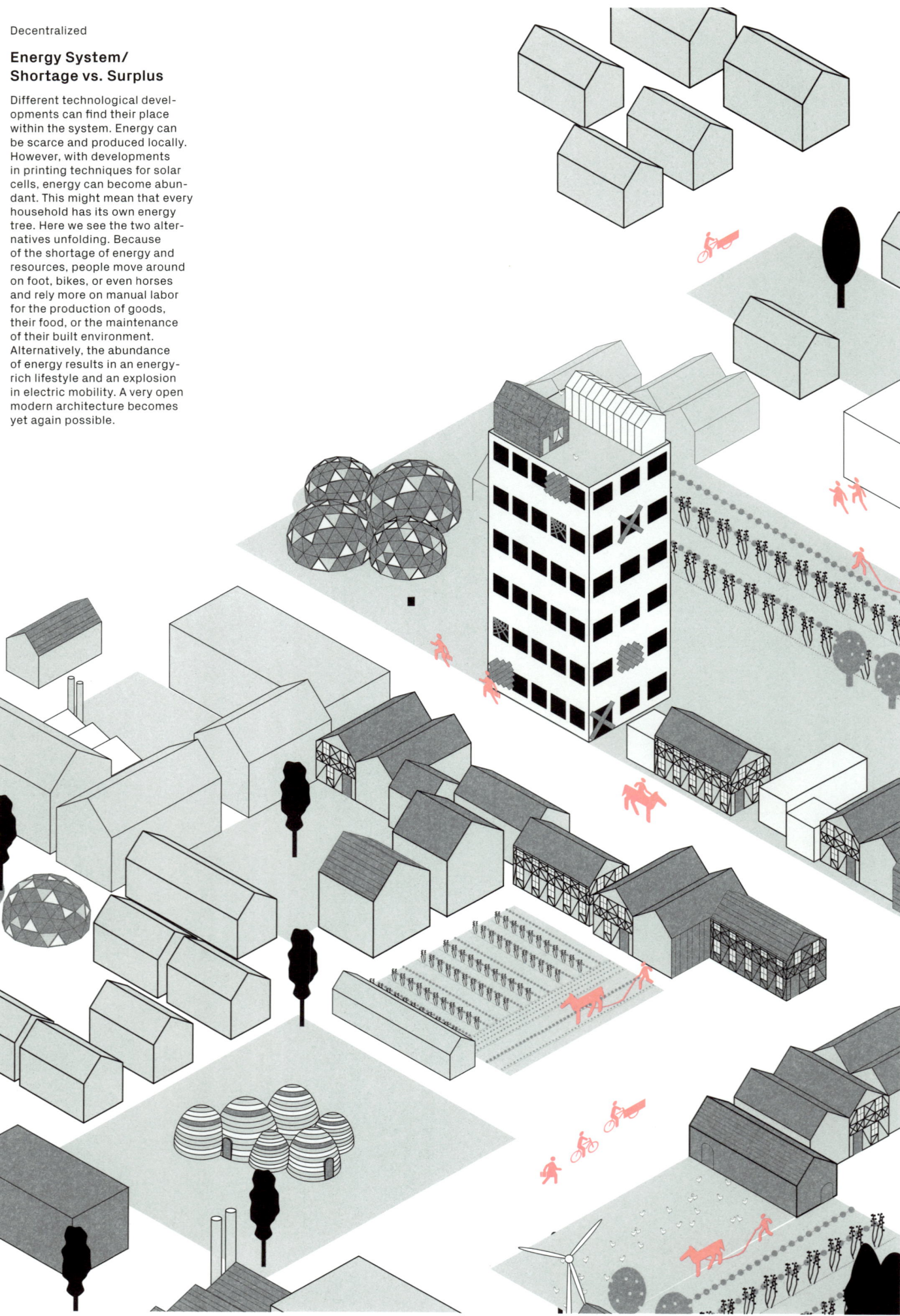

Decentralized

Energy System/ Shortage vs. Surplus

Different technological developments can find their place within the system. Energy can be scarce and produced locally. However, with developments in printing techniques for solar cells, energy can become abundant. This might mean that every household has its own energy tree. Here we see the two alternatives unfolding. Because of the shortage of energy and resources, people move around on foot, bikes, or even horses and rely more on manual labor for the production of goods, their food, or the maintenance of their built environment. Alternatively, the abundance of energy results in an energy-rich lifestyle and an explosion in electric mobility. A very open modern architecture becomes yet again possible.

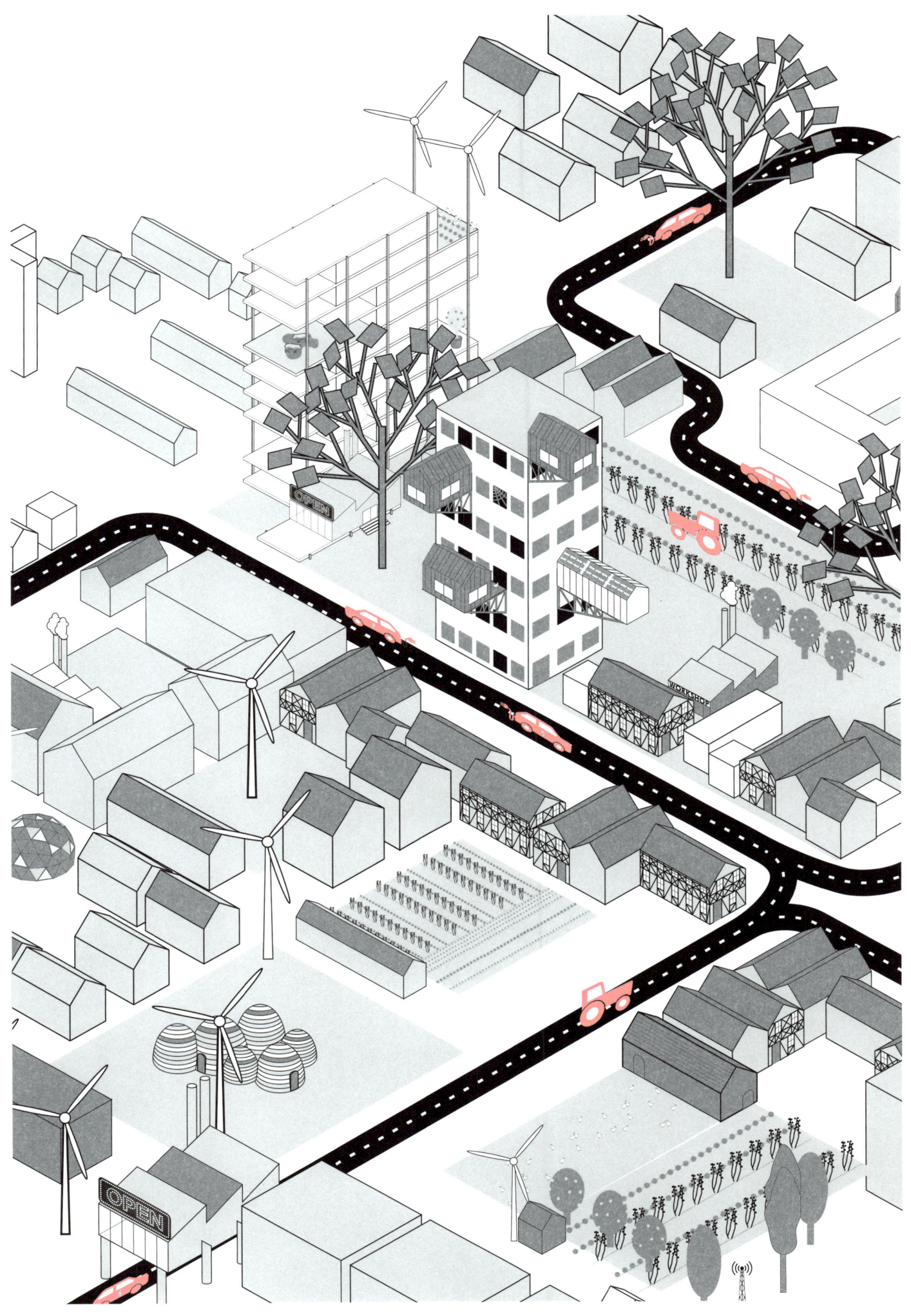

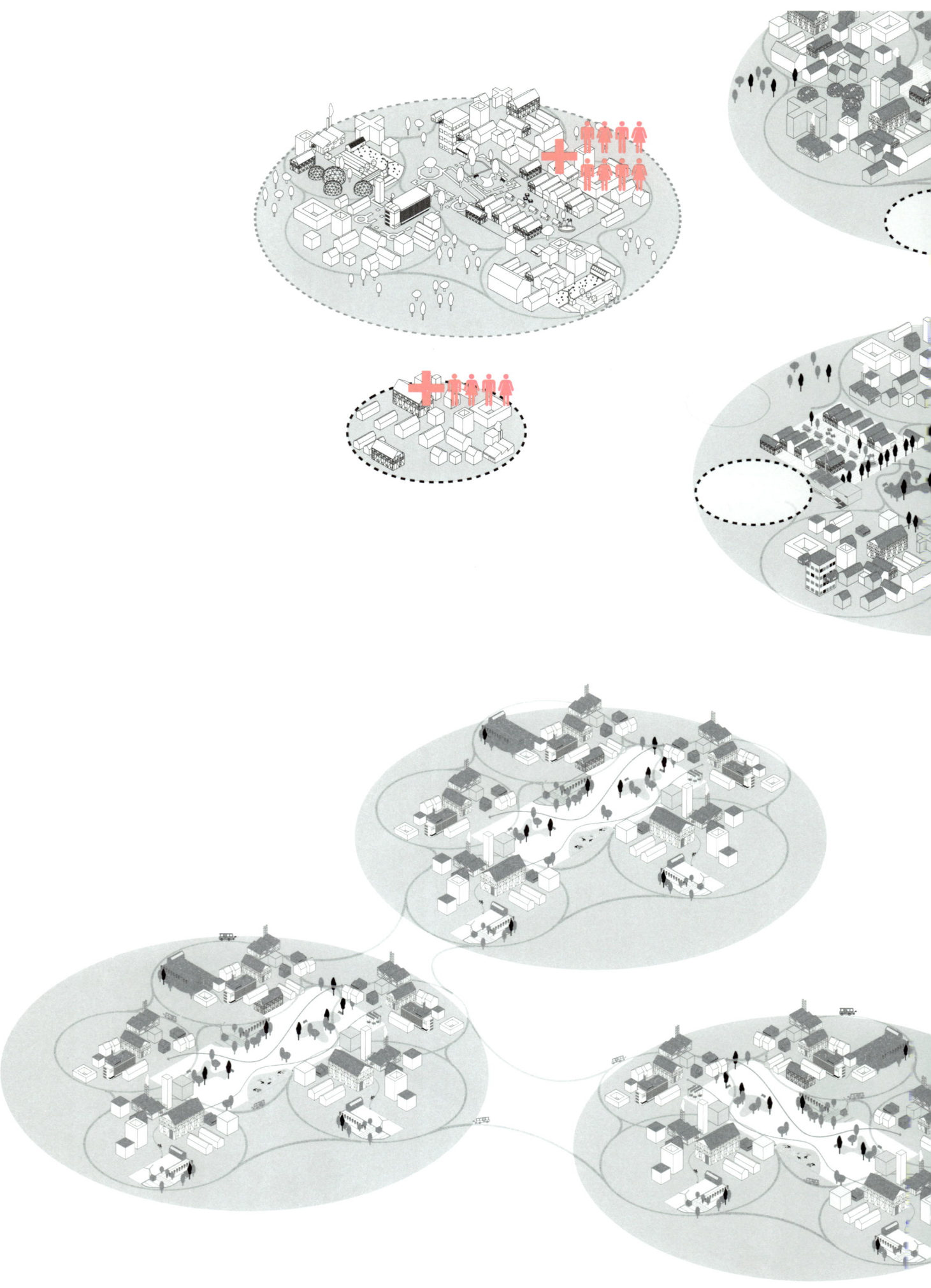

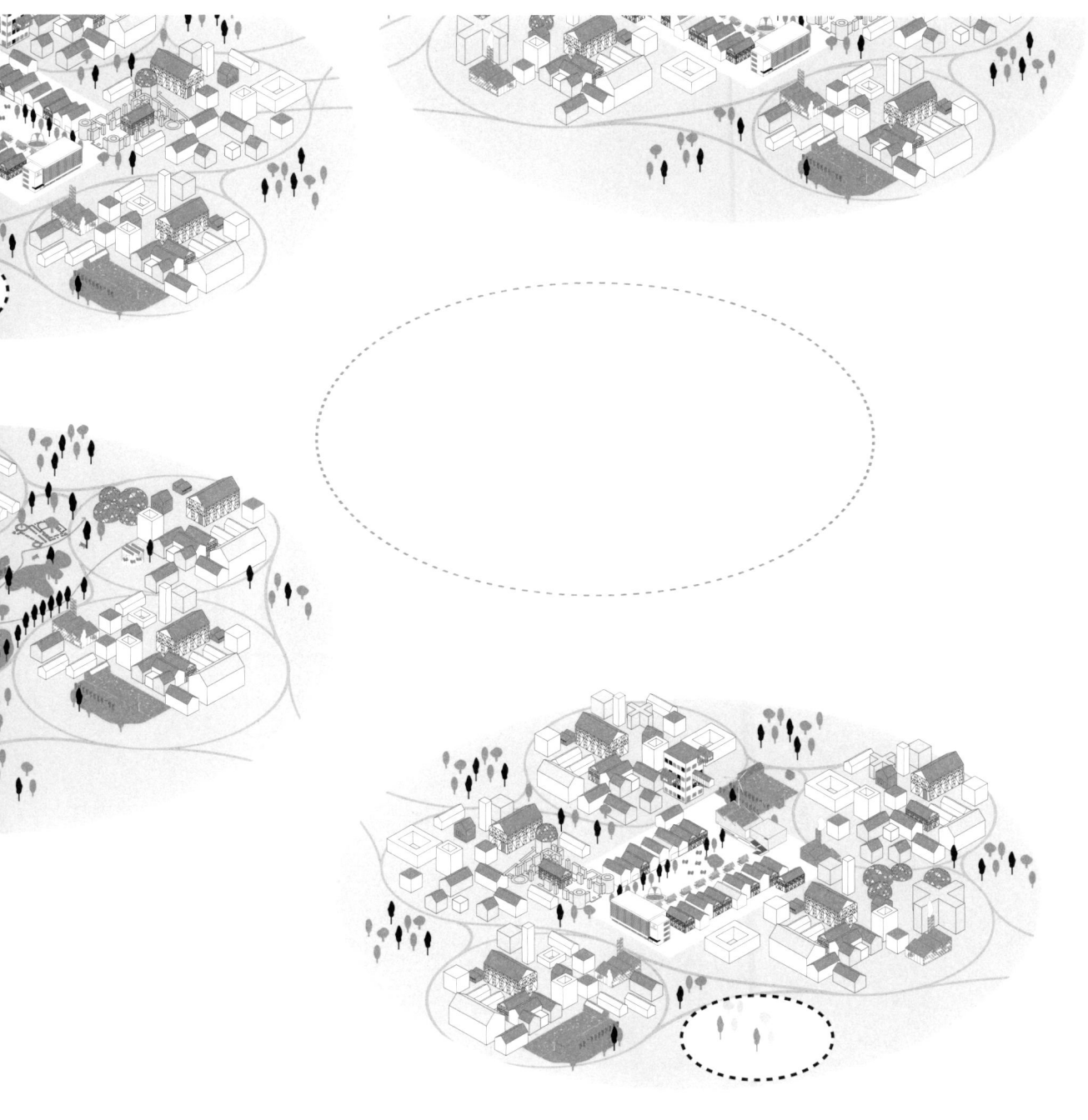

Cities/
Cities in Periphery

Demographic changes, both with regard to immigration as well as within a country, play a large role in any spatial development. Scale and size proves to be attractive to immigrants, who will settle in the few metropolitan areas. A critical mass of services, employment, and education will keep the metropolitan areas globally competitive. By the same token, internal migration will focus on these areas as well. Migration provokes settlements emptying out in favor of new settlement in or near the bigger metropolises. Growth takes place mostly in the big metropolitan regions; the peripheral cities and rural areas show a more balanced development.

Surroundings of Cities

Often, the landscape is thought of as complementary to cities, always close by, smoothly integrated in the lives of the city dwellers. Green belts extending into the urban areas feature small organic farms, recreational infrastructure, and well-preserved built and natural heritage. Further away, renewable energy landscapes and possibilities for sustainable tourism abound. The landscape is intertwined with the cities, such that together they form green metropolitan areas.

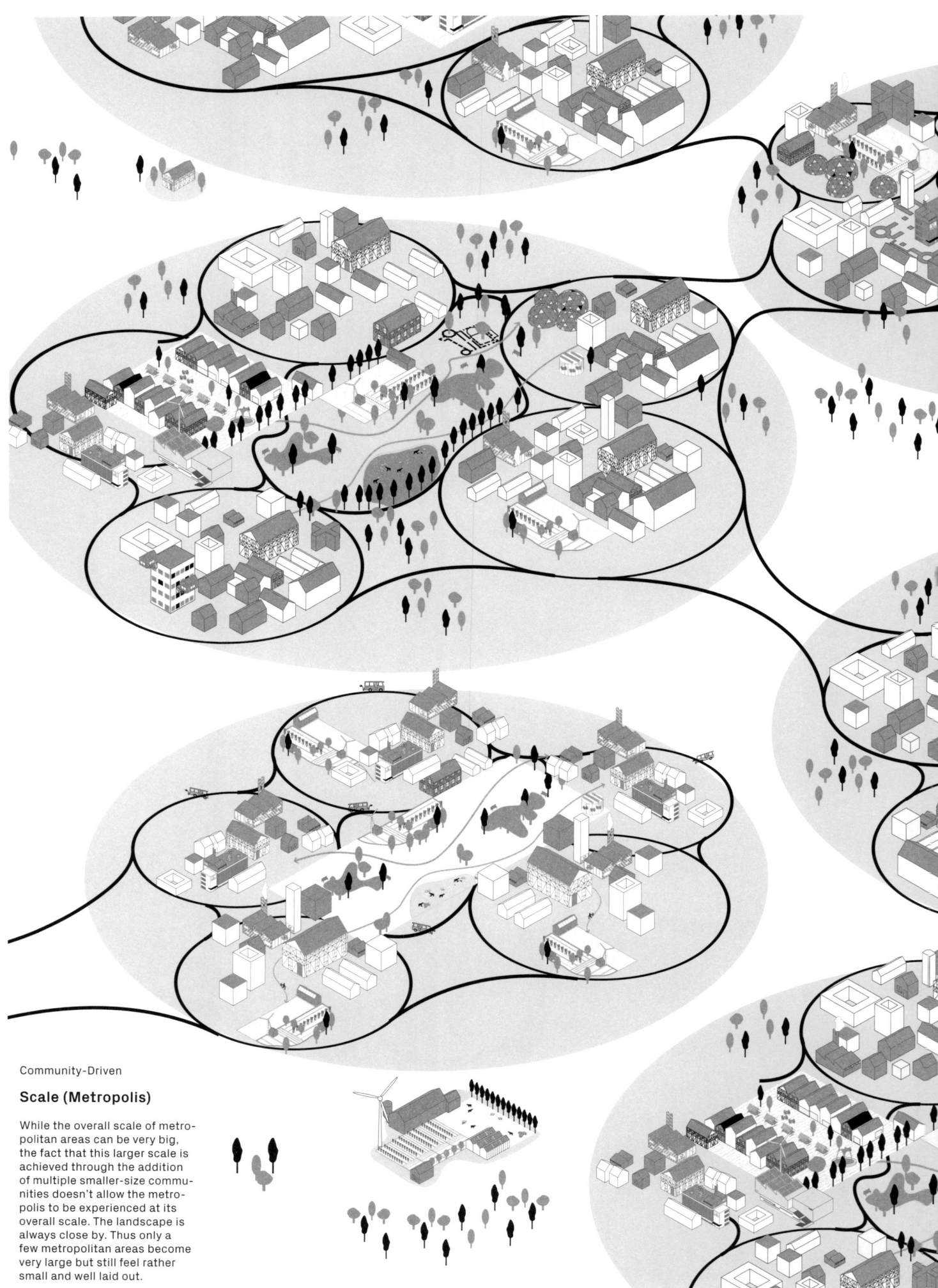

Community-Driven

Scale (Metropolis)

While the overall scale of metropolitan areas can be very big, the fact that this larger scale is achieved through the addition of multiple smaller-size communities doesn't allow the metropolis to be experienced at its overall scale. The landscape is always close by. Thus only a few metropolitan areas become very large but still feel rather small and well laid out.

157

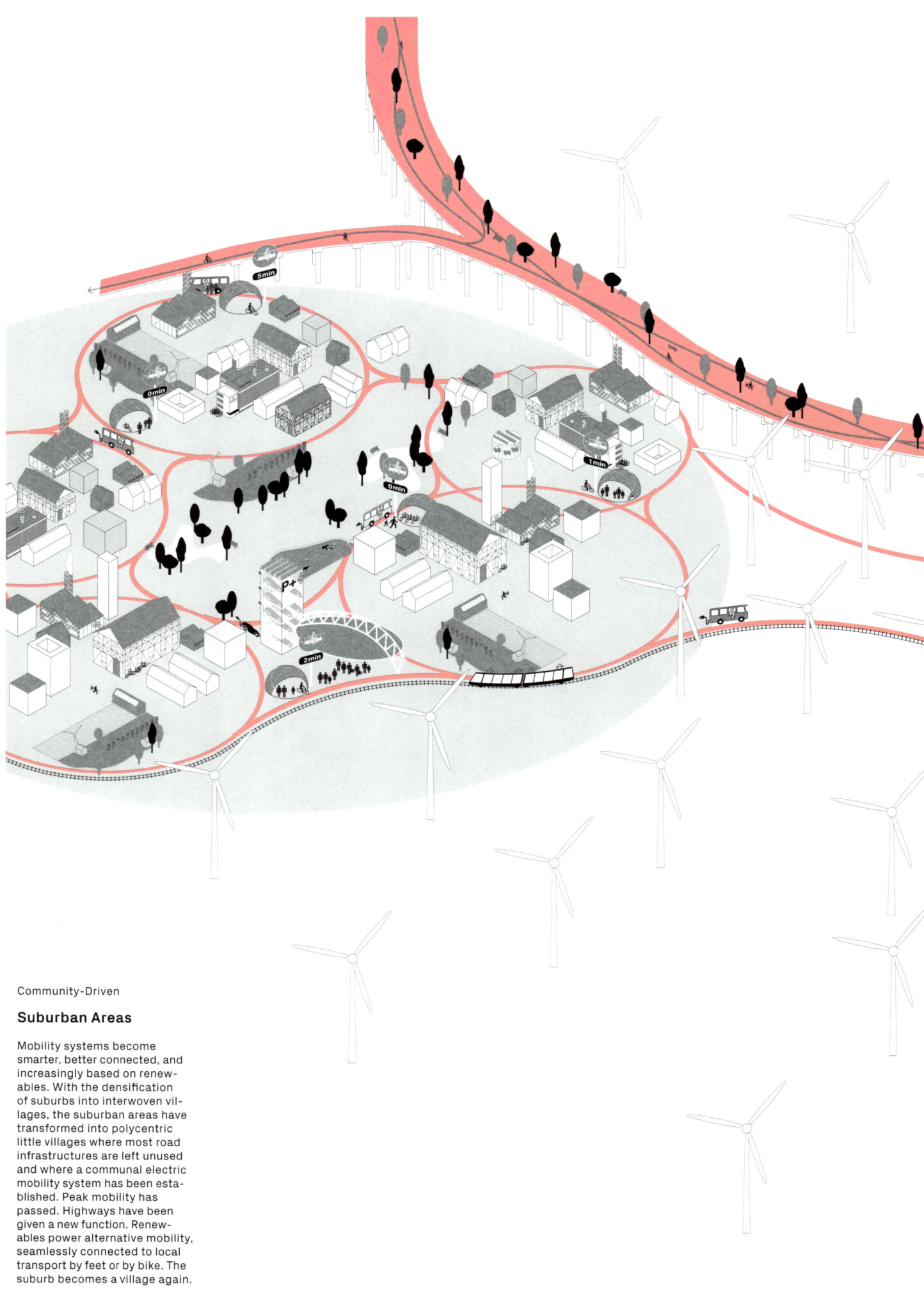

Community-Driven

Suburban Areas

Mobility systems become smarter, better connected, and increasingly based on renewables. With the densification of suburbs into interwoven villages, the suburban areas have transformed into polycentric little villages where most road infrastructures are left unused and where a communal electric mobility system has been established. Peak mobility has passed. Highways have been given a new function. Renewables power alternative mobility, seamlessly connected to local transport by feet or by bike. The suburb becomes a village again.

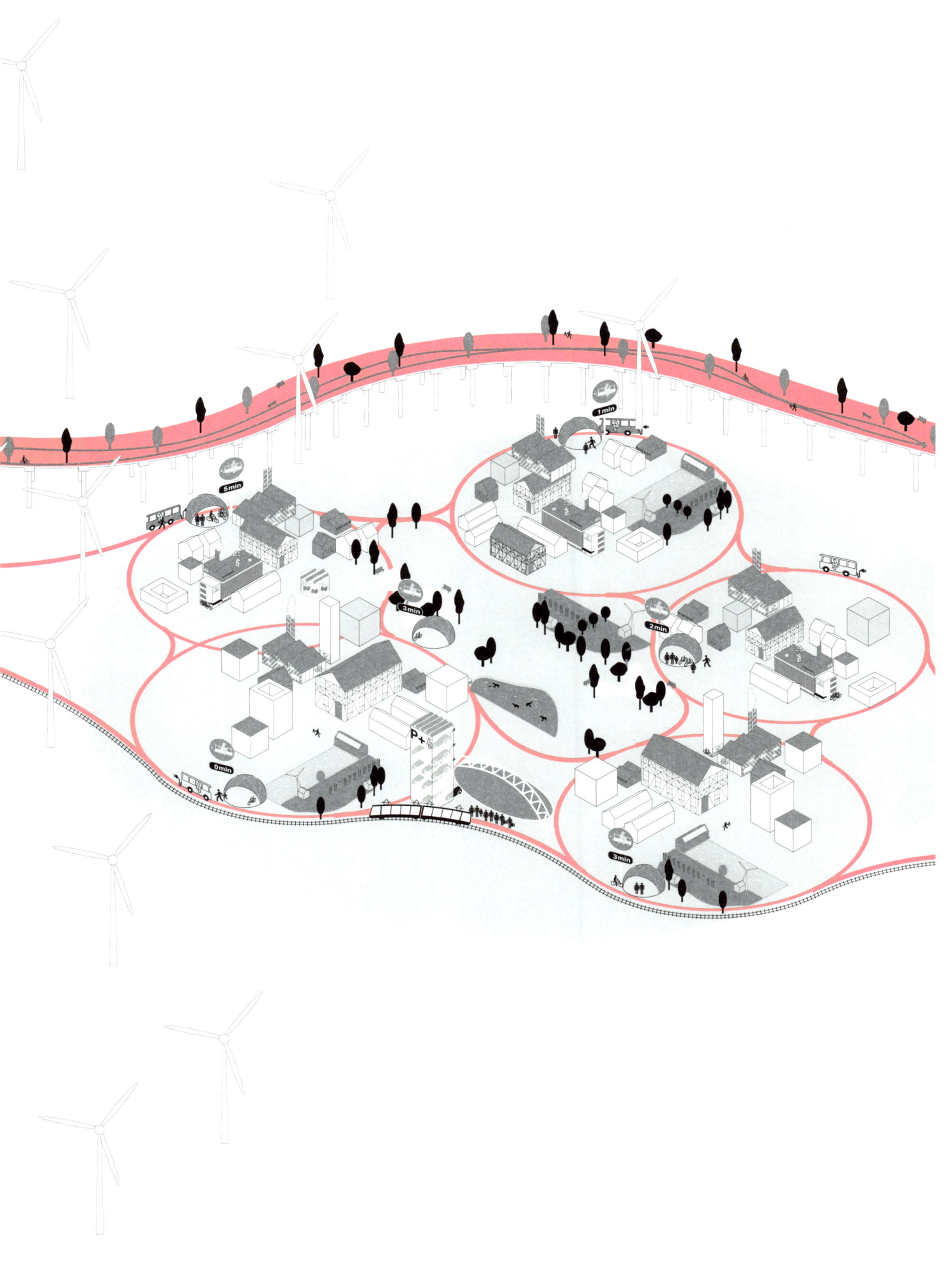

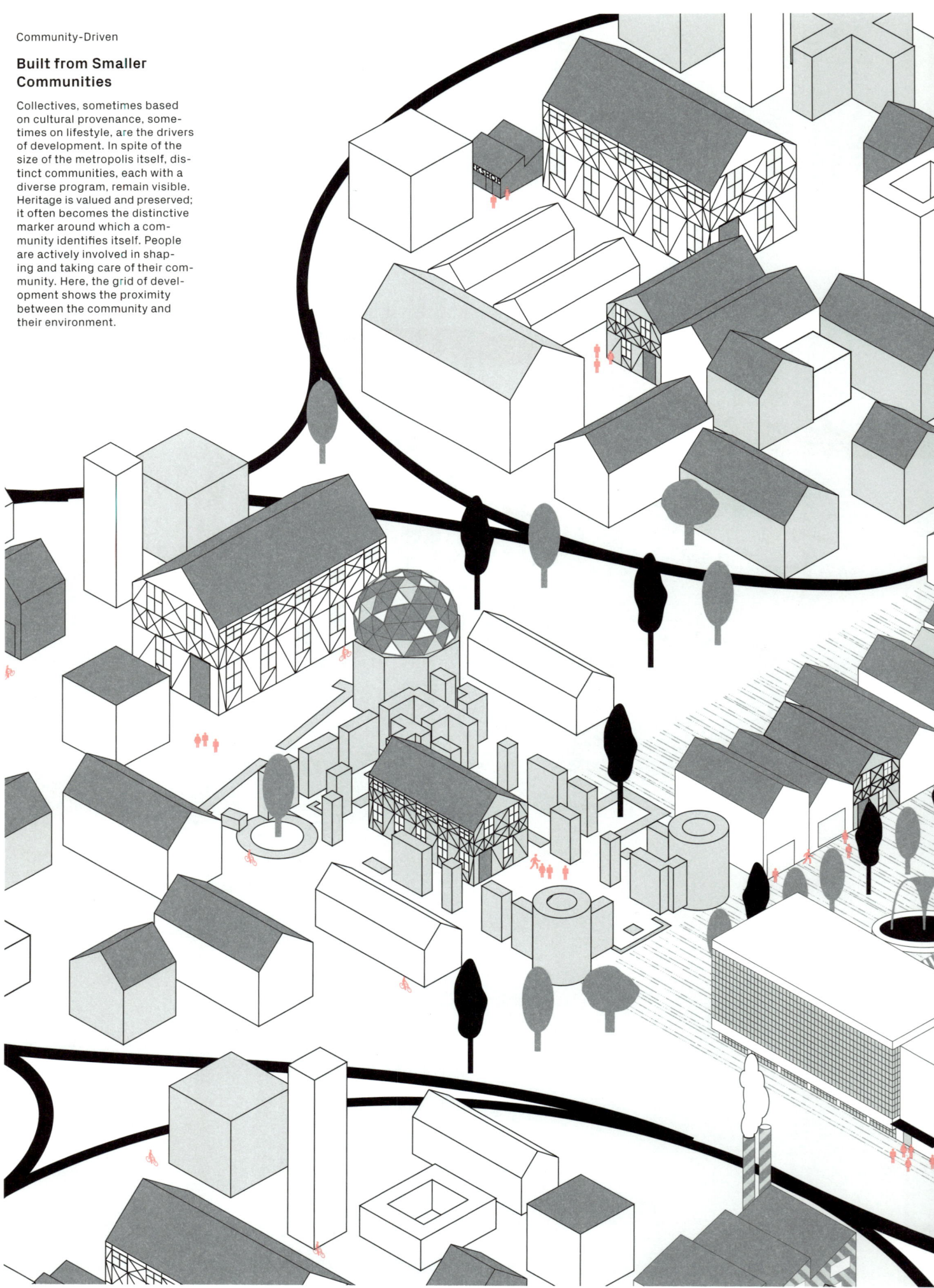

Built from Smaller Communities

Collectives, sometimes based on cultural provenance, sometimes on lifestyle, are the drivers of development. In spite of the size of the metropolis itself, distinct communities, each with a diverse program, remain visible. Heritage is valued and preserved; it often becomes the distinctive marker around which a community identifies itself. People are actively involved in shaping and taking care of their community. Here, the grid of development shows the proximity between the community and their environment.

Mixed Education, Business & Civic

Education, business, and civic life mix at the local level. Schools link with local companies and agencies into creative knowledge hubs where acquired skills and gained knowledge can directly be applied in real-time. Local knowledge and instruction are digitally connected to the global open knowledge base.

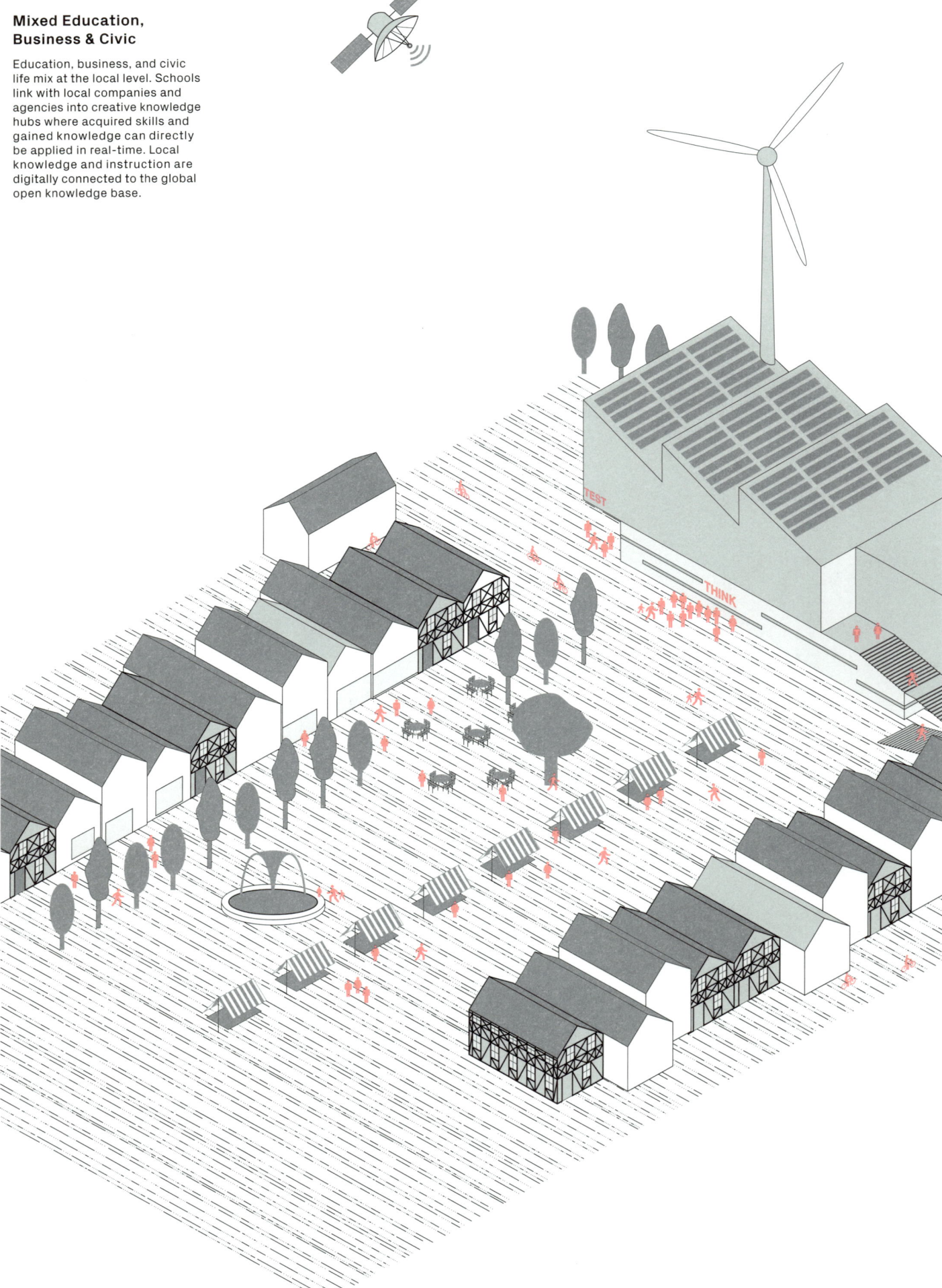

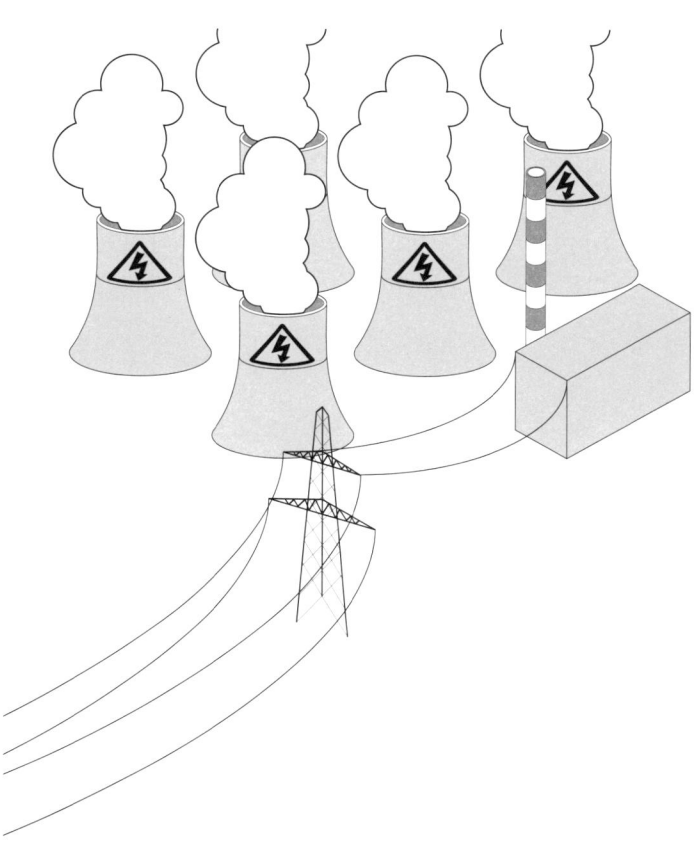

Exclusive

Large-Scale Landscapes

The accumulation of capital and maximum of spatial efficiency tend toward the large scale, in a process of ever-increasing aggregation and control in the hands of a few. Development is shaped by a few agents only; large corporations liaise with strong government, operating in large projects. Big empty spaces not served by the networks are considered inefficient by the scale of production and are largely ignored. Here we see an empty landscape as nuclear power and megafarming prevail.

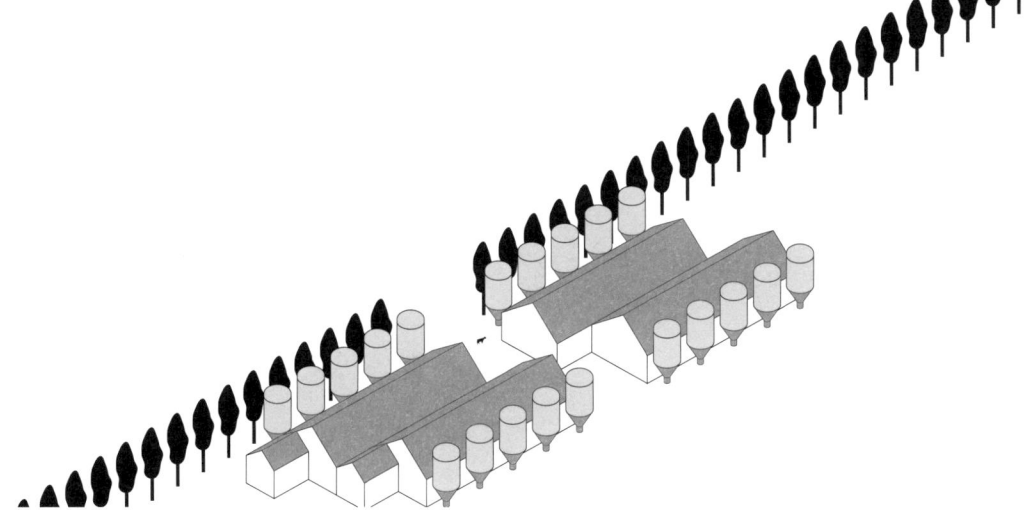

International
Energy Surplus

The energy networks are internationally intertwined. This
ensures that there are no capacity bottlenecks or energy short-
ages. Germany will become a
net exporter of energy. Hence,
energy production and distribution dominates the landscape.
Energy and goods are made
with maximum efficiency, at
locations that facilitate production. The organization of
the resulting flows forms the
mechanism behind the spatial
transformation.

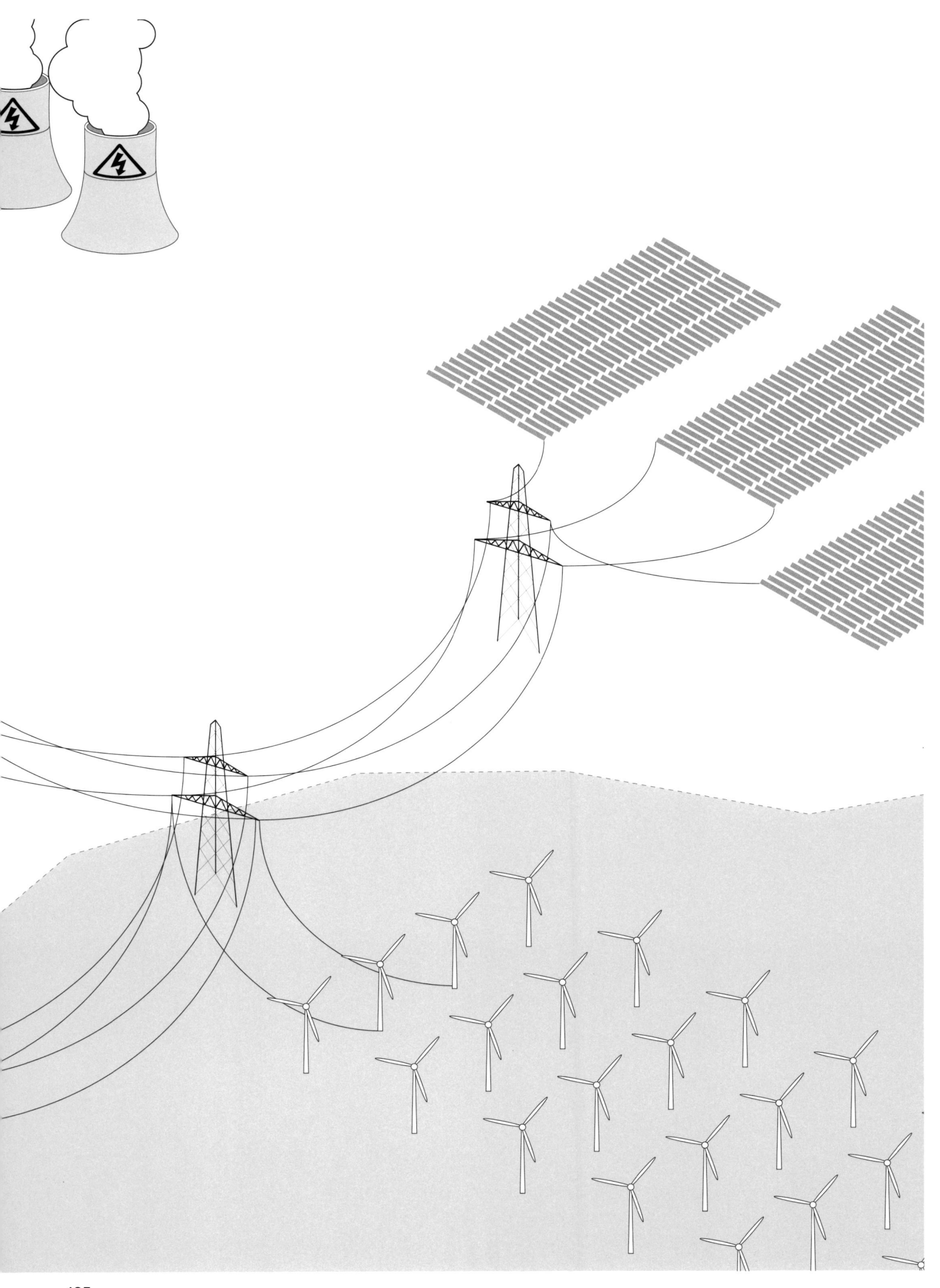

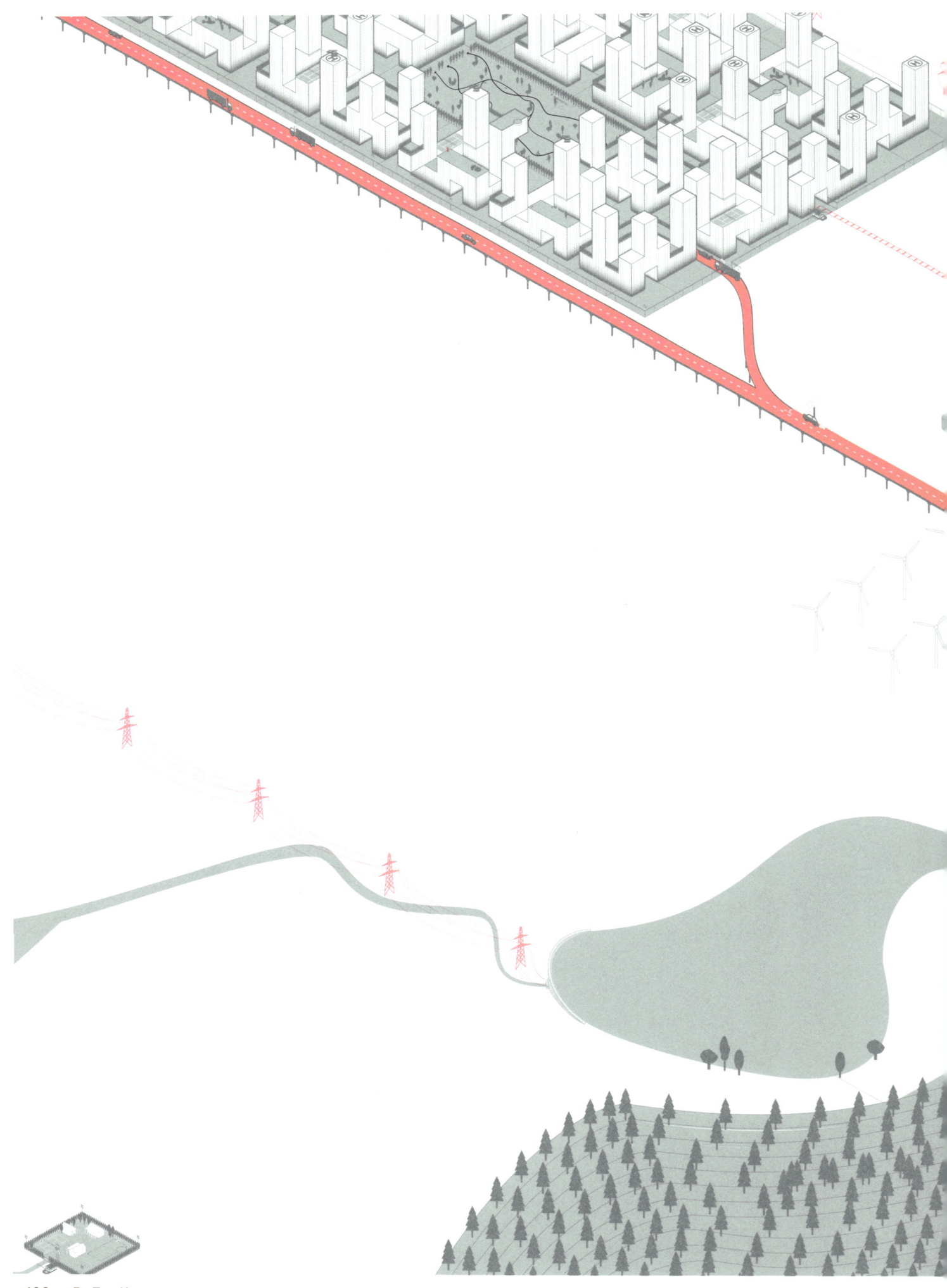

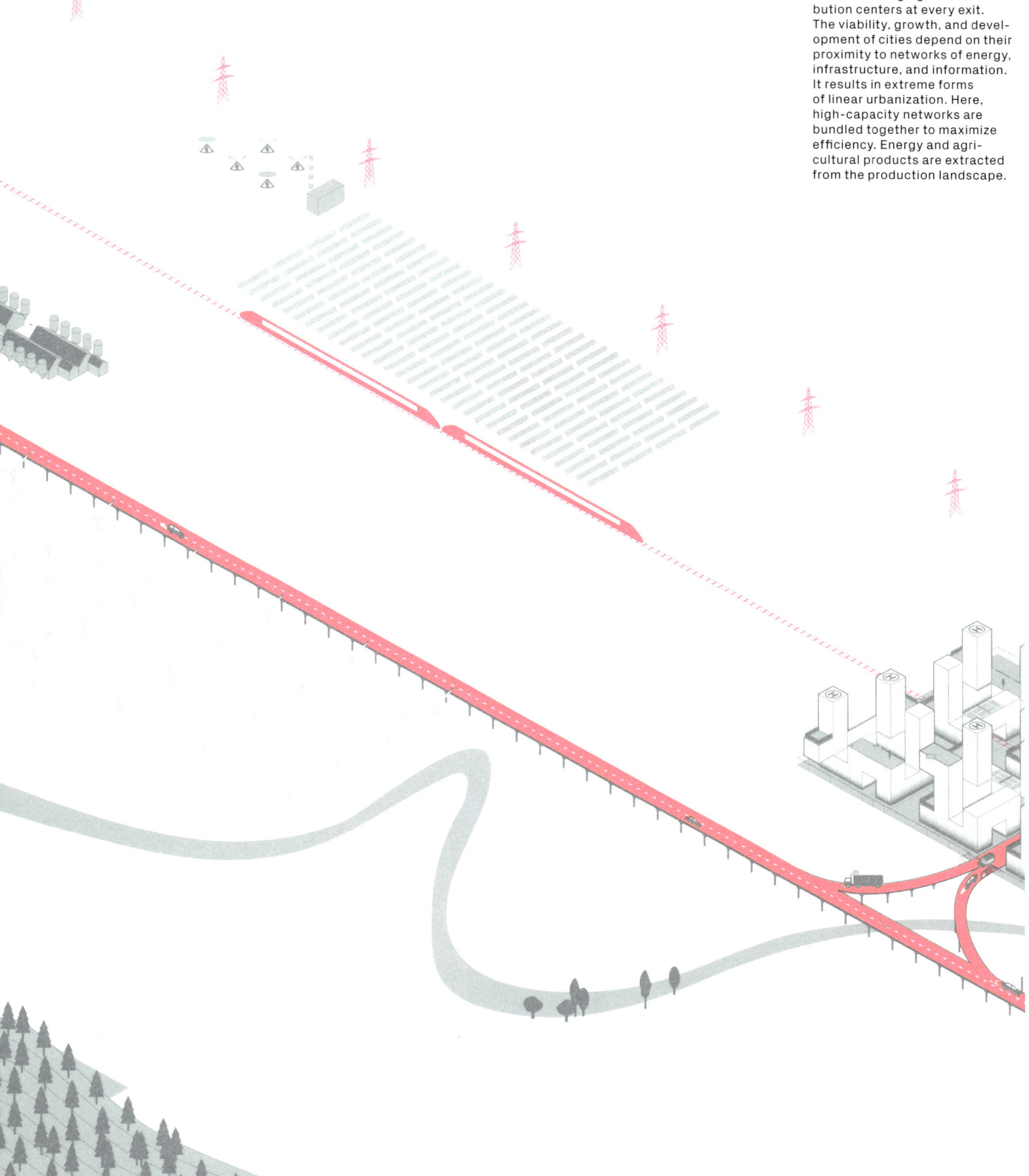

Proximity to Networks

Linear cities were once designed as emblems of modernization. In many countries, highways produced corridors with food, lodging, and distribution centers at every exit. The viability, growth, and development of cities depend on their proximity to networks of energy, infrastructure, and information. It results in extreme forms of linear urbanization. Here, high-capacity networks are bundled together to maximize efficiency. Energy and agricultural products are extracted from the production landscape.

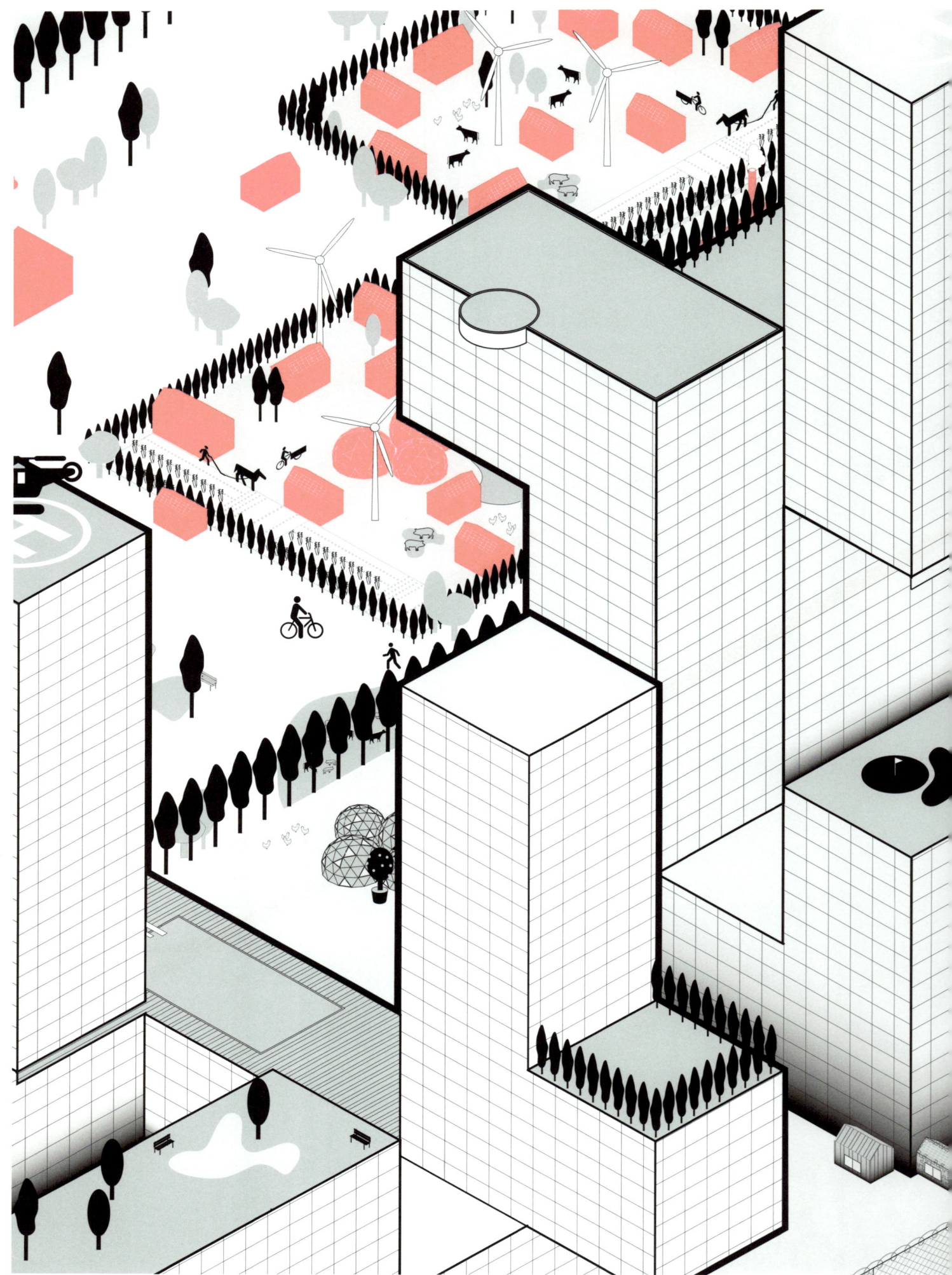

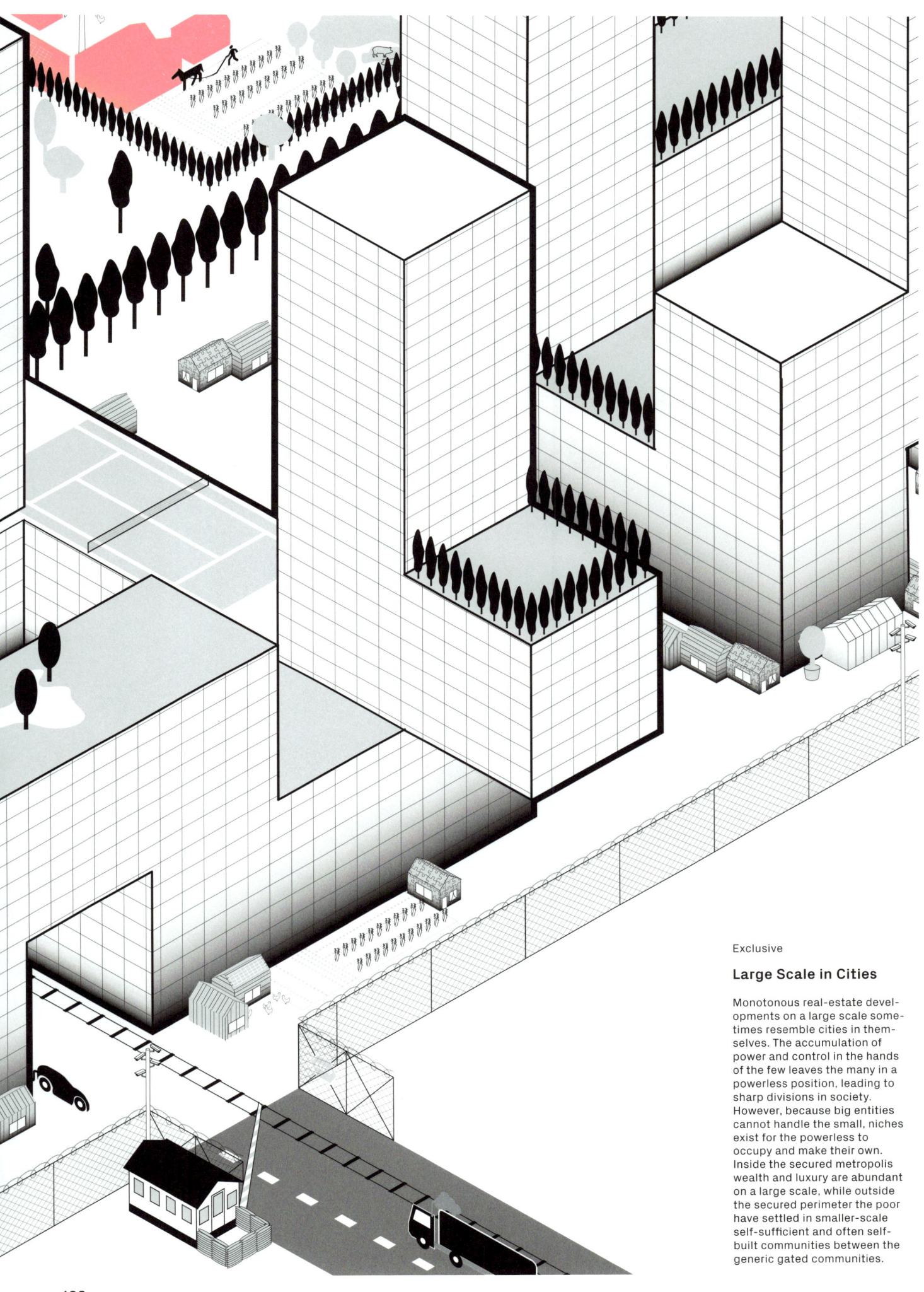

Exclusive

Large Scale in Cities

Monotonous real-estate developments on a large scale sometimes resemble cities in themselves. The accumulation of power and control in the hands of the few leaves the many in a powerless position, leading to sharp divisions in society. However, because big entities cannot handle the small, niches exist for the powerless to occupy and make their own. Inside the secured metropolis wealth and luxury are abundant on a large scale, while outside the secured perimeter the poor have settled in smaller-scale self-sufficient and often self-built communities between the generic gated communities.

Safety-Security Enclave

A large-scale networked landscape has its counterpoint in
emptiness outside the networks.
In these remote areas small
enclaves pop up where people
with plenty of resources retreat
and live in luxury, independently
in gated communities, digitally
connected to the rest of the
world. Here, people who can
afford it choose secluded living in
a small enclave, securely fenced
off from its surroundings.

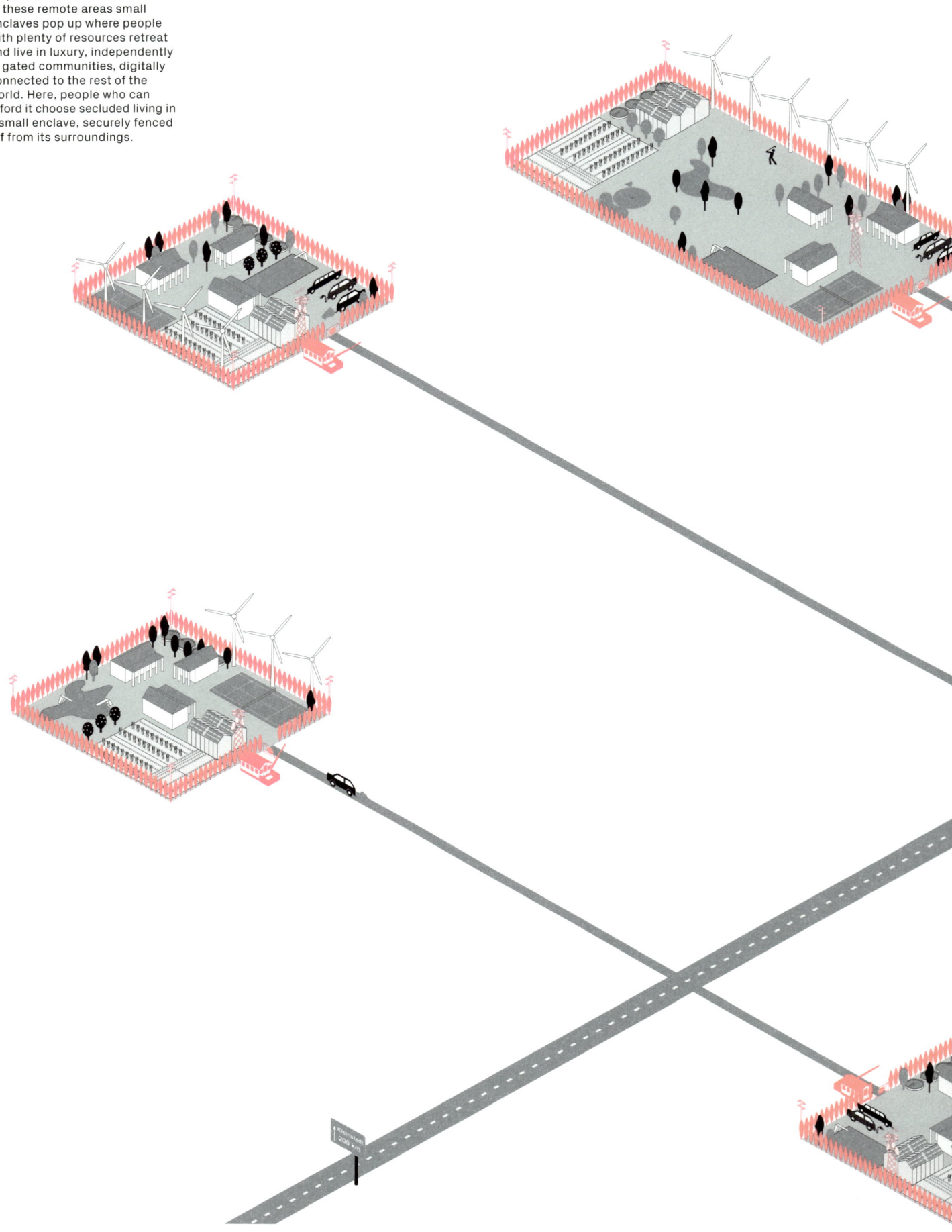

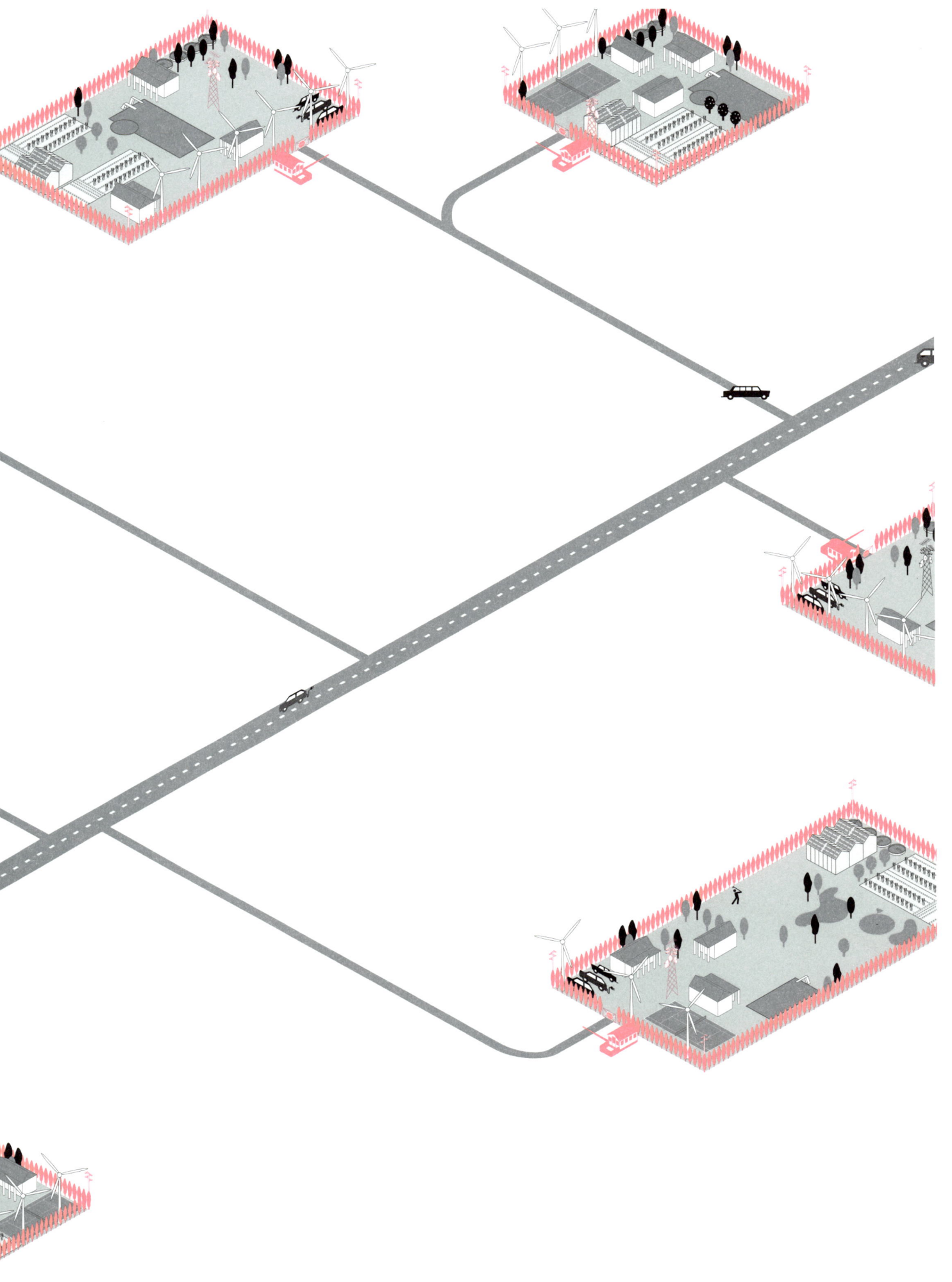

Flood Management

Ultimately, the *Baukulturkasten* allows for comparisons on many levels. One can imagine how issues of water management would be addressed in each of the explored scales and systems: "every man for himself"; collective solutions; or increasingly unequal mitigation, in which areas with insufficient protection flood. There might be individual flood protection measures on the scale of the built object in "Decentralized" versus collective measures taken by an entire community in "Community-Driven," and finally, in "Exclusive," pragmatic evacuation of flood-prone areas and rebuilding in safer areas.

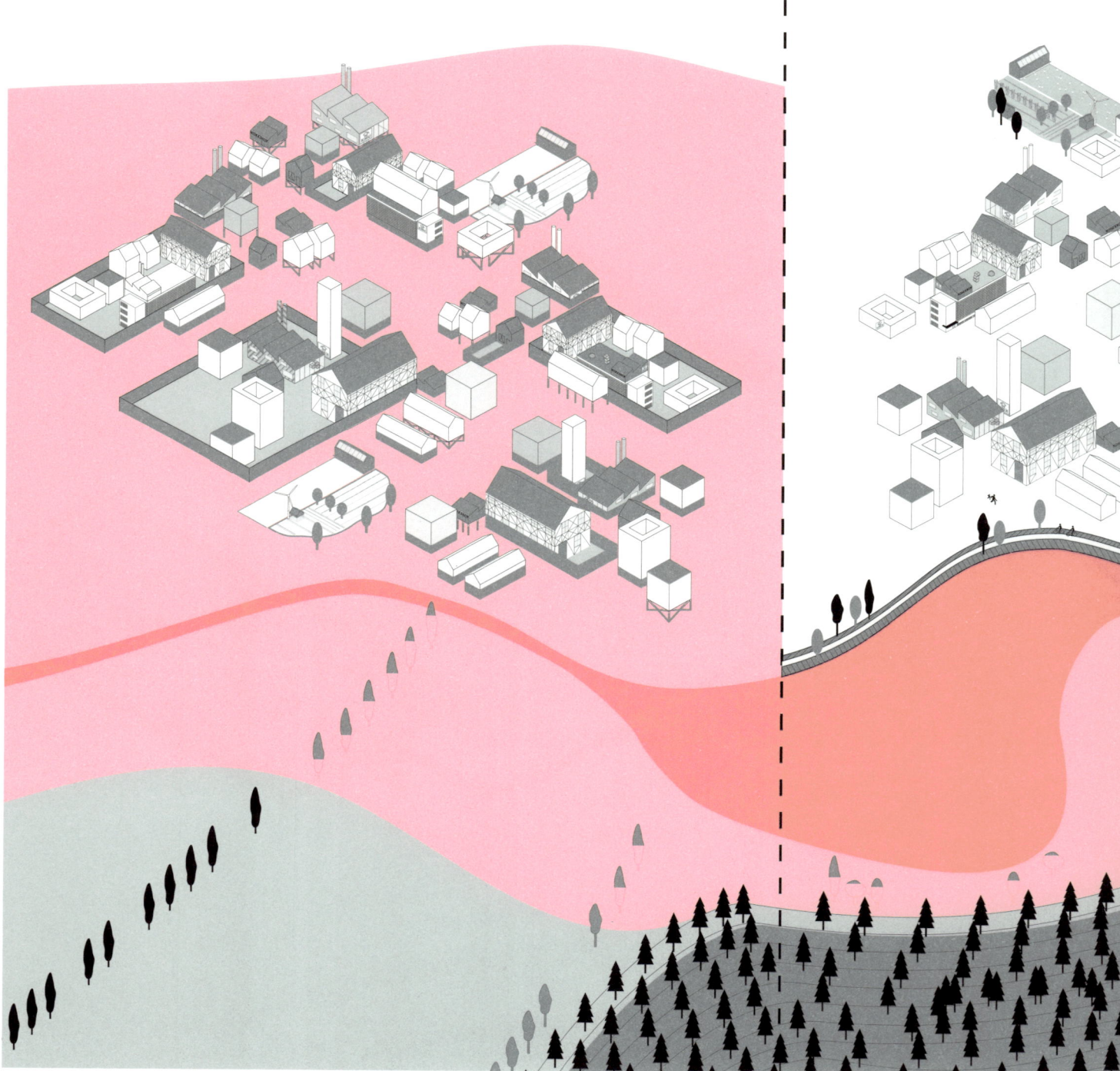

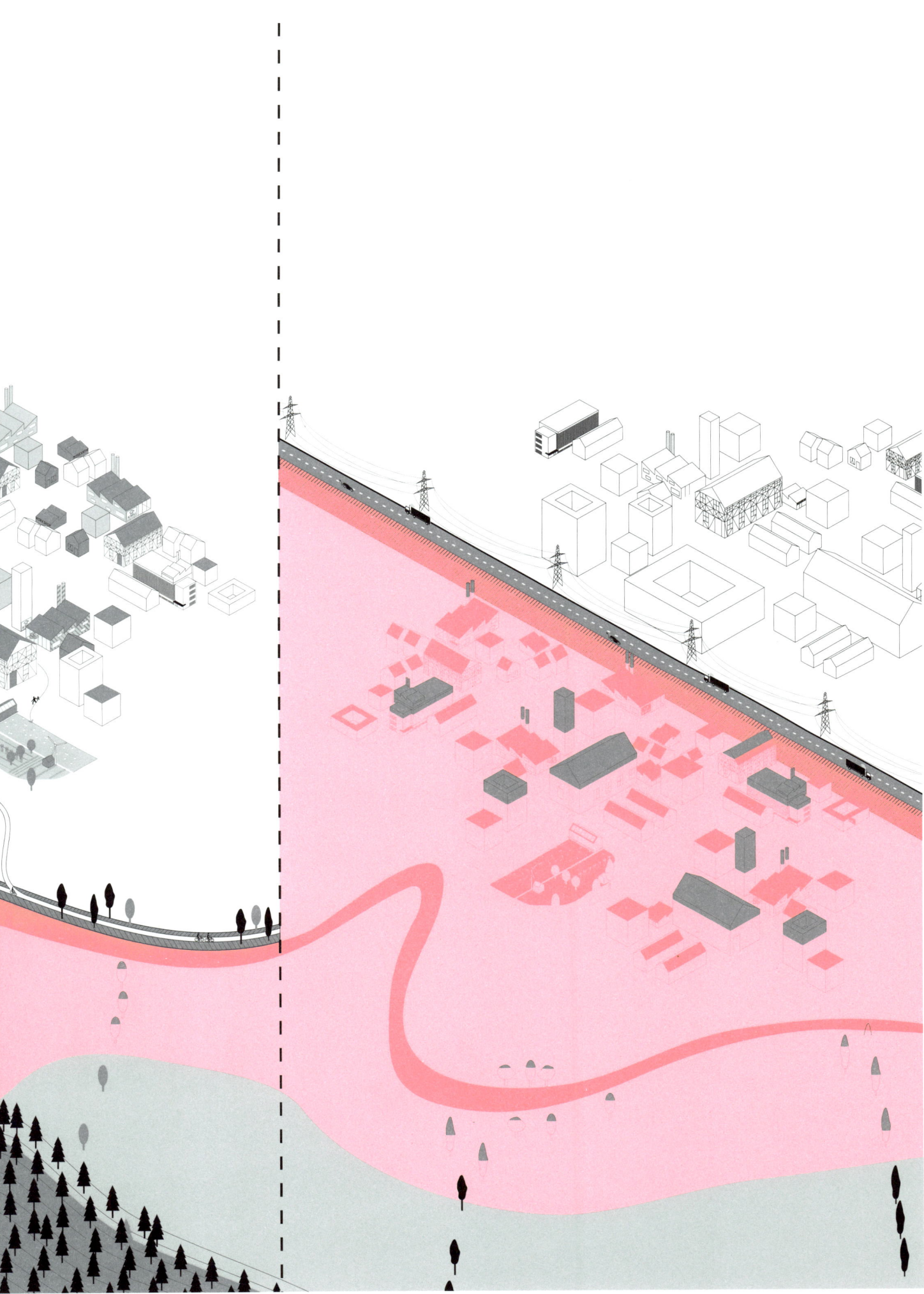

Public Spaces and Parks

In the different systems, the size and accessibility of the parks and recreational spaces differ greatly. In "Community-Driven," health and well-being are valued highly. Communities will invest in large, accessible parks with a variety of functions; the public spaces and parks are well maintained, easily accessible by bike, and form an important aspect of public life in the different communities. In "Decentralized," by contrast, parks are an anomaly: open space is either leftover space or filled in a very utilitarian way; open spaces will be "hacked" and used for things like urban farming. In "Exclusive," parks will be mostly private and fenced off for security reasons.

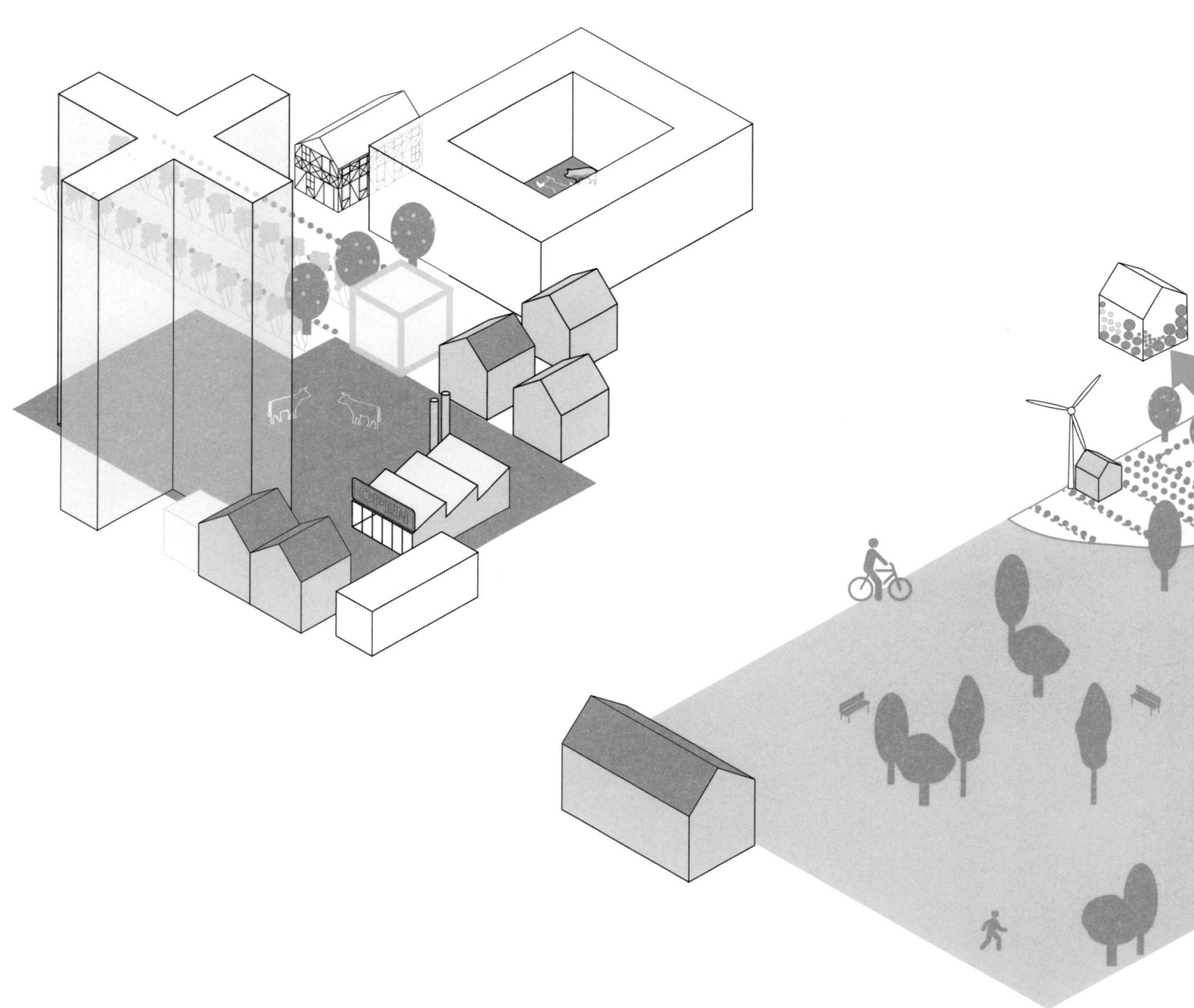

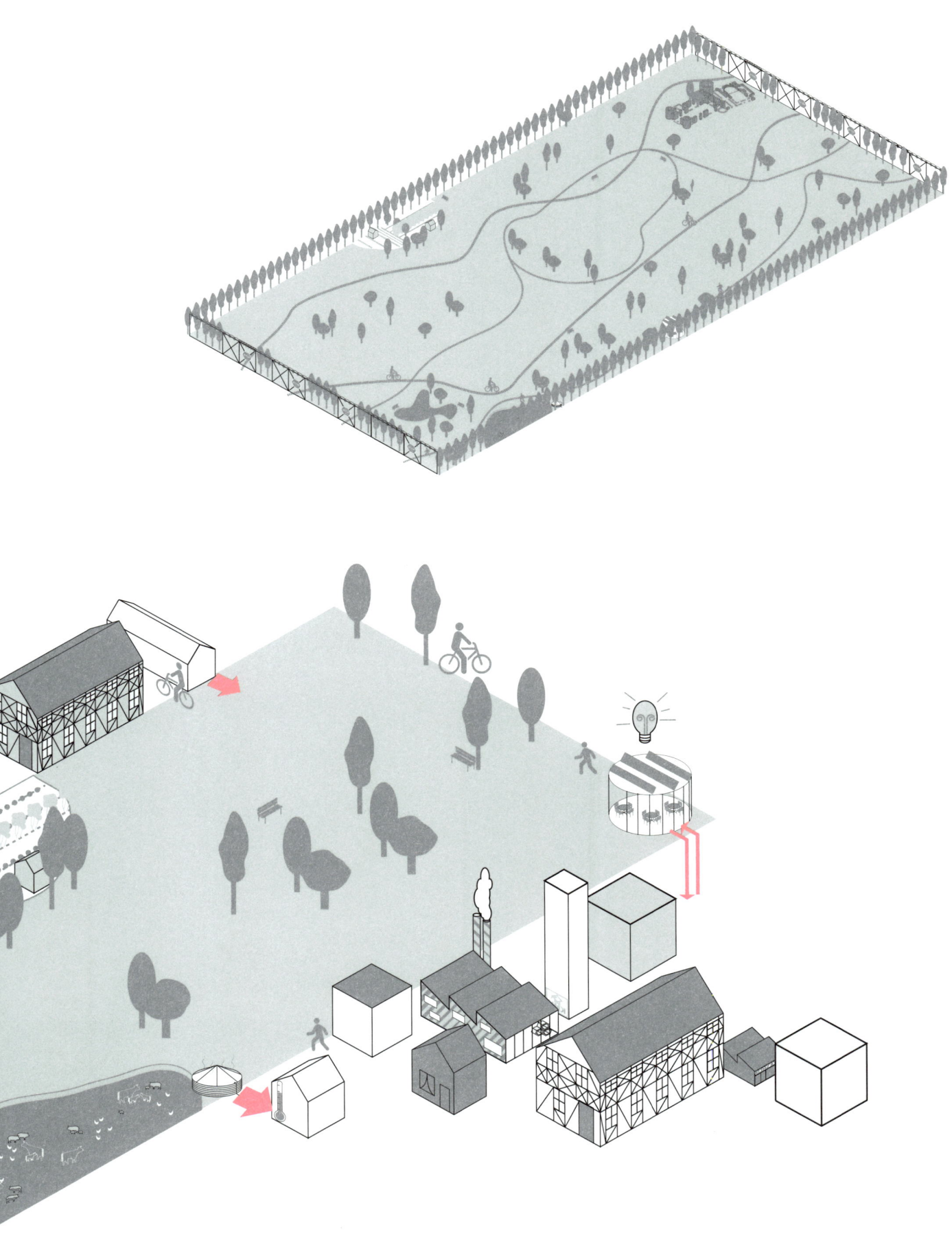

Building Modes

Developments in "Decentralized" happen on small isolated plots; in "Community-Driven" they happen communally; while in "Exclusive" there is an implementation of massive developments.

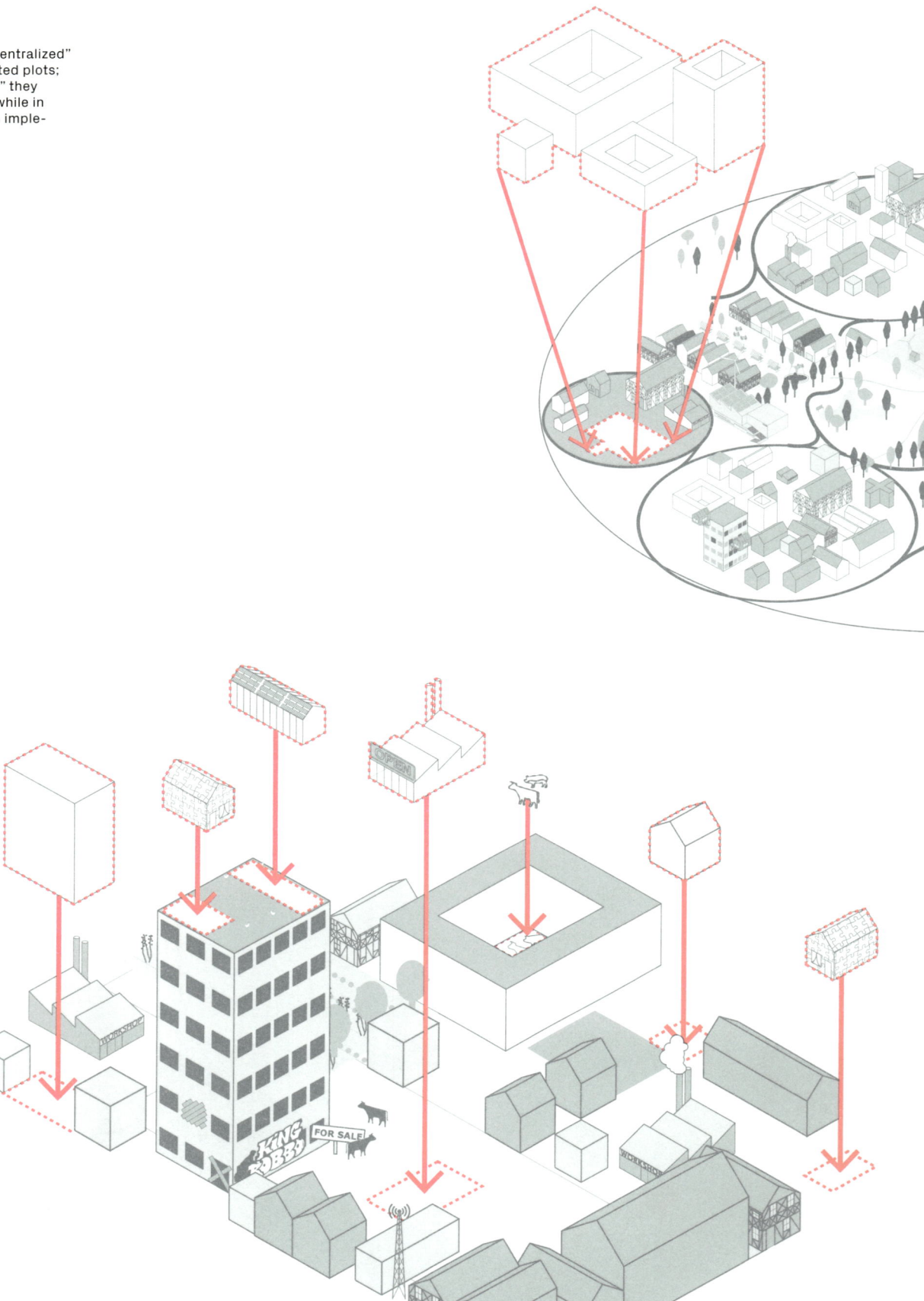

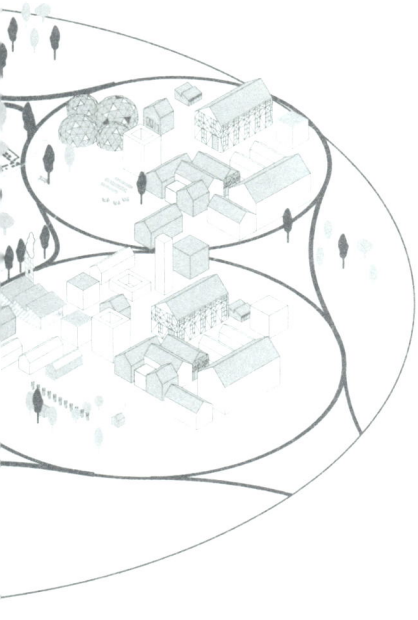

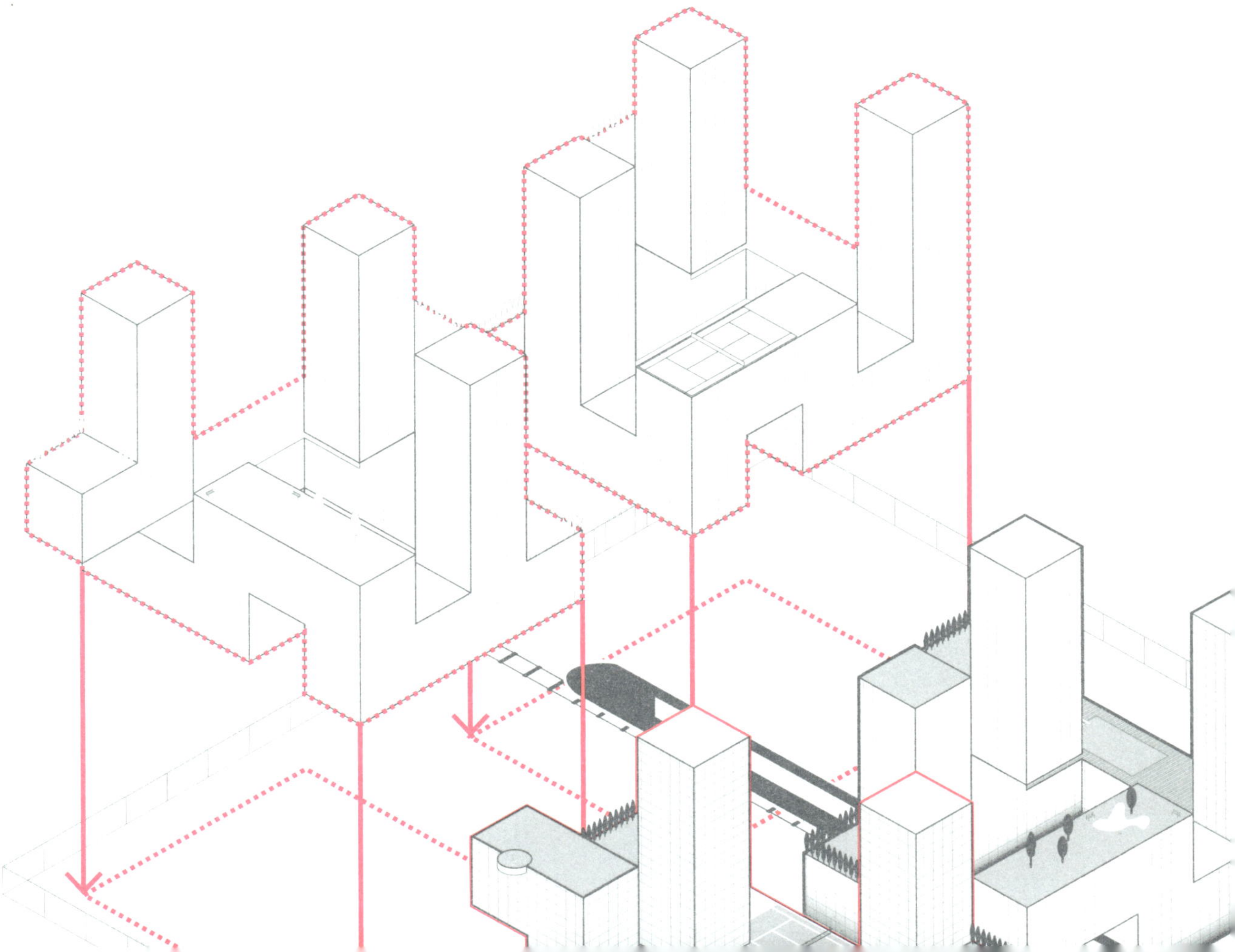

The Future Has Already Arrived:
Combined and Uneven Urban Catastrophe

Erik Swyngedouw

> "If the place isn't hotting up, we're fucked."
> "Here's the good news. The UN estimates that already a third of a million people a year are dying from climate change. Bangladesh is going down ... Methane is pouring out of the Siberian permafrost. There is a meltdown under the Greenland ice sheet. ... Two years ago we lost forty per cent of the Arctic summer ice. ... The future has arrived, Toby."
> "Yeah, I guess."
> "Toby, listen. It is a catastrophe. Relax."
>
> [Ian McEwan, *Solar*]

> "15. It is better to do nothing than to contribute to the invention of formal ways of rendering visible that which Empire already recognizes as existent."
>
> [Alain Badiou, "Fifteen Theses on Contemporary Art"]

Occasionally, a novel is written that captures better than most academic treatises the condition we are in. One of these is *Solar*, Ian McEwan's environmental testimonial novel that takes the perils of climate change as quilting point for its intricate plot. In the novel, a Nobel Prize–winning physicist teams up with a bunch of shady financiers to build a revolutionary solar-energy system that in one stroke would push back the terrifying prospect of irreversible and catastrophic climate change and return a more-than-healthy profit for the investors. Truly the technology of the elites' wet dream: saving the earth while making money. The realization of this phantasmagoria has only one catch: What if climate change is not happening? The scientist confidently reassures the wavering investors: "Toby, listen. It is a catastrophe. Relax." Indeed, the novel narrates how the "inconvenient truth" (in Al Gore's words) of the environmental condition we are in and the dystopian future it promises, if properly spun, can turn into a convenient truth that might spur a new "green" accumulation strategy while ensuring nothing really changes.

The feverish search for a prophylactic to deflect the anticipated apocalyptic reality of a disintegrating urban future propelled on by galloping ecological destruction, alleged pending resource depletion, and irreversible anthropogenic climate alteration has indeed nurtured a global urban design industry and urban intellectual and professional technocracy in search of a reinvented ecological urbanity that seeks out the healing qualities of a combination of eco-development, retrofitting, sustainable architecture, resilient urban governance, the commodification of environmental "services," and innovative technological design. This techno-managerial disposition has now been consensually established as the frontier of architectural, planning, and design theory and practice, presumably capable of saving both city and planet, while ensuring that civilization as we know it can continue for a while longer. Under the banner of radical techno-managerial restructuring, the focus of technical innovation and smart city design is now squarely on how to sustain capitalist urbanity so that nothing really *has* to change.

I shall argue in this contribution that the elevation of the environmental condition to the status of universal global concern that requires urgent techno-managerial attention is sutured by a particular phantasmagoric scripting, one that deflects attention from the socio-ecological predicament we are actually in, solidifies the very dynamics and processes that produce radically uneven and unequal urban socio-ecological outcomes, and prevents a politicization of the environment understood as the egalitarian-democratic dispute and struggle over the production of the socio-ecological conditions we wish to inhabit.

Ultimately, the intellectual challenge posed by the socio-environmental conditions of present planetary urbanization must be to extend the intellectual imaginary and the powers of thought and practice beyond the horizon of the contemporary cultural injunction identified by Fredric Jameson, that it is easier to imagine the end of the world than changes in the eco-capitalist order and its inequities [Jameson 2003]. This is the courage of the intellect that is now required more than ever, a courage that takes us beyond the impotent confines of a technocratic sustainability discourse and a(n)estheticized blueprints that radically disavow the political-ecological scripts underpinning their possibility and leave the existing combined and uneven, but decidedly urbanized, socio-ecological dynamics fundamentally intact. What is required today is to chart new politicized avenues for producing a new common urbanity.

The Future Has Already Arrived!

The German word for sustainable city or development is *nachhaltige Stadt* or *Entwicklung*. The signifier *nachhaltig*—which translates as "enduring" or "lasting"—should be taken literally indeed. Does it not refer to a city or development that "endures," that is maintained, does not change too much, that continues indefinitely into the future? And in the absence of questions that attempt to answer "for what" or "for whom," *nachhaltig* refers precisely to what is at stake today for the elites, namely how to make sure that the socio-ecological order we inhabit can continue a while further to ensure that the urban condition is adequate to support and guarantee the *Nachhaltigkeit* of the existing socio-ecological, or rather eco-capitalist, order.

In fact, techno-imagineered fantasies of sustainable future cities narrate and prefigure an imaginary of and for the future that is already embryonically here, that is already an integral part of the existing constellation of planetary urbanization. Consider the future city scenarios of Integralland, Netland, and Wattland, the three alternative possible futures for German urbanity. They reminded me of Alain Badiou's 15th and final thesis on contemporary art: "It is better to do nothing than to contribute to the invention of formal ways of rendering visible that which Empire already recognizes as existent" [Badiou 2008]. Is this not exactly what these future city representations actually do, to symbolize and represent in a formal manner what we already know to be an integral part of the contemporary urban condition? These scenarios recount what is already visible and lived in the practices of actually existing urbanity. Contemporary urbanization, as urbanists know very well, is kaleidoscopic and heterogeneous, conflicting and dynamic, producing restless spaces where both the possibilities of the future lurk in the interstices of actually existing practices and the whip of brutal repression and socio-ecological exclusion comes down masterfully on those caught in the infernal spiral of poverty and precarization. The practices prefigured in Integralland, for example, remind me of a monstrous combination of a Proudhonian anarchic urban-rural idyll with high-tech urban "metabolic vehicles" that permit the residents to live in an apparently consensual participatory democracy, blissfully ignorant in their cozy local arcadia of the feral geographies that drive their wind-turbines welded together in Chinese megafactories with their repressive labor practices and environmentally disastrous operations, or that power their laptops and mobile phones with the rare-earth coltan, sourced from the land-grabbed mines in central Africa, whose infernal political ecological dynamics perpetuate the social and ecological genocide around the Great Lakes, mainly by putting Kalashnikovs in children's hands. This is truly a cyborg-city, one hermetically sealed off in its phantasmagoric identitarian gated existence from the combined and uneven apocalypse that nonetheless sustains the very functioning of Integralland; it is a holistic urbanism predicated upon a global, but depressingly unequal, integration.

Netland represents of course Google-earth, an urbanism fully wired and networked. Here we see the Orwellian figure of Big Brother state and capital—the combination of a Kafkaesque Castle of disembodied yet permanent surveillance and meticulous pseudo-control, National Security Agency (NSA) style—with a globally networked yet utterly privatized and centralized mobilization of the world's ecologies. It is a city of flows, of seemingly dematerialized services and affective commodities, blissfully ignorant of the deeply material and physical conduits and power-laden infrastructure that sustains the flows of affect, water, energy, food, and other matter. It reminds me of Masdar City's post-carbon urban promise, Foster + Partners' designed networked zero-emission high-tech city that sets Abu Dhabi on course for a post-oil, but globally competitive, urban future. It is the "sustainable" gated community par excellence, constructed by a global precariat living in tent cities, and sustained by local and global social and physical circuits that not only reproduce but further intensify already existing profound socio-ecological inequalities. The few who decide to stay "off the grid," who exit from urban empire, who choose exodus above connectivity, can dwell happily in the intoxicating bliss of their anarcho-experimental lives in self-chosen local exile, perhaps mixed in with some guerrilla gardening to maintain the illusion of a still roaring rebellious spirit. This is the city of forced choice between connection as neurotic engagement or disconnection as impotent hysterical acting out.

And finally, Wattland is a sort of postapocalyptic *Mad Max* urbanity that too is already here, lurking in the interstices of actually existing urbanity. It is a combined urbanization where both energy-producing and -exporting places and those whose sustainability depends on the continued accumulation by resource extractivism and energy mobilization choreograph a socio-ecological condition of energy wealth and exclusion. One does not have to consider in this context the emblematic cases of cities that should not be where they are, like Las Vegas or Los Angeles, but also cities like London, Berlin, Athens, Paris, or Frankfurt show precisely how cyborg living in gated energy-intensive production and consumption hubs is paralleled by the energy-deprived living of the resource-poor. The latter do not roam the countryside, however. They sleep under the canopy of the heated entrances to high-class buildings or burn the leftovers of discarded urban organic matter in makeshift fires. Wintery Athens under conditions of enforced austerity by dogmatic neoliberal empire shows and reeks of the smog-filled atmosphere of indiscriminate burning by the energy-starved urban poor. The great invention of a future Wattland is that the elites do not need to have militarized gated communities if the disenfranchised and outcasts can be forcefully decamped to the desert of the rural. Is this not precisely what New York mayor Rudolph Giuliani already prefigured when he cleansed the city of its undeserving outcasts by decanting them to somewhere else [Smith 1996]?

The future has indeed arrived—each of the proposed city scenarios is already discernible within the interstices and heterogeneous dynamics that shape and choreograph present-day planetary urbanization. So, in the midst of their already existing reality, what is the actual ideological and political performativity of these aestheticized techno-natural utopian or dystopian representations that prefigure a city apparently still to come? Why do we not insist that these prefigured urban conditions *already* are the Real of our early twenty-first century urbanity?

"We Know Very Well, Nevertheless We Act as If We Do Not."

As Jacques Rancière has repeatedly pointed out, politics dwell in the domain of the aesthetic, understood as the registers of the sensible, of what can and cannot be said, what is rendered audible or mute, what is made visible or hidden from view. In this sense, scenarios as works of art are intrinsically politically charged. Of course, what Rancière has in mind is strictly opposite to the aestheticization of politics performed in these imagineered urban futures [Rancière 2000]. The aestheticization of politics is a central depoliticizing procedure at work in scenario construction, a process by which politics as an aesthetic practice is traversed by a tactic of aestheticizing politics—the standard trope of any form of authoritarian governing, as Walter Benjamin pointed out a long time ago. This is a process by which what is already sensible and visible, audible and intelligible, is rendered opaque, mute, and invisible; it is a procedure of foreclosing or disavowing the condition we, urbanites, are already in. The difference between politics as aesthetic and aestheticizing politics can be rendered clear by analogy with *The Matrix*, the Wachowski Brothers' sci-fi trilogy. The anesthetized virtual reality in which Neo, the film's hero, dwells— albeit with an uncanny sense of disorientation—and in which everyone has their assigned place and function in a seemingly seamless order, is utterly shattered when Morpheus, leader of the resistance, introduces Neo to the Real of the urban condition. The encounter with the "Desert of the Real," as Morpheus puts it, the plainly horrifying cyber-organic *thing* that functions as the bio-techno-material support structure for the virtual reality, the reel of life, disintegrates the frame of an unfractured cohesive real life.

The uncanny intrusion of the Real interrupts the fantasy of reality and provokes a revolution in and of Neo's senses and sensibilities, reconfiguring his coordinates of what is true or false, right or wrong, good or bad. The aestheticization of urban future scenarios produces precisely this kind of Technicolor illusion of a future whose horrifying and already acutely present underlying political and ecological coordinates remain foreclosed, "yet [such a vision's] principal aim is to make us forget that this is the case. It constructs us as passive consumers of assorted false promises and manages to keep us in its thrall by making us forget that we are the world's inmates rather than free agents" [Cavallaro 2000, 212].

Nonetheless, such urban fantasies disavow the unarticulated horror of the Real: that there is no Master in charge; the Matrix too is nothing but socially disembodied vampire-like cybermachines animated by digital circuits. Here resides the infernal illusion of the Matrix or other anesthetized simulations/simulacra, the perverse lie at the core of the simulacrum, its proper ideological performativity. It renders possible the forgetting, the amnesia of our situation, of the condition we are already in and which we know: there are all manner of power-laden political and socio-ecological relations, conflicts, and struggles already at work in the actual production of the already present urban condition. These scenarios are not just techno-natural horrors to come; they are already actively produced in and through political and other power relations that assemble new forms of urbanity.

This is precisely where the truly horrifying implications of Integralland, Wattland, or Netland are to be situated. In their a(n)estheticized formulation of already existing urbanities projected onto a future that will never be, their extraordinary performativity resides in the production of amnesia, a willful forgetting of what we already know but cannot act upon without radically altering our frame, disturbing and interrupting the common sense of the day, challenging the asymmetric power relations that infuse their production. Such performative forgetting of the present by fast forwarding to some distant future is vital to sustain the functioning of ideology today, one that, as Slavoj Žižek has repeatedly insisted, articulates around "despite the fact we know very well [the horrifying realities of the apocalyptic social and ecological processes that choreograph contemporary planetary urbanization], nevertheless we act as if we do not know" [Žižek 1989]. For Žižek, "ideology is not a dreamlike illusion that we build to escape reality; in its basic dimension it is a fantasy construction which serves as a support for our reality itself: an 'illusion' which structures our effective social relations and thereby masks some insupportable Real. ... The function of ideology is not to offer us a point of escape from our reality but to offer ... social reality itself as an escape from some traumatic, Real kernel." [Žižek 1989, 45]

Here we are faced with the deadlock inscribed in the radically depoliticizing disposition of urban techno-social scenario-building, one that disavows the infernal underbelly of the Real of the present combined and uneven urban socio-ecological catastrophe. We already live in the interstices of combined and uneven socio-ecological apocalypse but we act, dream, and imagine the future as if we do not (yet) know.

Combined and Uneven Urban Socio-Ecological Catastrophe

The production of urban environments, and the "metabolic vehicles" that make sure they function (the socio-technical infrastructure that permits the flow and metabolism of affect, energy, food, information, bodies and things) are of course mediated by political and socioeconomic arrangements that are often nominally democratic, but nonetheless deeply committed to ensuring the uninterrupted expansion of the capital circulation process. It is precisely this articulation between state, social power, and environmental translation that renders urban socio-ecological processes, including the question of "sustainability," highly conflictive, crisis prone, and subject to intense political and social struggle. Metabolic circulation as "value-in-motion—as the alienated product of human labour that comes to develop a quasi-autonomous, self-expansionary and crisis-ridden dynamic that increasingly imposes itself upon social reality as an abstract form of domination" [Wilson 2014, 305] remains as the Real that unhinges and interrupts any fantasy construction.

Despite the extraordinary leap forward in critical understanding of the urban socio-environmental condition and the consensual attention to "sustainable" and "smart" eco-technologies, ecological conditions continue to deteriorate at an alarming rate as planetary urbanization intensifies. This is a paradoxical situation that can only be rendered legible in strictly ideological terms. While the techno-managerial elites desperately attempt to micro-engineer socio-ecological conditions in ways that permit the phantasmagoria of both sustaining economic growth indefinitely into the future and turning environmental technologies into a "green" accumulation strategy, the depth and extent of environmental degradation gallops further in what Evan Calder Williams calls "a combined and uneven apocalypse" [Williams 2011]. It is indeed becoming abundantly clear that the early ecologists' clarion call, borrowed from the twentieth-century Italian communist Amadeo Bordiga, that "when the ship goes down, the first-class passengers drown too" is manifestly untrue. The earth's first-class urban passengers are busily building transplanetary metabolic rescue vessels in their "sustainable" gated eco-pods, while ecological and political refugees drown in the Mediterranean, and the world's megacity slum dwellers, often despite the mobilization of extraordinary creative energies to sustain their lives, continue to live in the proliferating socio-ecological wastelands of their degrading socio-ecological environments. Planetary urbanization, unfolding through the universalization of the commodification and accumulation of natures within a neoliberalizing political-ecological configuration, accelerates the process of combined and uneven ecological apocalypse, one increasingly sustained by the mythical promise of a technologically mediated sustainability accessible to all on the one hand and post-democratic forms of consensual governance that do not tolerate radical dissent or the pursuit of real urban political-ecological alternatives on the other. Rather, urban desires articulate around how to maintain the splendid isolation of the "sustainable" bubbles of elite urban life that only permit a highly selective percolation of its membranes to the Real of the world. Such depoliticizing techno-managerial endeavors elude foregrounding more politicized modes of producing a more egalitarian socio-ecological mode of governing and transforming the urban commons [Swyngedouw 2009].

As I have argued elsewhere [Swyngedouw 2007, 2011], consensually established concerns, like "sustainability," structured around ecologies of fear that nurture a reactionary stance and urge techno-managerial forms of intervention, are an expression of the current post-political and post-democratic condition, one that is arranged around distinct biopolitical and bio-immunological gestures. Post-politics refers to a politics in which dissensual contestation and agonistic struggles are replaced by techno-managerial planning, expert management and administration, "whereby the regulation of the security and welfare of human lives is the primary goal" [Žižek 2008, 34]. Such post-political arrangement signals a depoliticized public space (in the sense of the disappearance of the democratic agonistic struggle over the content and direction of socio-ecological life) whereby expertise, interest intermediation, and administration through governance defines the zero-level of politics [Marquand 2004].

Nonetheless, the very foundation of politics is intervention in order to change the given socio-environmental order in a certain manner, to order the distribution of the sensible, to reallocate times, places, and ecologies. Like any intervention, this is a violent act, erasing at least partly what is there so that something new and different becomes possible. It is of vital importance to recognize that political acts are singular interventions to produce particular socio-ecological arrangements and milieus and, in doing so, foreclose the possibility for others to emerge. Any intervention enables the formation of certain socio-ecological assemblages and closes down others; none is neutral with respect to their social and ecological embedding. The "violence" inscribed in such choice has to be fully endorsed. For example, one cannot have simultaneously a truly carbon-free city and permit unlimited car-based mobility. A "sustainable" wired high-tech urbanity that coincides with roaming the earth's most vulnerable ecologies in search of rare earths like coltan and the systematic decamping of its toxic e-waste (for "recycling") and other residues to the slums of Delhi, Accra, or Lagos just intensifies the horror of socio-ecologically combined and uneven planetary urbanization. Displacing climate change gases with solar cells or wind turbines produced under unbearable socio-ecological conditions in the world's new dirty manufacturing belts does not solve problems; it just moves them around. Even less can an egalitarian, democratic, solidarity-based and ecologically sensible urban future be produced without marginalizing or excluding those who insist on the private appropriation of the commons of the earth and its mobilization for accumulation, personal enrichment, sustained by mere philanthropic gestures to the social and ecological distress of the less fortunate.

Such violent encounters, of course, always constitute a political act, one that can be legitimized only in political terms, and not—as is customarily done— through an externalized legitimation that resides in a fantasy of sustainability and cozy post-democratic techno-managerial consensus, whereby political choice is refracted and straitjacketed in techno-natural managerial "alternatives" like Integralland, Wattland, or Netland. Politics, from this perspective, is about enunciating demands that lie beyond the symbolic order and socio-ecological realities of the urban present. These are demands that cannot be symbolized within the frames of reference, the "common sense," of what is already there, but would require a transformation in and of common sense, a change in the registers of the see-able, say-able, do-able, and hear-able to permit symbolization to occur. Nonetheless, these are demands that are eminently sensible and feasible when the frame of the symbolic order is shifted, when the parallax gap between what is (the constituted symbolic order) and what can be (the reconstituted symbolic order made possible through a shift in vantage points, one that starts from the partisan universalizing principle of equality) is acknowledged fully. These are the sorts of demands that "restructure the entire social [and ecological] space" [Žižek 1999, 208]. Politicizing urban environments democratically, then, becomes an issue of enhancing the democratic political content of socio-environmental construction by means of identifying the strategies through which a more equitable distribution of social power and a more egalitarian mode of producing urban techno-natures can be achieved. This requires foregrounding egalitarian but agonistic dispute as a foundation for and condition of possibility for more inclusive and democratic urban socio-ecological arrangements, and the naming of positively embodied ega-libertarian socio-ecological

futures that are immediately realizable. In other words, egalitarian ecologies are about demanding the impossible and realizing the improbable rather than sanitizing the already existing, and this is exactly the challenge the present combined and uneven urban catastrophe poses. In sum, the politicization of the urban environment is predicated upon the recognition of the political indeterminacy of nature, the constitutive split of the people, the unconditional democratic demand of political equality, and the real possibility for the inauguration of different possible public and collective socio-ecological urban futures that express the democratic presumptions of freedom and equality.

Politicizing Urban Presents

The Real of the political, the affirmation of radical heterogeneity that splits the social and fractures the illusion of oneness, can never be fully suppressed. If the political is foreclosed and the polis as political community is moribund in the face of the consensualizing post-political suspension of the properly democratic, what is to be done? What design for the reclamation of the polis as political space can be thought? How and in what ways can the courage of the urban collective intellect(ual) be mobilized to think through a design of and for dissensual or polemical spaces? I would situate the tentative answers to these questions in three interrelated registers of thought.

The first revolves around transgressing the fantasy that sustains the post-political order. This would include not surrendering to the temptation to act. The hysterical act of resistance ("I have to do something or the city, the world, will go to the dogs") just answers the call of power to do what you want, to live your dream, to be a "responsible" citizen, to symbolize what is already present. Hysterical acting out is actually what is invited, an injunction to obey, to be able to answer to "What have you done today?" The proper response to the injunction to take action, to design the new, to project the present into the urban future, to be different (but which is already fully accounted for within the state of the situation), is to follow Bartleby's modest, yet radically transgressive, reply to his Master, "I'd prefer not to" [Žižek 2006]. The refusal to act, to stop asking what they want from me, to stop wanting to be liked is not only an affirmation that the Master does not know or, at least, that the emperor is naked, but also an invitation to think, or rather, to think again. The courage of the urban intellect(ual) is a courage to be an organic intellectual of the city qua polis. This is an urgent task and requires the formation of new radical imaginaries and the resurrection of thought that has been censored, scripted out, suspended, and rendered obscene. In other words, is it still possible to think, for the twenty-first century, the design of a democratic, polemical, equitable, ecologically sensible, free common urbanity? Can we articulate what we really desire? Can we still think through today the censored metaphors of equality, living-in-common, solidarity, ega-libertarian political democracy? Are we condemned to rely on our humanitarian sentiments to manage socially to the best of our techno-managerial abilities the perversities of late capitalist urbanity, or can a different politics and process of being-in-common be thought and designed?

The second moment of reclaiming the polis revolves around recentering/redesigning the urban as a democratic political field of disagreement. This is about enunciating dissent and rupture, to recognize and register the hard bone of the Real that scratches the skin like a fish bone stuck in one's throat. It is centrally about the ability to literally open up spaces that permit acts that claim and stage a place in the order of things. This centers on rethinking equality politically and on foregrounding the urban as its stage; i.e., thinking equality not as a sociologically verifiable concept or procedure that permits opening a policy arena that will remedy the observed inequalities (utopian/ normative/moral) sometime in a utopian future (i.e., the standard recipe of left-liberal urban policy prescriptions), but as the axiomatically given and presupposed, albeit contingent, condition of democracy. This must include of course the constitution and construction of common spaces as collectivized spaces for experimenting and living differentially, to counter "the hyper-exploitation or the time that is imposed and that one tries to re-appropriate" [Kakogianni and Rancière 2013, 24]. Political space emerges thereby as the collective or common space for the institutionalization of the social (society) and equality as the foundational gesture of political democracy (as its presumed, axiomatic, yet contingent foundation). This requires extraordinary designs (both theoretical and material), ones that cut through the master signifiers of consensual urban governance (creativity, sustainability, growth, cosmopolitanism, participation, etc.) and their radical metonymic reimagination [Swyngedouw 2010]. Such metonymic re-registering demands thinking through the city as a space for accommodating egalitarian difference and disorder. This hinges critically on creating equalibertarian public spaces. Most importantly, the utopian framing that customarily informs urban visioning requires reversal to a temporal sequence centered on imagining concrete spatiotemporal socio-ecological utopias as immediately necessary and realizable. This echoes of course Henri Lefebvre's clarion call for the "right to the city" understood as the "right to the production of urbanization," one that urges us to think of the city as a process of collective human and nonhuman codesign and coproduction [Harvey 2012].

Thirdly, and most importantly, supporting a politicizing urban sequence poses the need to traverse the fantasy of the elites, a fantasy that is sustained and nurtured by the perverse imaginary of an autopoietic world, the hidden hand of market exchange that self-regulates and self-organizes, serving simultaneously the interests of the elite Ones and the All, the private and the common. The socialism for the elites that structures the contemporary city is really one that engages the common of social life and the commons of nature in the interests of the elite Ones through the mobilization and disciplinary registers of consensual post-democratic techno-management. It is a fantasy that is further sustained by a double fantastic promise: on the one hand, the promise of eventual enjoyment—"Believe us; our designs will guarantee your enjoyment." It is an enjoyment that is forever postponed, that becomes a veritable utopia, a no-place. On the other hand, there is the recurrent promise of catastrophe and disintegration if the elite's fantasy is not realized, if one does not surrender to the injunctions of the Master. This dystopian fantasy is predicated upon the relentless cultivation of fear (for ecological disintegration and ecocide, excessive migration, rapidly moving diseases, terrorism, failing energy security, economic and financial collapse), fears that are both relayed by and managed through technocratic expert knowledge and elite governance arrangements. This fantasy of catastrophe has a castrating effect—it sustains the impotence for naming and designing truly alternative cities, truly different emancipatory spatialities and urbanities.

Traversing elite fantasies requires the intellectual and political courage to imagine egalitarian democracies, the production of common values and the collective production of the greatest collective oeuvre, the city, the inauguration of new political trajectories of living life in common, and, most importantly, the courage to choose, to take sides. Traversing the fantasy of the elites means recognizing that the social, economic, and ecological catastrophe that is announced every day as tomorrow's threat is not a promise, not something to come, but *is* already the Real of the present.

Acknowledgment

I would like to thank Maria Kaika for critical reading and editorial help. All remaining errors of fact or reasoning are of course entirely mine.

References

Badiou, Alain. 2008. "Fifteen Theses on Contemporary Art." Online: www.lacan.com/issue22.php (accessed August 25, 2014).

Cavallaro, Dani. 2000. *Cyberpunk and Cyberculture: Science Fiction and the Work of William Gibson*. New Brunswick, NJ: Athlone Press.

Harvey, David. 2012. *Rebel Cities: From the Right to the City to the Urban Revolution*. London: Verso.

Jameson, Fredric. 2003. "Future City." In *New Left Review*, 65–79.

Kakogianni, Maria, and Jacques Rancière. 2013. "A Precarious Dialogue." In *Radical Philosophy*, 181, 18–25.

Marquand, David. 2004. *Decline of the Public: The Hollowing Out of Citizenship*. Cambridge: Polity Press.

McEwan, Ian. 2010. *Solar*. London: Nan A. Talese/ Doubleday.

Rancière, Jacques. 2006. *Le Partage du sensible: Esthétique et politique.* Paris: La Fabrique.

Smith, Neil. 1996. *The New Urban Frontier: Gentrification and the Revanchist City*. New York: Routledge.

Swyngedouw, Erik. 2007. "Impossible/Undesirable Sustainability and the Post-Political Condition." In *The Sustainable Development Paradox*, edited by Rob Krueger and David Gibbs. New York: Guilford. 13–40.

Swyngedouw, Erik. 2009. "The Antinomies of the Post-Political City. In Search of a Democratic Politics of Environmental Production." In *International Journal of Urban and Regional Research*, 33, 601–620.

Swyngedouw, Erik. 2010. "Trouble with Nature— Ecology as the New Opium for the People." In *The Ashgate Research Companion to Planning Theory: Conceptual Challenges for Spatial Planning*, edited by Jean Hillier and Patsy Healey, 299–320. Farnham, UK: Ashgate.

Swyngedouw, Erik. 2011. "Interrogating Post-Democracy: Reclaiming Egalitarian Political Spaces." In *Political Geography*, 30, 370–380.

Williams, Evan Calder. 2011. *Combined and Uneven Apocalypse*. Washington, D.C.: Zero Books.

Wilson, Japhy. 2014. "The Shock of the Real: The Neoliberal Neurosis in the Life and Times of Jeffrey Sachs." In *Antipode*, 46, 301–332.

Žižek, Slavoj. 1989. *The Sublime Object of Ideology*. London: Verso.

Žižek, Slavoj. 2006. *The Parallax View*. Cambridge, MA: MIT Press.

Žižek, Slavoj. 2008. *Violence*. New York: Profile Books.

Altermodern Architectures

Armen Avanessian

Accelerationism and Contemporary *Baukultur*

Times passes—in other words future exists. But what actually deserves to be called future in the emphatic sense? What the past conveys via a negative speculative concept can't be the future. What feeds on the experiences of the past, using algorithms to literally in advance prescribe the future to the present, forcing it down fixed paths, can't be the future. Present action is only possible if one views the present from the future and not the past. That is the emancipatory quality of a speculative view of time, or, to paraphrase J.G. Ballard: "science fiction of the next five minutes."

What interests me in this sense is accelerationism as a Promethean project, in other words a project conducted by theorists, political scientists, and economists who say: We're not helpless victims of developments—we can, we *must*, guide and control, because there's no going back. It is only at the level of the present in which we currently find ourselves that we can try (that's the Promethean bit) to gain control of the productive forces. That doesn't mean acceleration in the sense of "driving against a wall." We need to *accelerate*, meaning incorporate an emancipatory gesture into existing technologies and architectural know-how, as also into our urban planning and urban technological premises. So what interests me is how one can integrate particular architectures into what already exists. That is not the drawing-board logic of modernism, though it does inherit its Promethean enlightenment fury. Drawing-board planning based on a specific formal language that alone can promise salvation is conceived on a false, aesthetic model.

So it makes sense to contrast a recursive Promethean model and an aesthetic model based on reflexivity and hence on ever new stimulation, experiences, and atmospheres. I discern a poeticization in philosophy vis-à-vis its existing aestheticization, and I'd be no less interested in an altermodern architecture in architecture. The question becomes: What would a relevant poeticization in the sense of *poiesis*, i.e., the production or fabrication of something genuinely new, actually be? One reply to this question, or solution to this problem, could be: an architecture that is and will be a site of production. We need an architecture that is in line with the current state of technology. It needs to be an architecture confident it can realize modernism's utopian content of big-style planning. But that assumes an important condition, namely, that one is in a position to learn. It needs to be an architecture that arises trusting in technology and science. "No one has yet determined what the body can do," Spinoza said. The accelerationists say: "We don't yet know what the technosocial body can do." That we are still natural bodies has long since been an illusion. We have been a hybrid of technology, chemical additives, algorithms, electronic devices, digital interfaces for a good while now. That we're cyborgs isn't just a crude sci-fi hypothesis but has long since become everyday reality, though we don't much notice it. What counts now is to not let this insight faze us but to exploit it as an irreversible state of affairs. It is our only chance to better understand what our technosocial bodies are capable of and what our bodies can do in alternative architectural settings.

Fundamentally, I endeavor to work at a discursive level, at the level of philosophy, theory of art and literature; concretely, I endeavor to manipulate, alter, and transform at the specific institutional level. I would demand the same of an accelerationist architecture that is no longer fooled by the old answers and pseudo-approaches to problems. There can be no going back; neither hardcore urbanism nor decelerative fantasies such as allotment garden settlements are solutions if we want to maintain our level of civilization.

I don't believe in deduction or induction but in abductive reasoning, thought, and action. This concerns, for instance, how to handle the fact that one does not know in advance what the future is going to be like, or things generally, or how a certain house or a certain city is to be built. As we put it in *Metanoia*: "Abduction offers hypotheses and concepts for which we can't determine, at the time of the abduction, whether there are any objects that correspond to them. The important features of abduction appear if we contrast it with the other modes of reasoning. Deduction reasons from a law and a correlation to a particular case. Inductive reasoning proceeds from a particular case and a correlation to a general law. Conversely, in abduction we do not proceed from laws to particular cases or vice versa, but hypothetically from a particular case *and* a law to a correlation" [Avanessian and Hennig 2014, 169]. Proceeding abductively transforms the general by means of the particular. The temporal viewpoint is reversed and the question becomes: How can one organize a transformative or manipulative process so that the house, the city, the country functions differently? This raises the issue what kind and degree of complexity one wants to include in the planning process in the first place so that a part of the whole, within a recursive process, can begin to produce a transformation.

What does recursion mean at this level? That is the most interesting question. What would recursive reflection on architecture be, or what are the recursive processes in architecture? And not reflexive processes! It's not a question of people in a certain house starting to think differently about themselves and the world. It's far more a question of their forming different parts with a different whole and integrating things differently in the whole. In the Manifesto for an Accelerationist Politics by Nick Srnicek and Alex Williams, as also with

Laboria Cuboniks, the collective that wrote a manifesto for a new Xenofeminism, and other writers, for instance the design theorist Benedict Singleton, the concept of a "platform" plays an important role as a—two inseparable aspects!—theoretical and practical tool. Platforms create cooperative possibilities without one's being able to say in advance where the cooperation will lead. It's never a matter of idyllic sites of free communication, but of sites of outer constraints that must be overcome. But progress is not only achieved by having recourse to or adopting something but also by influencing and reorienting already existing platforms on which various subjects are collaborating.

Abductive thinking, so understood, is thinking that does not oppose theory to practice. Abduction is manipulative action and thought. It is not a question of sensitization or some aesthetic shakeup or reflection. We all have enough feelings, perceptions, and stimuli. We all feel and feel compassion. The problem is more that we all know that something is fundamentally off track. It's clear to everyone that things are economically off track. That's no big secret. It's also pretty evident in what ways the banks and financial policies in general are off track, what's off track in politics, and who is profiting from these conditions. We have all been hypersensitized to the misery there is. We live in a hypersensitized and aestheticized culture, and precisely that might be the problem. Instead, we must think the general and the particular differently; how are forms of practice that create and enable knowledge and change possible? And not using sensibility to make knowledge appliable. That's an aesthetic model that remains trapped in permanent reflection and meta-reflection and perpetual oh-so-critical self-reflection. And that's the aesthetic regime of thinking, of acting, of political action, and of building.

Rather, we need to assume that not everything is known, nor can be known, and that knowledge only arises in action, for instance in the act of building. What kind of building is it that manipulatively brings forth knowledge in the act of building, that produces something that has not previously and sensitively been appropriated to the weak of thought so that they begin thinking, acting, building correctly with their compassion? We need to break out of this sentimentalism, this aestheticization that's not only reflected in how our cities are but in how we experience ourselves and our creative, eventful, aestheticized cities. Which brings us to the final and decisive question: How are we to escape this aesthetic regime? How can the power of our imagination be incorporated into a rational calculus? How are we to develop a recursive model? And what might an altermodern architecture look like that allows itself strategies that, for the most part, are no longer referred to other than as utopian? I'm talking about recourse (not a postmodern leave-taking or ironization) and with it a shift of the original intentions of modernism's typical features and goals. Altermodernity is a transformative engagement with modernism by way of alternatives to the past-directedness of contemporary society. Emancipation, progress, enlightenment—these catchwords of modernism need to be taken up and taken further with a view to positively changing our future. We have to put together future again and imagine a future in which we actually want to live.

Revised transcript of a conversation with Armen Avanessian, April 26, 2014

Reference

Avanessian, Armen, and Hennig, Anke. 2014. *Metanoia: Spekulative Ontologie der Sprache*. Berlin: Merve. 169.

Trans-forma-tions

The analysis and speculations taken together bring out clear patterns for possible transformations. The three normative, condensed paradigms for the lived environment—quality of life, value creation, resources—are central trends in the social changes currently felt to indicate directions for the future. Common to all these trends is the fact that they are already discernible in a wide range of signals and are having concrete geographic effects. Photo essays by Armin Linke prefacing each of the transformations are a visual quest for traces of these paradigms in the global present.

Archive Armin Linke

El Cuello, nomad tent, Sahrawi Republic (SADR Territories), Western Sahara, 2004

Petrol tankers on the road to Jordan, Iraq, 2002

Moving cloud, Aosta, Italy, 2000

Three Gorges Dam, construction of a lift for ships, Yichang (Hubei), China, 1998

Three Gorges Dam project, model, Yichang (Hubei), China, 1998

Ghazi Barotha hydroelectric project, workers praying, Hattian, Pakistar, 1999

Tal-Oil Group transalpine pipeline, control room, Trieste, Italy, 2012

"We have no energy problem. What we lack is the imagination to conceive an alternative energy reality. Energy is not a question of resources but of logistics; in other words, the right interactions between energy production, storage, and use."

[Ludger Hovestadt, Lecture: Zukunftswerkstatt #3, Berlin, 27.11.2013]

Renewable Energies

Energy sources are key drivers behind the spatial organization of the economy, society, and mobility. The production and availability of energy, its transformation, distribution, and use can have powerful geographical effects—just as the transition to renewables that has already been politically endorsed will lastingly change Germany. The more thinly populated rural areas become increasingly important as regional producers of renewable energy. Their value is a function of their economically utilizable energy potential deriving from wind, sun, water, and soil. Simultaneously, areas that produce nuclear and fossil energy must be converted to new usage concepts or completely renatured. The transition from fossil to renewable energy takes place at both physical-geographical and socioeconomic levels. The new energy landscapes challenge our thinking about the man-made environment. It is a question of redefining our future cultural dedications of land and space. In addition to large-scale energy infrastructure, the focus will be on decentralized solutions that facilitate a return to small-scale energy systems organized close to their points of use. The distinction between producers and consumers will become progressively blurred, and decentralized energy supplies will break open the centralized structures of today's energy economy. What will the geographic and social consequences of these transformations be? How under these conditions will the relationship between city and country change?

122

130

60
100

52

Energy as Driver

Energy is a driver behind human development. Energy has been obtained from fire, water, wind, solar power, as well as from the exploitation of human beings, animals, fossil and nuclear fuels. A large number of social, technical, and cultural innovations and developments were only possible because of the availability and utilization of energy sources. Fossil energy sources, used in particular for driving the machinery of mass production and mobility, led to extreme acceleration in the nineteenth and twentieth centuries. Just how available and accessible energy is has always been determined by the geopolitical world order, a fact that, given our heavy dependence on fossil fuels, has time and again led to disagreements and war, right up to the present day.

Ultimately, the permanent and ubiquitous availability of electrical energy has led to changes that have radically influenced how cities are built and used. Electrical power is at work everywhere: street lighting, streetcars, elevators, household appliances, computers, cell phones, the Internet, and smart homes: "The impact of what electricity brought into being has fundamentally changed the geography of the city, and the way we live in it, and the way in which we interact with each other. Now we need to see what it can offer for the near future. It can encourage both anti-urban developments, and their antithesis. We need to find ways in which to emphasize the latter at the expense of the former. Electricity has made new spaces, both physical and virtual, possible. It has powered technologies that have shaped the grain of life in the city." [Sudjic 2012, 4]

● 107

Decentralized Post-Fossil Energy Production

The proportion of total electricity production from renewable energy has increased sharply in recent years. In the first half of 2015, some 34 percent of net electricity production in Germany was generated by renewable sources. [Burger 2015]

With an economy focused on renewable energy, the key resources in the future will be wind and solar energy. Water and biomass are not as important, being less scalable. [BMU 2012] At the same time, almost half the renewable-electricity production plants in 2015 are in the hands of citizen groups and cooperatives—civil society. Consumers are joining together in investment and consumer collectives, or in regional corporations, and are taking the energy supply into their own hands. This is a clear expression of the fact that citizens want to contribute toward shaping the transition to renewables, and it is commercially channeled.[1] Energy cooperatives are active locally. They use existing resources and can be effective on a small, local scale. Thanks to their regional focus, the approximately one thousand German municipal utilities services seem destined to organize this progressive decentralization of the energy supply. Energy politics remains closely tied up with societal politics, as seems to be confirmed by the re-communalization and/or foundation of new utilities services. Citizens' energy production is thus penetrating an industrial sector hitherto dominated by an oligopoly, taking into its own hands both the production and the supply of electricity. "Centralization and decentralization are dialectically related in shaping the transition to renewables: on the one hand, many centralized provisions, in particular the Renewable Energy Act (Erneuerbare-Energie-Gesetz), are geared to the decentralized implementation of the transition to renewables; on the other, certain of the decentralized actors are oriented toward centralized solutions, e.g., when municipal utilities services are involved in offshore windparks." [Gailing et al. 2013, 41] Frequently, these

63–69

68

36
41
60

36

66

130

1   By 2015, in the framework of the "100% Renewable Energy Regions" project, 149 regions had decided to convert their energy supply in the long term entirely to renewables. These regions account for some 26 million inhabitants; in other words, around one third of Germany's population.

operators are not interested in the short-term maximization of profit, but invest instead in sustainable energy supplies. Cooperative financing models function despite low return assumptions and contribute toward enhancing regional value creation. The local energy sovereignty thus achieved enhances resilience to systemic shocks. For Günther Ebert of the Fraunhofer Institute for Solar Energy Systems ISE in Freiburg, further regional-level experiments are indispensable: "In order to successfully effect the transition to renewable energies, we need a field for experimentation at the regional level. Only then can we see which approaches develop successfully in the face of competition." [Dilba 2013]

Climate Change

The connection between current world climate changes and anthropogenic emissions of climate-relevant gases is a matter of present-day scientific knowledge. These emissions are produced predominantly by the burning of fossil fuels. [Cf. WBGU 2011] Energy production issues today are thus not only defined by increasingly scarce resources, the conflicts to which this gives rise, and the challenge to adapt, but also by the necessity of avoiding, or limiting, both the predicted climate warming and the extreme weather events this entails, such as droughts, floods, and storms, and their social and economic corollaries. The international community of states has agreed in lengthy conferences that, in order to prevent humankind from being seriously damaged, the mean global temperature must not rise by more than two degrees.

● 30

● 104

● 37

In 2013, the Federal Environmental Agency (Umweltbundesamt) compiled a complete list of emissions sources and showed that Germany can reduce its greenhouse gas emissions by 95 percent against the figure for 1990. [UBA 2013] To attain this goal, three suggestions have been made: The use of fossil fuels must be approximated to zero by the year 2050 and replaced by renewable energy. Total energy consumption must be reduced. And consumer energy efficiency must be increased. [Klaus Müschen, Lecture: Zukunftswerkstatt/Workshop #3, Berlin, November 28, 2013] As a result of the transition to renewables in Germany there has already been a pronounced shift toward sustainable energy in the energy-producing sector. Developments in energy demand are variously assessed because increases in energy efficiency to date have been overcompensated by higher consumption, thus revealing a dilemma: "By 2030 energy demand compared to that of today could be reduced by 25 percent. This is also necessary if primary energy requirements are to be halved by 2050 as called for by the [Federal Government's] energy concept." [Eichhammer 2015]

● 35

Energy Landscapes

Simply because fuels derive from renewable sources does not make them environmentally neutral—their lateral spread is all the greater. The German transition to renewables will redefine the relationship between city and rural areas because the powerhouses for the generation of renewable energy are the thinly populated areas, while urban centers remain the chief customers.[2] Rural regions are especially important during the energy sector transformation because the surface areas that are required will be greater than in the era of fossil and nuclear-based energy supplies. [Brühne and Tempel 2013] Combining different types of energy production and other land uses will give rise to hybrid cultural landscapes: photovoltaic plants and wind parks coupled with food production, energy storage and distribution with

● 58

● 30
42

● 42
60

2   Cities today consume around 75 percent of the energy
     produced worldwide and in doing so cause some 80 percent
     of the world's CO_2 emissions.

communication and mobility infrastructures. Axial zones will shift and overlap, as will production and supply zones, natural landscapes, and producer and consumer spaces. "Centralized approaches to control will lead to the comprehensive restructuring of investment areas and the planned expansion of the supply network and renewables, which will in turn generate acceptance problems and lead to the formation of citizens' action and protest spaces." [Gailing et al. 2013, 21]

● 130

● 66

Facilities such as photovoltaic plants and wind parks shape our landscapes, making energy production more present, spatially and visibly, in the lived environments of growing numbers of the population. In many places, the changes and infrastructures necessary to exploit renewable energy conflicts with existing land use and with familiar landscapes. They can, on the one hand, enrich the appearance of the countryside; on the other, monotonous usage of land can destroy natural and cultural landscapes. Above all, a sociopolitical challenge is posed by the transfer of the products of the energy-rich productive centers, from the wind-rich north, for example, to the consumer centers in Germany's south.

● 68

Competition for the commodity of land is increasing and can have negative effects on existing landscape structures as well as on the diversity of biotopes and species. A result is new utilization and capitalization options for agricultural businesses, generating conflicts about whether land is to be used for producing energy, food, or animal feed.

● 36
52
62

Land that has been made unsuitable for other purposes can in future be used for solar and wind parks. At the same time, the question of the future of fossil fuels in Germany must be considered. Do large areas still need to be reserved for opencast mining? If not, new usages could be assigned to these locations. Abandoned open brown coal mines have already been successfully transformed into

● 64

nature reserves, reservoirs, or leisure parks. Power stations, including pipelines and transport infrastructures, can be converted and developed. Transformations of this kind could offer future prospects for localities in remote regions.

Storage

One of the biggest challenges posed by the transition to renewable energy is the question of storage. Depending on the weather, more wind or solar power is already being produced on certain days than is actually used, and the surplus is well above the current available storage capacity. On the other hand, when wind and sun are low, fossil fuels are still necessary today as a backup.

● 99

To guarantee enough energy production, new energy storage, regulation, and distribution technologies are necessary. "In the long term, electricity storage on a larger scale will be necessary to cope with surpluses and to shift energy over time. If we are going to aim at covering our entire energy supply with renewables, then seasonal energy storage will be indispensable." [Schill 2013, 85] In private households and commercial undertakings alike, the production, storage, and use of privately generated energy will grow in importance. What is at stake here, in addition to energy sovereignty, is the reduction of energy costs. The latest generation of electrical storage devices offers private households what they need to become largely independent of the big supply networks. These devices communicate in real time with the power grid, so electricity can be stored or fed into the grid as necessary—the owner of the storage equipment would be remunerated in both cases. Under optimal conditions, then,

● 131
● 32
● 39

● 132

different energy producers and energy consumers would be linked up and the electricity system kept decentralized and at the same time stable. Energy could always be accessed when available, or stored should the grid have a surplus; in the case of local surpluses, these could be fed into the grid.

These energy storage devices reveal how closely the actors are interconnected on the energy market. Decentralized energy production units such as combined heat and power plants and heat pumps, or electric-car batteries, could be built into this regulatory system and become part of a "smart grid." Originally designed with electro-mobility in mind, car storage devices might find extended use in households wishing to manage their privately produced electricity independent of the grid and trade it with the grid operators. Intelligent power grids can bridge the role change in private households from consumption-only to co-production. "Alternative growth logics geared to energy principles facilitate the extended integration of energy supply, use, storage, and saving in larger developmental contexts. It is seen that renewable energy needs to be integrated in other economic and materials cycles and that this can lead to a multiplicity of possible uses and spatial structures." [Andreas Dittrich and Daniel Czechowski, Lecture: Zukunftswerkstatt/Workshop #3, Berlin, November 28, 2013]

● 119

Electro-Mobility

Electric cars, scooters, and bicycles and the continually expanding use of local and nonlocal public transport will progressively challenge the axioms of the car-oriented city based on fossil-fuel propulsion. The mobility sector might

● 35
236

bring new urban planning actors into play: the energy industry, the information and communication industries, and the finance industry. New propulsion and storage technologies, for instance quieter propulsion, inductive charging systems, and less inactive traffic, will noticeably affect spatial, geographical, and transport planning. "In the future, the design of residential settlements, vehicle concepts, and users' needs and requirements must be oriented to long-term demands, since only then can present path dependencies be broken and the design of genuinely future mobility options effected." [Vallée 2013]

32

115

This is especially true of driverless mobility concepts, which of course are also based on alternative propulsion. Not only will driverless vehicles raise traffic safety considerably, they will also facilitate high-efficiency usage of space—this holds for street as well as parking space. Moreover, there are big differences in the acoustic emissions of electric and fossil-propelled cars. Even if wheel noise—the dominant noise source in street traffic—remains unchanged, with more 30-km-speed-limit areas and play streets, subprime locations could be opened up and busy main streets become again what they used to be: favored places for living and spending time.

78

Internet of Things

By the year 2020, according to an OECD report, there will be 50 billion networked devices, and their number will increase tenfold in the medium term. [OECD 2012] The "Internet of things" can make a lot of things possible and also easier. It will be possible to regulate buildings remotely; automation will not only be convenient, it will also contribute toward including people with limited mobility. And optimal control promotes energy savings. Nonetheless, these developments will themselves expend large amounts of energy and are reliant on constant availability of energy. The complex control and regulation technologies will make so-called smart homes more susceptible to breakdowns; control of a house can also be reversed to become control of its occupants. The control of this networked world will partly subvert the efforts

34

60

made to save energy, not least because the computer servers and routers that constitute the underlying infrastructures consume quantities of energy that are not to be underestimated.

Smart City

Several large industrial concerns have discovered the urban administrations as markets for technologies for regulating and optimizing the use of energy and resources: "Today, electricity is re-emerging as a common denominator of a new technological revolution as unprecedented advances in information and communication systems are matched by radical innovation in green-energy technologies and infrastructures. Much of this pervasive innovation nexus of power and information is, and will continue to be, centered in cities. Smart grid technology and the Internet of things, battery-powered vehicles and shared urban mobility, GPS enabled apps for smart phones and integrated mobility services, online retail and virtual consumption, digital collaboration and e-governance are already part of our everyday urban experiences." [Rode and Burdett 2012]

Technological solutions to urban problems are experiencing a boom quite apart from issues specific to *Baukultur*. Because of the commercial motives and the outright planning and control often pursued, cities are in danger of losing diversity and a certain unpredictability, two key features that make cities desirable places to live: "From experimentation, discovery, and open-source urbanism, we could slide into a managed space where 'sensored' becomes 'censored.' What stands out is how inadequately these technologies have been 'urbanized.' That is, they have not been made to work within a particular urban context." [Sassen 2012]

● 234

● 104

● 37

A central question is how the technologies implemented could be embedded in urban structures so as to genuinely serve people rather than downgrading them to control factors. The more cities are dominated by company-dependent intelligent infrastructures, the more the tasks of public administration fall into private hands and the less citizens are able to contribute. The current trend is to hide implemented technologies; in other words, to inhibit explicit interaction with their users. But only if the underlying data is visible and public will users be in a position to understand, interact, and contribute toward shaping their city. Summarizing: How can intelligent systems be implemented in cities without depriving cities of important defining features of the urban?

● 261

Energy Autarchy

Stricter regulations such as the Energy Saving Ordinance (Energieeinsparverordnung [EnEV]), investment incentives, and raised awareness among builders and owners, investors, banks, and tenants have led in recent years to more energy-efficient designs and methods of building and upgrading property. Buildings today can be designed to use solar and ground heat and hence to require practically no external thermal energy. The following are needed to achieve this goal: consistent orientation of buildings toward the sun, a radical approach to energy for new buildings, compactly designed structures, intelligent climate control, and good insulation. Smaller apartments and new communal types of habitation for certain groups (e.g., students, commuters, senior citizens) can reduce per person floor space while increasing the quality of life thanks to communal areas, and hence reduce energy and resource consumption. Experiments are being conducted with new layouts facilitating particularly extensive spaces for communal uses, or seasonally adaptable situations where different areas

● 35
39

● 108

have different room climates. The additional development of vertical concepts could be another alternative for the built environment. As green buildings they need to be capable of being energy-optimized and at the same time introduce mixed functions and vitality into their city districts. There are always urban conversion areas suitable for such apartment or office buildings on city outskirts. For Franz Josef Radermacher it is also a question of large international companies' social responsibility: "Energy-efficient buildings will define the cities of the day after tomorrow, especially in the premium segment. ... Companies with international charisma and brand power have a special role to play in the area of corporate social responsibility. They want to and they must reduce their carbon budget every year." [Radermacher 2013]

● 40

Energy-efficient buildings are the goal. Differing views as to the route to be taken influence the diversity and substance of the *Baukultur*. The one-sided focus on thermal insulation has led to losses for *Baukultur* as well as to new problems such as mold formation, fire hazards, and possible issues of subsequent disposal. The discrepancy between insulation and thermal gains can probably never be completely resolved, and the best solution will likely need to be sought for each individual case. Buildings in future will be able to produce more energy than they consume and so be active rather than passive buildings.

● 39

In addition to the efforts toward the reduction of energy consumption and climate-relevant emissions, adaptation strategies also exist to enable cities and settlements to continue functioning should it prove impossible to meet the politically negotiated two-degree limit, or should the climate nonetheless change drastically. In regions prone to flooding, certain areas are no longer being settled, or buildings are being constructed

● 36

on supports. Dikes and protection devices are being built against storm floods. To counteract overheating, new surfaces are being tested, while city ventilation and greening are priorities. Mitigation and adaptation are two aspects of future development and must not exclude each other. Both approaches already play an important role in the design of cities and buildings.

References

Bundesministerium für Umwelt, Naturschutz und Reaktorsicherheit (BMU). 2012. *Erneuerbare Energien in Zahlen: Nationale und internationale Entwicklung.* Berlin.

Burger, Bruno. 2015. "Stromerzeugung aus Solar- und Windenergie im ersten Halbjahr 2015." Freiburg. Online: www.ise.fraunhofer.de/de/downloads/pdf-files/aktuelles/folien-stromerzeugung-aus-solar-und-windenergie-im-ersten-halbjahr-2015.pdf (accessed July 28, 2015).

Brühne, Thomas, and Michael Tempel. 2013. "Postmoderne Energielandschaften in Rheinland-Pfalz." *Geographische Rundschau*, 65/1, 28–35.

Dilba, Denis. 2013. "Das autarke Dorf." *Die Zeit*, February 12, 2013. Online: www.zeit.de/zeit-wissen/2013/02/Autarkes-Dorf-Energiewende (accessed September 2, 2015).

Eichhammer, Wolfgang. 2015. "Weltmeister der Energieeffizienz? Wie gut ist Deutschland wirklich?" Workshop im Rahmen des EU-Projekts "ODYSSEE MURE." Fraunhofer Institut for Solar Energy Systems ISE. Berlin, April 20, 2015.

Gailing, Ludger, Frank Hüesker, Kristine Kern, and Andreas Röhring. 2013. *Die räumliche Gestaltung der Energiewende zwischen Zentralität und Dezentralität.* IRS Leibniz Institut für Regionalentwicklung und Stadtplanung. Working Paper, No. 51. Erkner.

German Advisory Council on Global Change (Wissenschaftlicher Beirat der Bundesregierung Globale Umweltveränderungen [WBGU]). 2011. "World in Transition—a Social Contract for Sustainability." Flagship Report 2011, Berlin.

OECD. 2012. "Machine-to-Machine Communications: Connecting Billions of Devices." *OECD Digital Economy Papers*, 192, OECD Publishing. Online: http://dx.doi.org/10.1787/5k9gsh2gp043-en (accessed July 28, 2015).

Radermacher, Franz-Josef. 2013. "Wie wollen die Menschen leben? Treiber und Risiken in der Stadtentwicklung – die globale Sicht. Klimawandel, Technikentwicklung, Wertewandel." Lecture: "The City of the Day After Tomorrow" ("Die Stadt von Übermorgen"). Documentation expert panel at the Federal Ministry for the Environment, Nature Conservation, Building and Nuclear Safety (Bundesministerium für Umwelt, Naturschutz, Bau und Reaktorsicherheit [BMUB]) and the Federal Institute for Research on Building, Urban Affairs and Spatial Development (Bundesinstitut für Bau-, Stadt- und Raumforschung [BBSR]), Bonn, December 11–12, 2013.

Rode, Philipp, and Ricky Burdett, 2012. "The Electric City." In Richard Burdett and Philipp Rode (eds.), *The Electric City Newspaper: Urban Age Electric City Conference, London.* The London School of Economics and Political Science, Alfred Herrhausen Society, London, 2.

Sassen, Saskia. 2012. "Urbanising Technology." In Richard Burdett and Philipp Rode (eds.), *The Electric City Newspaper: Urban Age Electric City Conference, London.* The London School of Economics and Political Science, Alfred Herrhausen Society, London, 12–14.

Schill, Wolf-Peter. 2013. "Systemintegration erneuerbarer Energien: Die Rolle von Speichern für die Energiewende." *Vierteljahrshefte zur Wirtschaftsforschung.* DIW Berlin, 82/3 (2013) 61–88. Online: http://ejournals.duncker-humblot.de/doi/pdf/10.3790/vjh.82.3.61 (accessed September 2, 2015).

Sudjic, Deyan. 2012. "Electricity: A Thing and an Idea." In Richard Burdett and Philipp Rode (eds.), *The Electric City Newspaper: Urban Age Electric City Conference, London.* The London School of Economics and Political Science, Alfred Herrhausen Society, London, pp. 4–5. Online: https://lsecities.net/media/objects/articles/electricity-a-thing-and-an-idea/en-gb/ (accessed September 2, 2015).

Umweltbundesamt (UBA) (ed.). 2013. *Treibhausgasneutrales Deutschland im Jahr 2050*, Umweltbundesamt, Dessau-Roßlau. Online: www.umweltbundesamt.de/publikationen/treibhausgasneutrales-deutschland-im-jahr-2050 (accessed September 2, 2015).

Vallée, Dirk. 2013. "Mobilität 2035 – wer? wie? wo? Emissionsarm, Geteilt, Vernetzt! = SMART." Lecture: "The City of the Day After Tomorrow" ("Die Stadt von Übermorgen"). Documentation expert panel at the Federal Ministry for the Environment, Nature Conservation, Building and Nuclear Safety (Bundesministerium für Umwelt, Naturschutz, Bau und Reaktorsicherheit [BMUB]) and the Federal Institute for Research on Building, Urban Affairs and Spatial Development (Bundesinstitut für Bau-, Stadt- und Raumforschung [BBSR]), Bonn, December 11–12, 2013.

Archive Armin Linke

Swimming pool, Kinshasa, Congo, 2002

Park, Hong Kong, China, 2001

Swimming pool at the settlement, Ma'ale Adumim, West Bank, 2003

Restaurant view, Cairo, Egypt, 2006

Occupy Frankfurt, camp in front of the ECB, Frankfurt am Main, Germany, 2011

"It is not necessary that the economy continue to grow for us to continue improving our quality of life."

[Maja Göpel, Lecture: Zukunftswerkstatt/Workshop #3, Berlin, November 28, 2013]

Alternative Prosperity

The "Alternative Prosperity" paradigm endeavors to overcome the inadequacies of the prevailing growth-oriented economic system, whose central target value is gross domestic product and its increase. At the core of this paradigm are Germany's growing social inequalities and simultaneous economic success. Against this background it describes the progressive detachment from conventional notions of wealth, success, and growth in cities and regions. What model of prosperity might initiate sustainable societal and economic aspects of social coexistence and genuinely improve the quality of life? What values, issues, and general principles structure the actions of society as a whole? Is a return to the local, to orientation on the immediately experienceable environment and its actors, sufficient to raise the quality of life? What scale can be used to measure these developments? Natural resources continue to be exploited and emissions released; the quality of life of many people is deteriorating; immigration—in particular refugee flows at the moment—is hitting communities whose means to adequately receive and integrate the newcomers are either severely reduced or nonexistent. How might spatial interventions and modifications encourage and facilitate the implementation of alternative prosperity—conversion of private into public spaces; care and safeguarding of commons; furtherance of alternative building and housing projects; maintenance of free spaces for urban agriculture, communication, and culture? What additional underlying conditions need to be created? How do these affect planning?

● 126

● 115

Growth—Prosperity—Quality of Life

Worldwide economic crises, social disparities, and ecological disasters are contributing to a growing critique of capitalism in Germany, as well as to a debate on new models of prosperity. For the sociologist Wolfgang Streeck three developments are responsible for capitalism's having become a "social system permanently in need of repair": "Firstly, the persistent fall in growth rates, exacerbated since 2008. Connected with this, the extreme rise in debt, both of states and private households and companies. Thirdly, the increased economic inequality in these societies." [Streeck 2015] Is exclusive orientation toward gross domestic product a sufficient indicator of growth, productivity, and economic dynamism so as to be able to define the well-being of society as a whole?[1] Hardly, seeing that the quality of life of large sections of the population is decreasing even in times of economic prosperity and that people in the wealthier countries are in no way more satisfied with their lives than the inhabitants of poorer countries. [Cf. OECD 2014] The issue as to what indicator to use is less important than the debate on common goals. According to Hans Diefenbacher and Roland Zieschank, the following questions need to become central: What ought German society to look like in the future? What exactly should be measured—and why? How useful, for example, is a "national welfare index?"

[Diefenbacher and Zieschank 2011]

> While the early growth phases of the industrial age were relatively modest, the development of the Fordist economic system after World War II, driven by reconstruction, cheap oil, and a consumption-oriented society, resulted in rates of growth unknown to the Western industrial nations until then. Growth in the capitalist system became a sign of social progress. [Seidel und Zahrnt 2015] In 1972, Club of Rome publications directed attention to the limits of our planet's resources: "If the present growth trends in world population, industrialization, pollution, food production, and resource depletion continue unchanged, the limits to growth on this planet will be reached sometime within the next one hundred years." [Meadows 1972] To this day, the debate concerning the

● 22

● 41

---

1   In *Die Macht der einen Zahl*, the economist Philipp Lepenies points out that a measure of prosperity such as the GDP is unable to negatively register losses to prosperity such as those caused by environmental pollution, noise, and road accidents. Indeed, losses like these, through their commercial impact (e.g., a car wrecked in a road accident has to be replaced), actually contribute to an increase in GDP and hence—purely mathematically—to the prosperity of society as a whole (cf. Lepenies 2013).

limits to growth has not let up. And the current demands of the post-growth and de-growth movement ought not so much to be seen as a social vision, but rather as a response to ecological necessities calling for modes of production "that are non-profit and need-oriented and based on solidarity; new product design and repair workshops that lengthen product life; the development of local, easily reproducible technologies of low ecological impact; the extension of exchange and sharing models for joint use of products and services; self-sufficiency and locally closed production cycles." [Muraca 2014, 10]

● 255

● 258

● 255

Social Commitment

Small application-related projects in the areas of collaborative learning, growing, shaping, and working are currently experiencing significant growth in Germany. Those involved are concerned with making social commitment a part of economic calculations as a desirable activity and a societal responsibility. [Ferguson 2014] Local initiatives are putting a wide range of ideas into practice: neighborhood cafés where people meet to repair or convert broken utility objects; jointly situated and run kindergartens and old people's homes; young designers drawing on the talents and resources of manually skilled elderly people for their knitwear collections; shared gardens where cooperation is practiced, from the arrangement of beds to the consumption of products; citizen-run energy supply businesses; and experiments in local currency systems.

● 92
   94

While these initiatives and their actors have had only limited social influence to date, they are nonetheless doing important spadework for political reorientation, providing some of the first working concepts for alternative prosperity outside the existing economic logic. Many of these initiatives must seek premises and sites where they can work close to the community. Hence, one of the central prerequisites for local structures is the availability of work spaces and meeting places. The projects referred to are often town-based, without any transfer of know-how or news of the projects taking place to the surrounding areas. This is an expression of geographical disparities in social accomplishments that must be broken down with suitable processes.

● 123

Inclusion

The social city and its accomplishments are in danger because social, ethnic, and demographic developments are arising in cities whose budgets in many cases allow little leeway to uphold the existing social protection systems. Hence, since at least 2008, when Germany ratified the UN Convention on the Rights of Persons with Disabilities,[2] the inclusion debate has become a prominent theme in urban development. It is a question here of cities and regions facilitating equal access for all, those with disabilities included, to education and work opportunities, as well as to high-quality housing and leisure activities. More specifically: "Inclusion means the coexistence and mutual acceptance of everyone within a particular living area. Inclusion also has an active aspect: public and private institutions must see that there is a potential place or room where inclusion can actually occur. Citizens mutually support each other according to their strengths and opportunities." [Strunk 2013] In a comprehensive sense, inclusion in cities has to do with partaking, with activating potential in the immediate, lived environment, and with people-friendly architecture. [Montag Stiftung Jugend und Gesellschaft 2011] Designing an inclusive society is a cross-generational project that necessitates fundamental changes in how people treat each other.

> Even where resources are short, innovative projects could lastingly modify the appearance of cities and regions, for instance through obstacle-free entrances, cooperative learning among disabled and nondisabled students, safe street crossings, or the provision of public spaces for all. Community living in cities and regions could thus be declared a common goal for development. This also covers, for example, how refugees and migrants are treated, insofar as suitable living space is found and everyone is socially integrated. The same holds for the inclusion of the elderly, for instance in the context of multigenerational housing.

17
94

103

114

115

---

2   Convention on the Rights of Persons with Disabilities, Art. 1: "The purpose of the present Convention is to promote, protect and ensure the full and equal enjoyment of all human rights and fundamental freedoms by all persons with disabilities, and to promote respect for their inherent dignity. Persons with disabilities include those who have long-term physical, mental, intellectual or sensory impairments which in interaction with various barriers may hinder their full and effective participation in society on an equal basis with others."

Role Models

A glance at the worlds of work and leisure among today's jobholders reveals contrasts and raises questions. Is job satisfaction, with appropriate career paths and remuneration, the top priority? What counts—money, career, power? Or is having more time for family, leisure, and life more important? The journalist Bettina Weiguny has even characterized Generation Y—those born after 1985—as the "Softie Generation": allegedly unwilling to take on responsibility or to work hard, yet demanding that what they do be meaningful. They would rather forgo high income than curtail their social networks, leisure time, and hobbies. [Weiguny 2012] The new debate on gender roles described by Ralf Bönt fits here. Men have evidently still not found their new role in society and family. "But, like soldiers, men continue to serve their employers, the state, and family, until they drop into the grave." [Bönt, 2012, 19] The findings include a suicide rate three times higher than for women, and regular complaints of fathers at having spent too little time with their children. The reason for this, in Bönt's view, is the inability of men to cope adequately with the new division of roles. Men of the younger generations must reorient themselves, learning new behaviors and values in work, family, and leisure. As values and relationship patterns change, the role of well-educated, highly flexible young women will also continue to shift in this process of social renegotiation, accelerated by fuller job-market participation that until now has often been denied to them.

23 31

Women's increasing employment rate, the altered roles of men and fathers, and the changing worlds of work are making life in a suburban "own home" increasingly unattractive for many young professionals. "Living in the suburbs was based on traditional work and family gender roles and on a family division of labor that has been progressively undermined by the growing professional orientation and employment of women. Living in a suburban own home was a 'housewife model,' i.e., a wife's unpaid work was necessary to organize life characterized by the all-round mobility of family members. Because young women's qualifications have reached the same standard as those of young men today, there are more and more couples where both are interested in working professionally. The suburbs are running out of staff, so to say." [Häußermann 2011, 30] A similar development is discernible regarding life in rural districts. Upholding rural

86

84

54 92

lifestyles is heavily dependent on multigenerational cohabitation. The exodus of the rural population to the cities has drastically impacted such types of living so that further depletion of rural areas can be expected.

Forms of Building and Living

Alternative prosperity makes it necessary to renegotiate living together. The return to downtown-close living in Germany has already reduced the supply of housing space. Real estate speculation is endangering social and spatial coexistence: "The real estate industry in modern cities today is a motor in a primarily negative sense. Powerfully driven by transnational actors, it is exceedingly intransparent, deregulated, and controlled by the financial markets." [Leggewie 2013] To counteract this trend, a variety of forms of alternative building and housing have been established. These include building groups and housing cooperatives and schemes where members agree on common interests and basic needs and together create new housing space.

● 76 88

● 99

As critics have pointed out, only a financially and culturally privileged social minority participate in the building group projects realized to date, but nevertheless they provide ideas and models of how urban housing can be reorganized and architecturally implemented. [Cf. Hummel 2011] This holds not only for new buildings but also for the refurbishing of existing properties. At the same time, new cooperatives are developing that function as holding companies administering the joint acquisition of buildings that then become autonomously organized common property. The idea is to create and secure living space that is affordable in the long term. The question is whether such models can be extended to housing construction on a larger scale and also whether they are feasible in suburban and rural contexts.

Combinations of private and public, interior and exterior, of house-in-the-city and city-as-house are springing up in densely populated places and could point the way to new forms of urban living. [Cf. Arch+ 2012] *Baukultur* here is determined by users' needs. Consequently, however, a central feature of cities is jettisoned: anonymity. On the positive side, this leads to

● 100

more neighborly-social commitment, closer-knit coexistence, more social solidarity. On the negative side, such developments could lead to a reduction of freedom and to small-scale totalitarian structures where those who reject sharing, the new community, or neighborly closeness are excluded.

Nutrition

The food-city-rural triad has hitherto played little role in urban planning processes. However, mutual interrelations here are being increasingly exploited. Slow food, for instance, has come to epitomize seasonal, regional, pleasurable nutrition that disassociates itself from industrial fast-food culture. Central to these initiatives are enjoyment, well-being, and nutritional autonomy through the consumption of local products. New forms of interdependence among producers and consumers, such as community supported agriculture (CSA), are arising to meet such requirements. Farmers and urban consumers coexist here in mutual-aid groups facilitating a nutritional culture outside of the existing food product markets.

● 130

Alternative consumption can help organic agriculture to diversify and balance the demands of city and country, consumer and producer. Spaces of jointly owned agricultural production could develop from industrially organized agricultural regions. At the same time, agriculturally utilized space is entering urban societies: public gardens, parks, or former waste land are being used for small-scale agriculture. These spaces are, above all, a locus of sharing that cuts across social divisions: "At the social level, the sharing of gardening strategies and crop cultivars can help build connections across neighborhood fences, and across cultures. Both increased self-reliance and stronger community connections lead to greater resilience in times of crisis." [Grubb 2012, 95]

● 62

● 40

● 122

Public Space

Increasing surveillance and misuse through commercialization and privatization have drawn attention to public space. In 2003, the director of urban development planning in Munich, Stephan Reiss-Schmidt, spoke of the significance of public space: "A European city is defined by public space. A city without public space is inconceivable. The character of European cities is more strongly determined by the various social and aesthetic qualities of their public spaces than by topographical peculiarities or the distinctive features of their types of building." [Reiss-Schmidt 2003] Putting this idea in the global context, the geographer Ash Amin has outlined possible problems: "What we're witnessing in many parts of the world is a grotesque privatization of public space. Squares are being sold because the sites are often highly popular, or they are taken over by commercial developments. It's very easy for a city to exclude the poor, or migrants, from public spaces. ... There are people who think that all will be friends in a multicultural public space. That will never happen. It's simply unrealistic." [Amin 2014]

Freely accessible public spaces with high amenity value function as meeting and contact places that could contribute to interpersonal solidarity and to an open, transparent society. Even when public spaces are constantly subject to consumerist pressures and the control of private firms, they differ in certain ways from the technologically optimized, commercialized routines of a "Smart City." Public places and squares are administered by the public authorities and, to be genuinely accessible to all, should never be permanently "appropriated." Temporary appropriations include outdoor advertising, evening entertainment programs, cultural and sporting events, Christmas markets, and other short-term forms of privatization such as weekly markets or sales events. In addition, they are sites for public negotiation processes with broad citizen participation, as well as for protest and resistance.

● 212

● 23

● 76

● 30
34

● 261/116

Basic Income

The topic of prosperity naturally includes how work is organized, lived, and remunerated, as well as the debate on how the state social systems could be altered. The basic-income guarantee is a controversial financial measure: a monthly transfer effected by the state without any specific preconditions and the simultaneous abolition of all other transfer payments.[3] The supporters point to self-fulfillment and the entrepreneurial aspects of a basic income that would enable individuals to shape their lives with some independence from financial constraints. Financially weak households could thus attain a new degree of freedom in the conduct of their lives, the more so as children would also benefit from the basic income. The basic-income guarantee could put recipients in a position to be active in shaping the future rather than just coping with day-to-day life.

23

Findings concerning the introduction of a basic income have been confined so far to the Canadian town of Dauphin, which offered a basic-income guarantee on an experimental basis for a few years in the 1970s. The social researcher Evelyn Forget later analyzed the experiment. "Above all, the basic income gave people a sense of security, thus eliminating the worries that afflict the poor and that also adversely affect their health. Income security gave the town's inhabitants, most of whom live from agriculture, economic stability and made them less dependent on vagaries of weather and global food prices. Participants in the program needed to see physicians less often—particularly mental health–related visits decreased. Further, a greater proportion of high school students continued on to grade 12." [Cf. Forget 2011] And against the backdrop of the capitalization of the real estate market, a basic income might also check the consequences of segregation discernible in the urban housing market.

127

---

3   In Europe, alongside Switzerland, Finland is a pioneer in the political discourse of implementing a basic income if only in a moderated form. See Roman Schatz, "Ein bisschen Grundeinkommen." *Zeit online*, June 30, 2015. Online: www.zeit.de/politik/ausland/2015-06/grundeinkommen-finnland-modellversuch (accessed July 23, 2015).

Mobility

The morphology of German cities and regions is heavily influenced to this day by the automobile planning paradigm and its traffic infrastructures. The value of owning one's own car in urban space, however, is continually declining. For many young people, the car is no longer a status symbol or proof of professional success. And in cities with a wide range of local passenger and mobility services it is no longer necessary. Ridesharing services, multimodal options, or on-demand bike and car sharing organized by service provider companies and private initiatives, rather than communally, bear witness to changing mobility structures. However, outside the cities the situation is different, particularly in sparsely populated and rural regions. Car mobility here still facilitates access and participation because provision of local transport services is often limited.

● 30
33
● 78

Cities and regions are faced with the challenge of abandoning a decades-old planning paradigm and of developing new mobility cultures. Mixed-use spaces with a high quality of living featuring short distances, local supply structures, and a concomitant orientation toward neighborliness and direct cooperation could evolve here. This needs to be implemented first and foremost by reducing car infrastructures (streets and parking space) while at the same time increasing the number of pedestrian facilities, bike paths, and amenity structures. This restructuring, the merits of electric mobility and of alternative mobility concepts being mutually complementary, will be accelerated by the parallel development of alternative forms of propulsion.

● 40
78
80

● 35
210

Commons

There is a distinction between commons and public goods: "While these public spaces and public goods contribute mightily to the qualities of the commons, it takes political action on the part of citizens and the people to appropriate them or to make them so." [Harvey 2013, 136–137] Unlike public spaces, commons are not necessarily subject to political power and administration, [Harvey 2013, 136] but are perpetually renewable, living social processes. They are not confined to small-scale niches, but are possible in all spheres of life, as for instance mobility or health care. But the commons can also be understood as a political process, an act of making and reclaiming that which we manage collectively.[4] [Ferguson 2014, 18]

24

The commons in today's cities are often co-produced and shaped by civic society: creative strategies of appropriation are employed in the use of public space, thus contributing to an at least temporary rededication of public land. New strategies are conceived, opening new perspectives. This invariably also means appropriation; the ability, that is, to reinterpret what is assumed to be useless and to dedicate it to new uses. According to the architect Olga Hungar, this creates a sense of well-being, especially in regard to one's perception of one's own life situation, and an awareness, also a feeling, of one's own efficacy: "I'm able to contribute toward actively shaping the space that I live in." [Lecture: Zukunftswerkstatt/Workshop #3, Berlin, November 28, 2013]

103
135

Advocates of these strategies of spatial appropriation, such as the spatial geographer David Harvey, point to the fact that the translatability of small-scale, local initiatives onto higher levels of the system is beset with

---

4   Since 2011, for instance, the Allmende-Kontor project has existed on the site of the former Tempelhof Airport in Berlin with the aim of reclaiming the airport ground commons. A garden with 300 raised beds is being developed here as an attraction and communications space (cf. Meyer-Renschhausen 2013).

far-reaching problems, and that their applicability to transforming society as a whole is uncertain. [Harvey 2013] Self-empowered shaping of space, on the other hand, radically alters one's relation to and responsibility toward a space: through his own involvement the "space user," now coproducer, establishes a personal and emotional connection to his environment. This could be the start of a movement toward sustainable, high-quality long-term usage of space. The coformative actor experiences his own efficacy in the space he lives in and can guide and control what creates and shapes his life foundations: "Space, as I see it, is a means to an end." [Olga Hungar, Lecture: Zukunftswerkstatt/Workshop #3, Berlin, November 28, 2013] Building becomes a constant process of appropriation under the altering basic conditions, where prosperity, the future, and the question as to how we want to live are continually being negotiated.

In times of shortage of available space, of loss of collectively shapable spaces, and of urban development based more often on profit rather than civic-oriented social principles, the debate on how to define and deal with the commons has gained in intensity. "It is precisely against the backdrop of 'austerity urbanism' that the public domain in its spatial dimension is a resource to be rethought, renegotiated, and reclaimed." [Ferguson 2014, 19] The right to the city manifests itself as a collective right to produce urbanization [Swyngedouw 2011] in that the city increasingly becomes commons again. These commons "are neither protected by the state nor by the

● 44

● 104

market. ... Communities of users alone can protect them. These can be collectives, neighborhood associations, or tenant communities that also receive resources for the purpose." [Leggewie 2013] This has an architectural corollary: "Architecture that successfully blends space and personal experience facilitates new images of the city in the imaginations of its users." [Olga Hungar, Lecture: Zukunftswerkstatt/Workshop #3, Berlin, November 28, 2013]

References

Amin, Ash. 2014. "Öffentlicher Raum: Guerillabewegungen können ein Funke sein," Interview with Katrin Nussmayr. *Die Presse* (August 5, 2014). Online: http://diepresse.com/home/99ideen/3850134/Offentlicher-Raum_Guerillabewegungen-konnen-ein-Funke-sein (accessed July 28, 2015).

Arch+. 2012. "Tokio: Die Stadt bewohnen." 208, 20–175.

Bönt, Ralf. 2012. *Das entehrte Geschlecht: Ein notwendiges Manifest für den Mann*. Munich.

Diefenbacher, Hans, and Roland Zieschank. 2011. *Woran sich Wohlstand wirklich messen lässt. Alternativen zum Bruttoinlandsprodukt*. Munich.

Ferguson, Francesca, and Urban Drift Projects (eds.). 2014. *Make_Shift City: Renegotiating the Urban Commons*. Berlin.

Forget, Evelyn. 2011. *The Town with No Poverty*. Manitoba. Online: http://public.econ.duke.edu/~erw/197/forget-cea%20(2).pdf (accessed July 28, 2015).

Grubb, Adam. 2012. "Permaculture as a Permanent Culture." In Peter de Rooden et al., *Food for the City: A Future for the Metropolis*. Rotterdam, 90–95.

Harvey, David. 2012. *Rebel Cities*. London/New York.

Häußermann, Hartmut. 2011. "Was bleibt von der europäischen Stadt?" In Oliver Frey and Florian Koch (eds.), *Die Zukunft der europäischen Stadt*. Wiesbaden: 23–35.

Hummel, Bernd. 2011. "Das Mietshäuser Syndikat: Eine Alternative zum Eigentumsprinzip." *Arch+*, 201/202, 124.

Leggewie, Claus. 2013. "Die Stadt von Übermorgen. Aus der Sicht Soziales." Lecture: "The City of the Day After Tomorrow" ("Die Stadt von Übermorgen"). Documentation expert panel at the Federal Ministry for the Environment, Nature Conservation, Building and Nuclear Safety (Bundesministerium für Umwelt, Naturschutz, Bau und Reaktorsicherheit [BMUB]) and the Federal Institute for Research on Building, Urban Affairs and Spatial Development (Bundesinstitut für Bau-, Stadt- und Raumforschung [BBSR]), Bonn, December 11–12, 2013.

Lepenies, Philipp. 2013. *Die Macht der einen Zahl – Eine politische Geschichte des Bruttoinlandsprodukts*. Berlin.

Meadows, Dennis, et al. 1972. *The Limits to Growth: A Report for the Club of Rome's Project on the Predicament of Mankind*. New York, 23.

Meyer-Renschhausen, Elisabeth. 2013. "Das Allmende-Kontor auf dem Tempelhofer Feld." *eNewsletter Wegweiser Bürgergesellschaft*, 23/2013, (December 6, 2013). Online: www.buergergesellschaft.de/fileadmin/pdf/gastbeitrag_meyer-renschhausen_131206.pdf (accessed July 29, 2015).

Montag Stiftung Jugend und Gesellschaft (ed.). 2011. *Inklusion vor Ort. Der kommunale Index für Inklusion – ein Praxishandbuch*. Bonn.

Muraca, Barbara. 2014. "Postwachstumsökonomie." *Böll. Thema* (1/2014): "Seitenwechsel. Die Ökonomien des Gemeinsamen." Online: www.boell.de/sites/default/files/boell-thema_1_2014_v08_kommentierbar.pdf (accessed July 27, 2015).

OECD. 2014. "All on Board: Making inclusive growth happen." Online: www.oecd.org/inclusive-growth/all-on-board-making-inclusive-growth-happen.pdf (accessed July 27, 2015).

Reiss-Schmidt, Stephan. 2003. "Der öffentliche Raum: Traum, Wirklichkeit, Perspektiven." Lecture in the context of "Zukunft Stadt – urbanauten-Debatte," Munich, September 30, 2003.

Seidel, Irmi, and Angelika Zahrnt. 2015. "Postwachstum – Kern der großen Transformation." *Movum* 5: "Wachstum." Online: www.movum.info/themen/wachstum/189-postwachstum-kern-der-grossen-transformation (accessed July 27, 2015).

Streeck, Wolfgang. 2015. "Das kann nicht gutgehen mit dem Kapitalismus," Interview with Ferdinand Knauss. *Wirtschaftswoche*, (January 8, 2015). Online: www.wiwo.de/politik/konjunktur/soziologe-wolfgang-streeck-das-kann-nicht-gut-gehen-mit-dem-kapitalismus/11195698.html (accessed July, 2015).

Strunk, Andreas. 2013. "Die inklusive Gemeinde." Website Heinrich Böll-Stiftung, March 12, 2013. Online: www.boell.de/de/node/277142 (accessed 28, 2015).

Swyngedouw. Erik. 2011. *Designing the Post-Political City and the Insurgent Polis*. Civic City Cahier 5, London.

Weiguny, Bettina. 2012. "Work-Life-Balance: Generation Weichei." *Frankfurter Allgemeine Zeitung* (December 22, 2012). Online: www.faz.net/aktuell/wirtschaft/work-life-balance-generation-weichei-12002680.html (accessed July 27, 2015).

Archive Armin Linke

Bibliothèque Science Po, server room, Paris, France, 2012

Bloemenveiling Aalsmeer, flower auction, Amsterdam, Netherlands, 1998

Mountain with antennas, Kitakyushu, Japan, 2006

Psigot settlement, Psigot, West Bank, 2011

Dej. Jote Street, Addis Ababa, Ethiopia, 2012

Chorsu Bazaar, Tashkent, Uzbekistan, 2001

DKRZ Deutsches Klimarechenzentrum, archives, Hamburg, Germany, 2013

Computer dump, Guiyu, China, 2005

"Under the conditions of decentralized modes of production, physical mobility of products and people will be limited; virtual mobility, on the other hand, will be unlimited. As a result, compartmentalized, individualized developmental regions will spring up in Germany."

[Matthijs Bouw, Lecture: Zukunftswerkstatt/Workshop #3, Berlin, November 27, 2013]

Decentralized Production

New technologies and the progressive digitization of daily life are changing patterns of production and consumption. Globally available knowledge and automated processes are already making possible modes of production that are more compartmentalized, more collaborative, less linear, and less hierarchically organized. Hand in hand with these changes, a geographic shift of forces is occurring: certain regions are attaining a new kind of centrality, while others are drifting into a digital nowhere. Against this backdrop, the shaping and development of networks and infrastructures continues to be a question of political power. Moreover, the new modes of production are turning consumers into prosumers who no longer only consume but are actively involved in processes of development and production. How are the products and services of the digital avant-garde, the makers and the hackers, changing the world in which we live? How will this decentralized production alter our cities and geographic regions? To whom do the products and ideas generated by these processes belong? Whom do they benefit? Over- and undercapacity, over- and undersupply will determine ownership options, how exactly and with whom one works, as well as the exact configuration of forms of usage and design, not just virtually, but in "real geographic" terms. Are we only talking about a privileged digital elite here who will benefit from the new options, or are there prospects for the broader population? These negotiative processes call for a new ethics because destructive exploitation is all too easy. What is required is extensive discussion of the options and limits in dealing with these modified socio-technological conditions.

● 118
● 136

● 107
● 104

Production and Geography

The production of goods, merchandise, and knowledge is always a powerful developmental factor for the built environment as well as for town and country. "Urbanization is not a fixed state; it stands in close relation to modes of production and their history and can only be understood in terms of them." [Dell 2014, 38] Modes of production play a vital role in the development and diversification of cities, geographic regions, and the countryside. In Germany, a national economy with value creation still heavily based on the industrial sector, the question of future modes of production is of far-reaching importance for geographic developments.

At the start of the nineteenth century, before the industrial revolution, population and labor density were low, and determined primarily by natural geographic conditions. At 3 percent worldwide and around 25 percent in Germany, the degree of urbanization was extremely low [Bähr 1997, 75 ff.] and the organization of production, supply, and marketing was geographically unfocused. Resources and what needed to be known about them were tied to localities and spread only slowly. Consequently, the growth of the population at the start of the nineteenth century still had no big impact on geographic developments, because the population was still agrarian. [Cf. Häußermann and Siebel 2004] Not until the industrialization of the mid-nineteenth century, and particularly in Germany's era of rapid industrialization (1870–1914), did production start to become centralized and mechanized while labor-divided society and its geographic regions underwent further diversification. Fordist-organized industry depended on cities providing large numbers of workers. Because living and housing conditions could not keep up with this rapid growth, the socially segregated city became a "hotbed of disease and vice." [Lindner 2004, 19 ff.] While in 1871 only 36 percent of the population in Germany lived in cities, by 1910 the figure had risen to 60 percent. [Cf. Bergmann 1970]

● 75

The paradigm of decentralized production marks a new phase characterized by increasing digitization and virtualization, cornerstones of the next society for the sociologist Dirk Baecker: "The next society and modern society are as different as electricity and mechanics. Circuits supplant levers; instantaneity renders mediation superfluous. While book-printing entails distribution, computers already think in resonances. The dynamics of modernity that could still be read in terms of history, progress, and decadence breaks up into turbulences where only singularities are discernible." [Baecker 2011, 8] The geographic upshot of this is a simultaneity of the local and the global, where everyone, thanks to digitization, virtualization, and autonomization, is able to join in and play a shaping role. The question will be whether this emancipatory force really embraces all sections of society. Will only a few individuals participate formatively using the available options? Or will the production spaces of the future depend yet more on the artificial intelligence of robots and drones generating autonomously operating production units? To what extent are man and machine still distinct when technological developments are increasingly turning the human body into a cyborg? Finally: How will our cities and regions function then? What geographic conditions will they confront under the impact of decentralized production?

● 32

Three-Dimensional Printing Systems

New information, communication, and production technologies are changing how development, manufacturing, and consumption interrelate. Three-dimensional printing systems that bring together local production and international generation of knowledge have become symbolic of a new decentralization of modes of production and betoken yet greater transformations ahead. Given today's technological developments, it is already possible to print highly sophisticated products such as cars and houses.

The widespread distribution of three-dimensional printing systems could entail a new wave of industrialization in Germany and powerfully affect the existing value-creation chains of processing industries and their workers. Will such developments be so widespread as to lastingly jeopardize established industries and their business models? In the future, cars, for instance, could be produced, or printed, in local workshops instead of in big central factories. [Kilimann 2015] Digitization of production could facilitate the individualization of even highly complex products, since requirements and matters of taste can be integrated right to the very last into development processes.

According to the architect Ludger Hovestadt, three-dimensional printing systems could lead not only to changes in forms of production and components but also, in the long term, to a rethinking of both architecture and *Baukultur*. Starkly reduced costs in the individualized production of customized building materials, in his view, are indicative of a potential widespread future development. The introduction of three-dimensional printing systems, according to Hovestadt, could also mean "that the construction of buildings and the building site in future will have to be organized on a cross-trade basis, whereas today the various onsite trades work additively. Building components, then, would be so fabricated that they can easily be transported and assembled trade-independently. This would entail a complete inversion of construction processes that would also affect the structures of building supplies stores, the building trade, and architectural practices." [Lecture: Zukunftswerkstatt/Workshop #3, Berlin, November 28, 2013]

● 56
74

● 107
127

Regional Material Cycles

Given the continuing growth in demand for raw materials worldwide, the exploitation and maintenance of local resources is becoming increasingly important. [Cf. Konrad-Adenauer-Stiftung 2014] Independence from global developments and sustainable access to raw materials could become a significant driving force behind decentralized production. Particularly at the local level, in combination with community waste management and sewerage, raw materials paths can be advantageously and efficiently organized and regulated. [Deutsches Institut für Urbanistik 2014] The more materials are recycled and reused, and the more these materials reenter the product cycle, the more necessary expert knowledge in the efficient use of raw materials becomes. Forty-seven percent of communal waste in Germany today is already being recycled and made available again as materials. [Europäische Kommission 2014]

229
41
104

> Identifying existing buildings and structures as utilizable resource stores could become an important task for communities. This could lead to an upgrading and refunctioning of urban industrial estates as sites for the storage and recovery of resources. Developmental potential could also be activated in suburban and peripheral areas insofar as natural geographic conditions and local cooperation abet the creation of integrated material cycles.

118
100
130

Individual Developer-Producers

If consumers become developers and producers, then individual design and production options with no need for highly specialized expertise become possible. The "maker culture," in this sense, is a technologically induced sphere of potential embracing the evolution and spread of development and production sites, tools, and collaborative appliances, combined with globally available knowledge and data for the production of physical products. The new actors exploit the digital potential of collaborative design to develop alternatives to existing processes of product-development and production in the established industries. Here the designer Susanne Stauch would welcome "more trust [being] placed in the individual, participatory prosumer, who responsibly confronts what he has brought into the world. The result would be the natural development

229
119

of a critical capacity and of mindfulness to self, others, and the environment." [Lecture: Zukunftswerkstatt/Workshop #3, Berlin, November 28, 2013] Traditional industries and lines of business will be challenged by these less hierarchical, flexible network structures, at least where entire trades are undergoing transformation in the wake of digitization.

For these possibilities to become feasible, sites must be available where three-dimensional printers or similar devices are located and can be used. [Tierney 2015] Susanne Stauch considers it necessary to develop and extend the specialized production facilities that today are mainly found in universities and design agencies, while at the same time elaborating suitable Internet distribution systems to enable "new designers" to step out of their current local confinement into the limelight. Hence, goods that are partly locally produced are distributed via centralized platforms. Decentralization, in Stauch's eyes, implies that "the distribution of tools and raw materials required is decentralized in the sense that goods are produced and stored according to respective local requirements and/or that greater variety is on offer as a result of de-monopolization. Decentralization here must also be understood in terms of the internet's ubiquity and non-local nature (= access to resources)." [Lecture: Zukunftswerkstatt/Workshop #3, Berlin, November 28, 2013]

Collaboration

Increasing numbers of online providers enable customers to provide independent data on the basis of which computer-assisted local production processes are controlled. Products and designs can be developed and improved as joint projects via net-based platforms and file-sharing sites. According to Norbert Palz, collaboration in development and production can lead to the creation of new, individualized products, for instance by adding nanotechnological materials. [Lecture: Zukunftswerkstatt/Workshop #3, Berlin, November 28, 2013]

● 56

● 107

Hence, collaboration presupposes taking into account the new conditions in design, modified concepts of authorship and intellectual ownership, and the intellectual, economic, and legal utility of individual productions within coproductive contexts. At the same time, the legal conditions must be created to thwart potentially destructive developments such as providing blueprints for making firearms. [Cf. Rötzer 2012 and 2013]

Availability and wider access are transforming the Internet into a genuinely local community. Standardized license contracts and the deregulation of usage rights by nonprofit organizations such as Creative Commons is a start that sets a potential example. Patents and monopolies must be challenged if the goal is a society where production is individualized and decentralized.

Sites will develop where a wide range of communally usable technologies is available. These will be sites for communicating about products and production, sites by and for makers and designers where local collaboration is possible. They are not insular systems but incubators for transparently transmitting knowledge to other local contexts and production centers. The openness of the sites can also contribute to spatially organizing cities and communities. Building components can be custom-produced, not only for private homes but also for mass-produced housing. This could lead to further diversification in the design of visible urban structures, of facades and public squares, or to the development of completely different local spatial configurations. There is, however, a danger of increasing monotony, when houses can be indefinitely replicated by standardized printing processes.

Exchange and Sharing

Digitized, platform-based communication processes have extended exchange and sharing options to central areas of life—the sharing of cars, apartments, houses (chiefly for vacation purposes), or the loan and exchange of clothing, books, tools, or furniture, is already regular practice for parts of society today. Values such as community, creativity, and variation are more important to the practitioners of these types of consumption than property is, although social trust and socio-demographic features such as age, education, and income also play a role. [Heinrichs 2013, 101 ff.] Transparency in regard to suppliers and consumers, products and services is instrumental for the development of the relevant Internet services.

● 229

● 119

In work, living, mobility, and leisure, transparency leads to complementarity. The borders between use and ownership are shifting. They have disappeared completely in some areas because what users expect of consumption and environment is changing: cost, sustainability, and the social are gaining in importance; conspicuous ostentation is declining. The social process of sharing has given rise to new perspectives on an "economy of sharing" geared to formulating a culture of "use over ownership" within economic parameters.

In many places, self-organized initiatives such as urban gardening communities, local exchange rings, and housing projects are experiencing an upswing. [Heinrichs 2013, 100] Cities and vicinities are changing, having become central localities for exchange and liaison as well as personal networks. More and more locations are arising specifically for nonlocal visitors whose common interest is work, livelihood, and temporary living space. Working on local or entirely nonlocal projects, they finance themselves by renting their own apartments while paying significantly less for their temporary accommodation, which they share with like-minded people. The market for these vacation apartments has been growing rapidly in recent years. Under these conditions, concepts such as "work," "vacation," and "visitor" are becoming diluted. At the same time, functionally definable, distinctly visible spatial units within cities are disappearing. Is every place simultaneously a place for dwelling, working, and living? For a highly

● 34

mobile group of city dwellers this breakdown is not confined to one specific urban space but holds for every city they visit. "In this sense we are always and everywhere tourists." [Rogers 2015]

Not only are distinct language zones developing in the affected cities but also specific options for the laboring tourists: there are translocal spaces where English is used as a lingua franca regardless of the native language. Existing patterns of residence are being transformed, not least because rising rents are displacing long-time residents. Differing motives for sharing reflect income disparities—sharing is fun and an experiment for some, while for others it is economically necessary.

Socio-Digital Disparities

Progressive digitization will give rise to painful adjustment processes. "Many workers will be unable to keep up with the pace of digitization and will drop behind. This is a serious problem and we need to address it. But we cannot react by stopping technological development. It cannot be stopped." [McAfee 2015] In the eyes of Robert Shiller, economist, there must at least be a new form of insurance for those who, because of digitization, permanently drop out of the work environment. Simultaneously, new work environments and activities of which we have no idea today will be created. [Shiller 2015] Yet not only labor market developments but also geographic and demographic issues will present a challenge. For Gesche Joost of the Design Research Lab, Berlin University of the Arts, there are deep gulfs to be bridged in this adjustment process: "We are effectively creating a digital division into those who are online and those who have hardly a clue. It's not just a question of age but that many people have no computer, no technical ability, or no interest in the issues. We cannot afford to leave these people behind. We have to keep creating forms of access for them." [Quoted in von Gagern 2015]

● 90

● 108

As Jeremy Rifkin pointed out in *The Age of Access* (2000), access to a large extent determines the possibility of participating in the digital society's transformation processes. In the words of the geographer Claus-Christian Wiegandt: "The danger of a digital gulf between cities and communities is imminent in Germany. Existing ● 137 disparities are increasing as a result of digitization, making it difficult for shrinking cities and communities to keep up with intercommunal competition."[Pricewaterhouse-Coopers 2015, 4] Is this synonymous with the death of villages and peripheral regions? "Likely this is a time when Germany ● 54 and a lot of other countries have once again entered a phase of geographical reorientation. Smaller settlements are dying out and society as a whole must see to it that this occurs with as little friction as possible." [Miegel 2015] The digital opening of cities and regions may prove more important than their opening via highways, air- and seaports in the future.

Analog Counterworlds

Will the growing digitization of our entire living space ● 108 encourage the development of analog counterworlds? After all, data networks are ever susceptible to misuse for purposes of surveillance, espionage, or sabotage. Moreover, Internet viruses and epidemic system failures reveal the almost uncontrollable nature inherent in decentralized networks. Perhaps this is why local, ● 120 complementary worlds might develop: islands of deceleration, places for recreation and encounter such as parks and gardens, mom-and-pop stores, libraries. Are they the analog counterparts to the digital world? Rural ● 56
74
123 spaces might continue to exist and function without being technologically networked and yet, or for just that reason, offer high living quality. These areas might further diversify, supplying themselves and surrounding communities with recreational space, food, and energy. Small and large cities, villages and isolated farms would still be evenly distributed across Germany, because there would be no need in these analog counterworlds to compete for scarce resources such as space and housing—the supply situation everywhere would be equally favorable.

Smart City

Data is to be collected, evaluated, and used to make cities more intelligent, efficient, and individualized. This covers areas such as housing (air-conditioning, energy flows), energy and the environment (emissions, immissions), health (bodily functions, fitness), transport and logistics (traffic flows, park management), industry and production (goods and production logistics). In the first place, it is a question of technically improving communication, as well as the regulation and control of urban and household infrastructures.

For Rem Koolhaas digital developments present architecture with a particular challenge: "Architecture has entered into a new engagement with digital culture and capital—which amounts to the most radical change within the discipline since the confluence of modernism and industrial production in the early twentieth century. Yet this shift has gone largely unnoticed, because it has not taken the form of a visible upheaval or wholesale transformation. To the contrary: It is a stealthy infiltration of architecture via its constituent elements. ... We became increasingly sensitive to the constant acceleration of architecture's 'smartness' in the form of embedded devices, sensors, and systems. Looking at the traditional elements of architecture through a microscope, we saw the extent to which they had been penetrated, if not completely transformed, by new kinds of 'intelligence.'" [Koolhaas 2015]

The goal of these concepts is the same for all cities and communities: to raise the quality of life by means of improved planning based on the collecting and analyzing of data. This goes hand in hand with elaborate forms of surveillance and control: sensors collect and evaluate data according to principles of efficiency. However, is this consistent with the attainments of the European city that has always been characterized by civil liberty, freedom, and anonymity? [Cf. Siebel 2012] The truly far-reaching effects of "smartness" will likely only be found, in the medium term, in new, planned cities in Asia and Africa, where blueprints for digital options will impact planning and design processes to create radical contrasts to the informal city.

● 213

Autonomization

Autonomization processes are part of digital developments and are diffused through ever-ramifying areas of industry and society: "Sooner or later, whatever can be automatized will be automatized." [Geuter 2015] Transformation through autonomization is particularly evident in the production sector. The networking of machines, robots, and human beings by means of protocols and processes can contribute to increased efficiency in production flows.

The transport sector, in addition to the production sector, will be a potential field of application: "We are on the eve of another mobile revolution. Driverless vehicles will play an active part in road traffic in future. The necessary data will be generated by means of cameras and/or sensors and computer processed in real time in a fraction of a second. Vehicles will also continuously exchange information with each other and with the transport infrastructure. Driver robots will take over more and more of the car driver's tasks." [Maurer et al. 2015] Related functions will likewise be tested using drones. Drones are already being used today to deliver medicines to remote districts. Particularly in the logistics sector they could be used as efficient modes of transport.

35
99

118

40
58
78
126

Autonomization would allow existing traffic infrastructures to be much more efficiently used. Consequently, were the volume of urban traffic to remain constant, or even to rise, the entire structure of streets and parking lots could be cut back, giving rise to new possible uses for the freed-up areas. Streets, parking garages and lots could be transformed into recreational, educational, and residential spaces. The beginnings of this remodeling are already observable in Berlin, Copenhagen, New York, and Seoul. Several questions crop up here: What new spaces will arise and how will cities use them to indicate future directions? Will this lead to new specializations developing? How will cities change given the "raised quality of life" planning concept? Quality of life today is still often connected with accessibility and cars to tie up with local retail trade or to enhance tourism. Conceivably, such requirements, driverless vehicles, and new mobility services will no longer be contradictory concepts, and traditional solutions such as beltways and large-scale parking lots will become obsolete.

Digital Appropriation of Space

● 107

The use of information and communication technologies leads to interactional changes with the built environment, especially in cities. There are many reasons for this: permanent mobile phone availability, announcements at site-specific services (supermarkets or department stores), use of GPS software in unfamiliar places, urban exploration with digital map information, spatial appropriation via geo-games. These applications simultaneously familiarize themselves with user routines and behaviors to make further planning suggestions for the day or for mobility/transport.

The built environment today is already a hybrid combining interfaces and outlets, surveillance cameras and tracking systems. This means that options for action in architecture and urban planning will also change as a result of how data is used. Processes that are only implicit at the moment will be made visible in the form of data flows.

● 116

Hacking

Development and production in the lived environment are not individual but a result of collaborative processes that obey definite rules. To break this conventionality it is sometimes necessary to play against the rules. Hacking, in this context, for Markus Huber (2013), becomes significant as an urban development design strategy. A wide range of experimental practices in art already address this phenomenon. It is not a question of destruction or manipulation, but of exploring technology: "In dismantling, examining, and then reassembling technologies, ideas, expectations, and formats, the goal is not so much to solve a problem as to discover unexpected paths and strategies by means of curiosity, creativity, and skill. The question arises here: How can the activities of hacking and critical engineering be rendered fruitful for the development of the lived urban environment?" [Lecture: Zukunftswerkstatt/Workshop #3, Berlin, November 28, 2013]

Hacking as an urban development strategy aims at the creative transformation of local data and the discovery of potential for improvement: "The variation, the alternative, is the quintessential structural feature of a 'hack.' The hacker knows that there is not just one way of using a device, software, service, or other technical artifact, but that there are always alternatives. There is always an unforeseen route.

That is the politics of hacking: the identification and creation of alternatives." [Seemann 2015] Communities release data with increasing frequency so that it can be used by programmers and those with an interest in urban development.

Willingness to collaborate openly with open sourcing is a prerequisite for data transfer at the communal level. Open sourcing, for Andreas Gebhard (2012), is a kind of social contract agreed on by the participants. "It is an idea, independent of people and institutions, that can be used by everyone. The software (the source code) is available for people in a readable and comprehensible form. It can be copied at will, distributed, and used, and it can be altered and distributed in its altered form." [Lecture: Zukunftswerkstatt/Workshop #1, Berlin, September 26, 2012] The more data that is made available and can be used in this way, the sooner it will be possible to tackle complex problems collaboratively. Communal problems can thus be addressed and converted into specific, local solutions. The process raises new issues: Who bears the responsibility, including for possible misuse? The people who make data available, or those who search for applications and uses?

● 94

References

Baecker, Dirk. 2011. "Zukunftsfähigkeit: 16 Thesen zur nächsten Gesellschaft." *Revue für postheroisches Management*, 9, 8–9.

Bähr, Jürgen. 1997. *Bevölkerungsgeographie*. 3d ed. Stuttgart.

Bergmann, Klaus. 1970. *Agrarromantik und Großstadtfeindschaft*. Meisenheim am Glan.

Dell, Christoph. 2014. *Das Urbane. Wohnen, Leben, Produzieren*. Berlin.

Deutsches Institut für Urbanistik. 2014. *Hemmnisse und Potentiale zur Ressourceneffizienzsteigerung durch Optimierung regionaler und lokaler Stoffkreisläufe und Stoffströme*. Research project, Berlin, 2014–2017.

Europäische Kommission. 2014. "Deutschland führend bei Recycling." (March 25, 2014). Online: http://ec.europa. eu/deutschland/press/pr_ releases/12216_de.html (accessed June 22, 2015).

Gagern, Stefan von. 2015. "Gesche Joost: Die Politik versteht zu wenig von der Digitalisierung," *Xing Spielraum* (March 13, 2015). Online: https:// spielraum.xing.com/2015/03/ gesche-joost-die-politik-versteht-zu-wenig-von-der-digitalisierung (accessed June 23, 2015).

Geuter, Jürgen. 2015. "Machines of Loving Grace/Wen überfährt das selbstfahrende Auto?" *Wired* (March 19, 2015). Online: www.wired.de/collection/tech/ wen-soll-das-selbstfahrende-auto-uberfahren (accessed 22, 2015).

Häußermann, Hartmut, and Walter Siebel. 2004. *Stadtsoziologie: Eine Einführung*. Frankfurt/Main.

Heinrichs, Harald. 2013. "Im Zeitalter des Homo Collaborans: Sharing Economy." *Politische Ökologie*, 135, 9–106.

Kilimann, Susanne. 2015. "Community, entwickle ein Auto." *Die Zeit* (August 3, 2015). Online: www.zeit.de/mobilitaet/ 2015-08/local-motors-auto-regionale-produktion-berlin (accessed August 6, 2015).

Konrad-Adenauer-Stiftung. 2014. "Globale Megatrends (III): Rohstoffe – Alternativen erschliessen und neue Paradigmen schaffen." *Analysen & Argumente*, 147, (May 2014).

Koolhaas, Rem. 2015. "The Smart Landscape". *Artforum* (April, 2015). Online: https:// artforum.com/inprint/ issue=201504&id=50735 (accessed June 22, 2015).

Lindner, Rolf. 2004. *Walks on the Wild Side. Eine Geschichte der Stadtforschung*. Frankfurt/Main, New York.

Maurer, Markus, J. Christian Gerdes, Barbara Lenz, and Hermann Winner (eds.). 2015. *Autonomes Fahren. Technische, rechtliche und gesellschaftliche Aspekte*. Berlin.

McAfee, Andrew. 2015. "Die Digitalisierung gefährdet die Routine-Jobs der Wissensarbeiter." *Netzökonom*, (May 9, 2015). Online: https:// netzoekonom.de/2015/05/09/ die-digitalisierung-gefaehrdet-vor-allem-routine-jobs-der-wissensarbeiter (accessed June 22, 2015).

Miegel, Meinhard. 2015. "Mit dem Dorfsterben leben lernen." *The European – Das Debatten-Magazin* (May 19, 2015). Online: www.theeuropean .de/meinhard-miegel/10105-doerfer-sind-relikte (accessed June 22, 2015).

PricewaterhouseCoopers (ed.). 2015. *Deutschlands Städte werden digital*. Online: www.pwc.de/de/publikationen/ paid_pubs/pwc-studie_ deutschlands-staedte-werden-digital.pdf (accessed June 22, 2015).

Rifkin, Jeremy. 2000. *The Age of Access*, New York.

Rötzer, Florian. 2012. "Herunterladen, Drucken, Schiessen." *Telepolis* (December 7, 2012). Online: www.heise.de/tp/ artikel/38/38145/1.html (accessed July 10, 2015).

Rötzer, Florian. 2013. "Waffen für alle mit dem 3D-Drucker." *Telepolis*, February 11, 2013. Online: www.heise.de/tp/ artikel/38/38537/1.html (accessed July 10, 2015).

Rogers, Thomas. 2015. "Berlin Is the 'Post-Tourist' Capital of Europe." *nymag.com* (March 17, 2015). Online: http://nymag.com/ next/2015/03/berlin-is-the-post-tourist-capital-of-europe. html (accessed June 22, 2015).

Seemann, Michael. 2015. "Der Hacker und die nächste Politik" (April 20, 2015). Online: http://mspr0.de/?p=4284 (accessed June 22, 2015).

Shiller, Robert. 2015. "Das gefährdet die Identität des Menschen," Interview with Ulrich Schäfer. *Süddeutsche Zeitung*, 78 (April 4–6, 2015), 25.

Siebel, Walter. 2012. "Die europäische Stadt." In *Handbuch Stadtsoziologie*, edited by Eckardt, Frank, Wiesbaden, 201–212.

Tierney, John. 2015. "How Makerspaces Help Local Economies." *The Atlantic* (April 17 2015). Online: www.theatlantic.com/ technology/archive/2015/04/ makerspaces-are-remaking-local-economies/390807 (accessed June 22, 2015).

Speculative Planning?

In-migration and out-migration, shortage of resources and climate change, digitization and individualization, the limits to growth and societal crises of identity, refugee influxes, the transition to renewable energies and the distribution of prosperity are challenges currently under discussion, the consequences of which we sense but are unable to assess with any exactitude. What seems to be clear is that they will change Germany's built and lived environment for years to come. As a means toward coping with this uncertainty, we have examined how optional futures can be used for planning processes in cities and regions. *Speculations Transformations* is an introduction to methodical aspects of planning and strategic forecasting that facilitate a constructive handling of weak, and sometimes also strong, signals that could develop into increasingly prominent phenomena. The book is both stimulating and, in a sense, perplexing because it raises awareness of the plurality and diversity of possible futures, both large-scale and small-scale, and converts otherwise incompatible planning approaches—abstract theory, short-term pragmatism—into a speculative practice.

The limits to this kind of speculative approach are obvious. Speculations can only be based on present conditions, and the transformations suggested endeavor to provide viable future applicability for present action on this basis. Thus, the three transformation paradigms presented in this book take as their starting point the assumption that planning is possible and they relate primarily to the challenges in Germany and to the specifically German understanding of planning and *Baukultur*. We are well aware that the idea of the necessity of planning and quantifying life in data and cartographically is based on a Western worldview and that this, too, needs to be critically examined in the context of fundamental transformations. Consequently, alongside technocratic top-down professionalism, the paradigms also draw on actor-based, bottom-up movements, because in our view these two poles will shape the future: scalability of abstract models on the one hand, social acceptance on the other.

Present in every hope, or positive view of the future, is always the no less relevant counterposition. The transition to renewable energies can be a chance to rethink city and countryside. Renewable energies may entirely meet Germany's power requirements by the year 2050. Reduced geopolitical dependencies and falling energy prices would facilitate radically new options for action. But is not the logic according to which the transition to renewables is to be accomplished—precisely if it is successful—a confirmation of the existing system, a cloak that hides economic growth of the current kind from radically new ideas?

The search for alternative prosperity today generally assumes the form of protest against the existing order. Participative processes are sensors of possible societal change, on the one hand, giving users of the built and lived environment the chance for their needs and ideas to flow into planning processes. But a culture of participation, off or online, if it is to be genuine, goes beyond purely procedural criteria, seeking dialogue on an equal footing with those who wish to contribute and be active in jointly shaping their environment. But where is participation genuine and where, for the sake of social stability, does it merely delegate responsibility away from institutions to individuals who thereby increasingly become nonpaid actors and self-exploiters of their own social participation?

This is particularly clear in those models of production and value creation that, based on the digital world and its putative achievements, are increasingly decentralized. Here, for those able to take part in this way, there is a wide range of options for participating in political, social, and economic processes, precisely because top-down delegating is no longer possible: action is decentralized. To avoid social and regional segregation in the form of a digital divide, the networking of *all* would be necessary here. But do not current marketing and surveillance trends bolster a contrary development where networking is leading, not to more participation, but to greater dependence and manipulation? Nor is digital sharing always emancipatory—often enough it simply shifts the risks to society's weakest members. Digitization's socio-technical appropriation will, at all events, change and mold our cities and municipalities, regions and landscapes. It is indispensable, therefore, that we look at the ways in which people can contribute and give shape to a networked society.

The conclusions drawn from these phenomena in this book with regard to *Baukultur* remain abstract because, as explained in the preface, we have avoided using "images of the future"; we have tried, instead, to place the possible future conditions affecting *Baukultur* on a broad foundation of knowledge. The developments, ideas, and approaches concentrated here are intended to orient and guide others in thinking through possible future developments. The results that these might entail for particular decision processes need to be corroborated in local workshops, planning processes, and participatory procedures. Only then can all the actors involved in the shaping of cities and regions become aware of the possible consequences of the developmental trends that have been outlined.

Sources

Interviews

Klaus Hurrelmann in conversation with
Stefan Carsten, July 9, 2012, phone call

Ralf Schüle in conversation with Stefan Carsten,
July 16, 2012, phone call

Konrad Götz in conversation with Stefan Carsten,
August 3, 2012, Frankfurt/Main

Frauke Burgdorff in conversation with
Matthias Böttger, August 7, 2012, Cologne

Armin Grunwald in conversation with
Stefan Carsten, August 17, 2012, Berlin

Tanja A. Börzel in conversation with
Stefan Carsten, September 7, 2012, phone call

Fritz Reusswig in conversation with
Matthias Böttger, September 10, 2012, Potsdam

Heinz Bude in conversation with Stefan Carsten,
September 11, 2012, Berlin

Michael Krautzberger in conversation with
Matthias Böttger, September 12, 2012, Berlin

Local Experts

Hamburg Metropolitan Region
Barbara Engelschall – Wedeler Au Regional Park
Katrin Fahrenkrug – Institut Raum & Energie
Jörg Knieling – HafenCity University Hamburg
Michael Koch – HafenCity University Hamburg
Fred Niemann – Town of Wedel
Petra Pelster – Urban Planning and Environment
Bureau Hamburg
Julian Petrin – Nexthamburg
Tobias Preising – HafenCity University Hamburg
Jakob Richter – Hamburg Metropolitan Region
Bureau
Simona Weisleder – International Building
Exhibition Hamburg

Kitzscher
Frank Amey – Urban and Regional Planner
Andreas Berkner – City of Leipzig
Kai Braun – City of Leipzig
Sigrun Kabisch – Helmholtz Centre for
Environmental Research, Leipzig
Petra Köpping – SPD Sachsen
Dieter Rink – Helmholtz Centre for
Environmental Research, Leipzig
Rainer Wünsche – District of Leipzig

Ludwigsburg
Albrecht Burkhardt – City of Ludwigsburg
Peter Fazekas – City of Ludwigsburg
Albert Geiger – City of Ludwigsburg
Martin Haas – Haas Cook Zemmrich, Architect
Christian Holl – Architect
Ulrich Pantle – Architect

Offenbach
Andrea L'Abbate – Fabbrica Latticini
Loimi Brautmann – Hochschule für Gestaltung
Offenbach
Erdogan Cavus – Cavus GmbH
Tobias Kurtz – City of Offenbach
Marcus Schenk – Area manager, Mathildenviertel,
Offenbach
Kai Vöckler – Hochschule für Gestaltung
Offenbach

Saale-Orla-Kreis
Katja Fischer – International Building Exhibition
Thuringia
Juergen Klimpke – Town of Schleiz
Manfred Klöppel – Thuringian Schiefergebirge/
Upper Saale Nature Park
Christine Kober – Thuringian Schiefergebirge/
Upper Saale Nature Park
Sören Kube – Action group leader
Heike Ramon – Cabka GmbH

Völklingen
Heinz Beck – Town of Völklingen
Meinrad Grewenig – Völklinger Hütte World
Cultural Heritage Site
Knut Quinten – Hochschule der Bildenden Künste
Saar
Igor Torres – Baubar Urbanlaboratorium
Georg Winter – Hochschule der Bildenden Künste
Saar
Michael Zimmer – Town of Völklingen

Maps

Cover

Orographic map of Germany and Western Europe, blank edition, scale ca. 1:5,000,000, Lambert conformal conic projection with two isometric parallels of latitude 48°40' and 52°40' and a central meridian of 12° East, ellipsoid: geodetic reference system WGS84, version: M. Ruhstorfer, Huber Kartographie

Einwohnerdichte, population per km² (grid square) 2012. Based on Laufende Raumbeobachtung des BBSR, Bevölkerungsfortschreibung des Bundes und der Länder, geometric basis: BKG, Kreise, December 31, 2012; version: G. Krischausky, R. Klütsch.

Topography and Water Surfaces, p. 49

Orohydrographic map of Germany, blank edition, scale 1:2,500,000, Lambert conformal conic projection with two isometric parallels of latitude 48°40' and 52°40', ellipsoid: geodetic reference system 1980 (GRS 80), Federal Agency for Cartography and Geodesy (Bundesamt für Kartographie und Geodäsie [BKG]), Frankfurt/Main, 2015

Population Distribution, p. 50

Einwohnerdichte, population per km² (grid square) 2012. Based on Laufende Raumbeobachtung des BBSR, Bevölkerungsfortschreibung des Bundes und der Länder, geometric basis: BKG, Kreise, December 31, 2012; version: G. Krischausky, R. Klütsch.

Gemeinden ab 2000 Einwohner, klassifiziert nach BIK. Based on Laufende Raumbeobachtung des BBSR, Bevölkerungsfortschreibung des Bundes und der Länder, geometric basis: BKG/BBSR, Einheitsgemeinden und Gemeindeverbände, December 31, 2013, version: R. Klütsch, G. Krischausky.

Transport and Energy Axes, p. 52

Bundesrepublik Deutschland – Fernstrassen: Federal Agency for Cartography and Geodesy (Bundesamt für Kartographie und Geodäsie [BKG]), Frankfurt/Main, 2012.
Bundesrepublik Deutschland – ICE Bahnhöfe mit Streckenlauf: Federal Agency for Cartography and Geodesy (Bundesamt für Kartographie und Geodäsie [BKG]), Frankfurt/Main, 2013.
Kraftwerke und Verbundnetze in Deutschland: German Environment Agency (Umweltbundesamt), Dessau, 2013.

Population Development, p. 54

Regionale Alterung 2010 bis 2030, average age 2030. Based on Laufende Raumbeobachtung des BBSR, BBSR-Bevölkerungsprognose 2009–2030/ROP, geometric basis: BKG Prognoseräume, 2010.

Kleinräumige Bevölkerungsdynamik in Vergangenheit und Zukunft 2010 bis 2030, changes in population numbers 2010 to 2030, in percent. Based on Laufende Raumbeobachtung des BBSR, BBSR-Bevölkerungsprognose 2009-2030/ROP, geometric basis: BKG Prognoseräume, 2010.

Employment Patterns, p. 56

Erwerbstätige sekundärer Sektor, employed in secondary sector (WZ 2008) per hundred employed 2012. Based on Laufende Raumbeobachtung des BBSR, Volkswirtschaftliche Gesamtrechnung der Länder, geometric basis: BKG, Kreise, December 31, 2012, version: R. Klütsch, G. Krischausky.

Erwerbstätige tertiärer Sektor, employed in tertiary sector (WZ 2008) per hundred employed 2012. Based on Laufende Raumbeobachtung des BBSR, Volkswirtschaftliche Gesamtrechnung der Länder, geometric basis: BKG, Kreise, December 31, 2013, version: P. Kuhlmann, G. Krischausky.

Impervious Surfaces, Woods and Forest, p. 58

Siedlungs- und Verkehrsfläche, proportion of grid 2013, in percent. Based on Laufende Raumbeobachtung des BBSR, Flächenerhebung nach Art der tatsächlichen Nutzung des Bundes und der Länder, geometric basis: BKG, Kreise, December 31, 2013, version: G. Beckmann.

Regionalatlas Deutschland. Indikatoren des Themenbereichs "Gebiet und Fläche." Anteil Waldfläche an Gesamtfläche, proportion of total area 2013, in percent. Information basis: Statistische Ämter des Bundes und der Länder, geometric basis: BKG, 2014.

Potential Renewable Energies, p. 60

Biomassepotenzial und Stromproduktion aus Bioenergie, potential. Based on Laufende Raumbeobachtung des BBSR, geometric basis: BKG, Kreise, 2008, Bonn, 2011.

Potentialermittlung für den Ausbau der Wasserkraftnutzung in Deutschland als Grundlage für die Entwicklung einer geeigneten Ausbaustrategie, potential. BMUB, Final Report, 2010.

Windkraftnutzungseignung gemäss Referenzertragskriterium nach EEG in der Bundesrepublik Deutschland. Information basis: Statistisches Windmodell 1981–2000. Germany's National Meteorological Service, 2005.

Solarenergiepotential Deutschland. Deutscher Fachverband Solarenergie.

Biomass, Status Quo and Potential, p. 62

Biomass energy, status quo. Information basis: Energieerzeugung in Deutschland (OpenStreetMap). Online: www.tappenbeck.net/osm/maps/deu/index.php?id=1019 (2014).

Biomassepotenzial und Stromproduktion aus Bioenergie, potential. Based on Laufende Raumbeobachtung des BBSR, geometric basis: BKG, Kreise, 2008, Bonn, 2011.

Hydro, Status Quo and Potential, p. 64

Hydroelectric energy, status quo. Information basis: Energieerzeugung in Deutschland (OpenStreetMap). Online: www.tappenbeck.net/osm/maps/deu/index.php?id=1019 (2014).

Potentialermittlung für den Ausbau der Wasserkraftnutzung in Deutschland als Grundlage für die Entwicklung einer geeigneten Ausbaustrategie, potential. BMUB, Final Report, 2010.

Wind, Status Quo and Potential, p. 66

Wind energy, status quo. Information basis: Energieerzeugung in Deutschland (OpenStreetMap). Online: www.tappenbeck.net/osm/maps/deu/index.php?id=1019 (2014).

Windkraftnutzungseignung gemäss Referenzertragskriterium nach EEG in der Bundesrepublik Deutschland. Information basis: Statistisches Windmodell 1981–2000. Germany's National Meteorological Service, 2005.

Solar, Status Quo and Potential, p. 68

Solar energy, status quo. Information basis: Energieerzeugung in Deutschland (OpenStreetMap). Online: www.tappenbeck.net/osm/maps/deu/index.php?id=1019 (2014).

Solarenergiepotential Deutschland. Deutscher Fachverband Solarenergie.

Empty Apartments and Net Migration, p. 70

Wohnungsleerstand. Number of empty apartments in residential buildings 2011, in percent. Information basis: BBSR-Wohnungsmarktforschung. Statistisches Bundesamt: Zensus 2011, Gebäude und Wohnungszählung, geometric basis: BKG, Kreise, December 31, 2012, version: J. Nielsen.

Aussenwanderungssaldo, Net migration per thousand population. Based on Laufende Raumbeobachtung des BBSR, Wanderungsstatistik des Bundes und der Länder, geometric basis: BKG, Kreise, December 31, 2012, version: R. Klütsch, G. Krischausky.

Hospital Accessibility and Population Density, p. 72

Erreichbarkeit von Krankenhäusern, car distance to nearest hospital for primary medical care, in minutes 2008. Information basis: Erreichbarkeitsmodell des BBSR, Krankenhausverzeichnis des wissenschaftlichen Instituts der AOK (WidO), independent surveys, geometric basis: BKG, Länder, December 31, 2008.

Einwohnerdichte, population per km² (grid square) 2012. Based on Laufende Raumbeobachtung des BBSR, Bevölkerungsfortschreibung des Bundes und der Länder, geometric basis: BKG, Kreise, December 31, 2012; version: G. Krischausky, R. Klütsch.

Secondary-Sector Employment, p. 74

Erwerbstätige sekundärer Sektor, employed in secondary sector (WZ 2008) per hundred employed 2012. Based on Laufende Raumbeobachtung des BBSR, Volkswirtschaftliche Gesamtrechnung der Länder, geometric basis: BKG, Kreise, December 31, 2012, version: R. Klütsch, G. Krischausky.

Einwohnerdichte, population per km² (grid square) 2012. Based on Laufende Raumbeobachtung des BBSR, Bevölkerungsfortschreibung des Bundes und der Länder, geometric basis: BKG, Kreise, December 31, 2012; version: G. Krischausky, R. Klütsch.

Community Debts and Real Estate Prices, p. 76

Kommunale Schulden, community debts, in euros per inhabitant, 2012. Based on Laufende Raumbeobachtung des BBSR, Statistik über Schulden des Bundes und der Länder, geometric basis: BKG, Kreise, December 31, 2012, version: R. Klütsch, G. Krischausky.

Kaufpreise für gebrauchte freistehende Ein- und Zweifamilienhäuser, average purchase prices for used, vacant single- and two-family houses, in thousands of euros, 2012. Information basis: BBSR-Wohnungsmarktbeobachtung, survey of experts, committee of experts and upper committee of experts work group 2012, source supplemented by estimated regression values, version: T. Held, J. Nielsen.

Car Ownership and Population Density, p. 78

Pkw-Dichte, cars per thousand population, 2012. Based on Laufende Raumbeobachtung des BBSR, vehicle statistics of the Federal Motor Transport Authority (Kraftfahrtbundesamt), Federation and Federal States debt statistics, geometric basis: BKG, Kreise, December 31, 2012, version: G. Krischausky, R. Klütsch.

Einwohnerdichte, population per km² (grid square) 2012. Based on Laufende Raumbeobachtung des BBSR, Bevölkerungsfortschreibung des Bundes und der Länder, geometric basis: BKG, Kreise, December 31, 2012; version: G. Krischausky, R. Klütsch.

Commuting Distances and Purchasing Power, p. 80

Pendeldistanzen, average commuting distances of all socially insured employees in a location, in kilometers, 2013. Information basis: Pendelverflechtungsmatrix der Bundesagentur für Arbeit, geometric basis: BKG, Gemeinden, December 31, 2013, version: T. Pütz.

Kaufkraft, purchasing power, in euros per inhabitant, 2012 (population = census projection). Based on Laufende Raumbeobachtung des BBSR, GfK, geometric basis: BKG, Kreise, December 31, 2013, version: P. Kuhlmann, G. Krischausky.

Voter Participation and Hartz IV, p. 82

Wahlbeteiligung Bundestagswahlen, voter participation in Bundestag elections 2013. Based on Laufende Raumbeobachtung des BBSR, Allgemeine Bundestagswahlstatistik des Bundes und der Länder, geometric basis: BKG, Kreise, December 31, 2012, version: G. Krischausky, R. Klütsch.

SGB II-Quote, quota of employable and non-employable receiving money from Social Insurance Code II (SGB II) per hundred population under 65 years, 2012. Based on Laufende Raumbeobachtung des BBSR Statistik der Grundsicherung für Arbeitssuchende nach dem SGB II der Bundesagentur für Arbeit, geometric basis: BKG, Kreise, December 31, 2012, version: R. Klütsch, G. Krischausky.

Births and Graduates with Academic Degrees, p. 84

Allgemeine Geburtenziffern 2011 für kreisfreie Städte und Landkreise, live births per thousand population. Information basis: Statistisches Bundesamt, Fachserie 1, Reihe 1.1, 2011.

Bevölkerung mit Hochschulabschluss, proportion of graduates with academic degrees (over 15 years old), in percent. Information basis: Statistische Ämter des Bundes und der Länder, 2014, geometric basis: BKG, 2013 (data adapted).

Female Graduates with Academic Degrees and Fathers Taking Parental Leave, p. 86

Akademikerinnen, proportion of female graduates with academic degrees (over 15 years old), in percent. Information basis: Statistische Ämter des Bundes und der Länder, 2014, geometric basis: BKG, 2013 (data adapted).

Elterngeldbezug Väter, fathers who received paternity pay, per child born, in percent, 2012. Based on Laufende Raumbeobachtung des BBSR, Statistisches Bundesamt, Elterngeld für Geburten, 2012, geometric basis: BKG, Kreise, December 31, 2012, version: G. Krischausky, R. Klütsch.

Population with Migratory Background and Rents, p. 88

Anteil der Einwohner mit Migrationshintergrund an den Einwohnern, 2011, ratio of population with migratory background, in percent. Based on Laufende Raumbeobachtung des BBSR, provided by Statistisches Landesamt Baden-Württemberg, geometric basis: BKG, Kreise, December 31, 2013, version: G. Krischausky, R. Klütsch.

Angebotsmieten für Wohnungen, new rental and re-rental prices excl. running costs, in euro/m², 2014. Information basis: BBSR-Wohnungsmarktbeobachtung, IDN ImmoDaten GmbH, geometric basis: BKG, Kreise, December 31, 2013, version: A. Schürt, J. Nielsen.

Youth Joblessness and Employment of Older Persons, p. 90

Erwerbslosenquote in der Altersklasse "15 bis 24 Jahre" für Deutschland, youth joblessness, jobless rate in the 15- to 24-year-old age group. Information basis: Statistische Ämter des Bundes und der Länder, 2014, geometric basis: BKG, 2013 (data adapted).

Ältere SV-Beschäftigte, persons of 55 years and over, employees liable to social insurance, per hundred population, 2012. Based on Laufende Raumbeobachtung des BBSR, Bevölkerungsfortschreibung des Bundes und der Länder, geometric basis: BKG, Kreise, December, 2012, version: G. Krischausky, R. Klütsch.

Young and Old People, p. 92

Einwohner 6 bis unter 18 Jahren, ratio of 6- to 18-year-olds in population, in percent, 2012. Based on Laufende Raumbeobachtung des BBSR, Fortschreibung des Bevölkerungsstandes des Bundes und der Länder, geometric basis: BKG, Kreise, December 31, 2013, version: P. Kuhlmann, G. Krischausky.

Haushalte im Rentenalter, households whose head is 60 or older, per hundred households, 2010. Based on Laufende Raumbeobachtung des BBSR, GfK Nuremberg, geometric basis: BKG, Kreise, December 31, 2012, version: G. Krischausky, R. Klütsch.

Community Debts and Hartz IV, p. 94

Kommunale Schulden, community debts, in euros per inhabitant, 2012. Based on Laufende Raumbeobachtung des BBSR, Statistik über Schulden des Bundes und der Länder, geometric basis: BKG, Kreise, December 31, 2012, version: R. Klütsch, G. Krischausky.

SGB II-Quote, quota of employable and non-employable receiving money from Social Insurance Code II (SGB II) per hundred population under 65 years, 2012. Based on Laufende Raumbeobachtung des BBSR Statistik der Grundsicherung für Arbeitssuchende nach dem SGB II der Bundesagentur für Arbeit, geometric basis: BKG, Kreise, December 31, 2012, version: R. Klütsch, G. Krischausky.

Biographies

Thomas Auer is the managing director of Transsolar and a professor of building technology and climate responsive design at the Technical University of Munich.

Armen Avanessian studied philosophy and political science in Vienna and Paris and literary studies in Bielefeld. He has been a visiting fellow at the German departments of Columbia University and Yale University, and a visiting professor and lecturer at the art academies in Nuremberg, Vienna, Basel, Copenhagen, and California (CalArts). He is the founder of the www.spekulative-poetik.de research platform and chief editor at Merve Verlag.

Stefan Bergheim is the director of the nonprofit think tank Center for Societal Progress, founded in Frankfurt/Main in 2009. His work involves the development of new ways and methods to improve the quality of life in Germany.

Tanja A. Börzel is a professor of political science. She currently holds the Jean Monnet Chair and is the director of the Center for European Integration at the Freie Universität Berlin. Her main spheres of interest lie in institutional and governance research, European integration, and comparative governmental research, especially of western and southern Europe.

Matthias Böttger is an architect and artistic director of the Deutsches Architektur Zentrum (DAZ) in Berlin. He is a professor of sustainable architecture and future tactics (SAFT) and the director of the Institut für Raum und Design der Kunstuniversität Linz. With raumtaktik—office from a better future—he works on spatial intelligence and intervention.

Gerhard Bosch is a professor of sociology at the University of Duisburg-Essen. His specialties are the sociology of work and economic sociology.

Matthijs Bouw is an architect and urbanist. He is the founding principal of One Architecture, with offices in Amsterdam and New York. One Architecture's work includes many long-term planning projects for the Dutch government as well as the protection of Lower Manhattan against floods (the Big U/Dryline). He is also the Rockefeller Urban Resilience Fellow at the University of Pennsylvania. He is particularly interested in the strategic role design can play in planning with risk and uncertainty.

Heinz Bude is a professor of macrosociology at the University of Kassel. His specialties are generational, exclusion, and entrepreneur research.

Frauke Burgdorff is an urban and regional planner and has been a board member of the Montag Stiftung Urbane Räume since 2006. Her specialty is projects at the interface of education, housing, and urban renewal.

Stefan Carsten is a futures researcher and urban geographer. His work brings together the subjects of the future, the city, and mobility. He is an adviser for futures and strategy design and among other things has been a visiting professor for socio-scientific futures research at the Braunschweig University of Art.

Ludwig Engel is a futures and urban researcher. Until 2011 he worked in the futures research department (Society and Technology Research Group) at Daimler AG in Berlin. He is currently teaching at the Technische Universität Berlin (Architecture Innovation Design Program) and at the Berlin University of the Arts (social and business communication) in the fields of urban planning and development, urban futures, and strategic futures planning.

Konrad Götz is a coordinator for strategic counseling and has worked with the Institute for Social-Ecological Research in Frankfurt/Main since 1995. His main spheres of interest are mobility research, social empiricism, and lifestyle concepts.

Armin Grunwald has been the director of the Institute for Technology Assessment and Systems Analysis (ITAS) at the Karlsruhe Institute of Technology (KIT) since 1999, director of the Office for Technology Assessment at the German Bundestag since 2002, and a professor of the philosophy of technology and ethics of technology at KIT since 2007.

Klaus Hurrelmann is a professor emeritus of social and health sciences at the University of Bielefeld and a senior professor of public health and education at the Hertie School of Governance in Berlin. His fields are socialization and educational research, specializing in family, childhood, youth, and school, as well as research into health and preventative medicine. He has been the director of both the Shell Youth Study and the World Vision Children's Study since 2006.

Michael Krautzberger was president of the Deutsche Akademie für Städtebau und Landesplanung until 2013 and vice president of the Deutsche Stiftung Denkmalschutz until 2014. He is a member of the Board of the Deutsche Stiftung Denkmalschutz and of the Board of Europa Nostra. He is an honorary professor at the Faculty of Spatial Planning at Dortmund University and an honorary professor of the Faculty of Law at the Humboldt-Universität zu Berlin.

Claus Leggewie is a professor of political science and the director of both the Institute for Advanced Study of the Humanities in Essen and the Center for Global Cooperation Research in Duisburg. His specialties are climate and interculture and democracy research in inter- and cross-disciplinary contexts.

Armin Linke is a professor at the Hochschule für Gestaltung Karlsruhe. As a photographer and filmmaker, he combines a range of contemporary image-processing technologies in order to blur the borders between fiction and reality. His artistic practice is concerned with different ways of dealing with photographic archives and their respective manifestations, as well as with the interrelations and transformative powers between urban, architectural, or spatial functions and the human beings interacting with these environments.

Julian Petrin is an urbanist from Hamburg, the proprietor of the consultancy practice urbanista, and the founder of the participative think tank Nexthamburg. From 2013 to 2015 he was a visiting professor of urban development and urban management at the University of Kassel. He is a member of the Deutsche Akademie für Städtebau und Landesplanung and a member of the board of experts of the Nationale Plattform Zukunftsstadt.

Fritz Reusswig is a sociologist at the Potsdam Institute for Climate Impact Research. He studies how lifestyles and consumption influence climate change and how cities are becoming climate-political protagonists.

Ralf Schüle is co-director of the Energy, Transport, and Climate Policy research group at the Wuppertal Institute for Climate, Environment, and Energy. His spheres of interest include climate protection and urban development, energy efficiency politics at EU, national, and regional levels, socio-ecological research, international climate politics, and Kyoto mechanisms.

Erik Swyngedouw is a professor of geography at Manchester University. His intellectual contributions have set the academic agenda in a range of fields, including political ecology, hydro-social conflict, urban governance and urban movements, democracy and political power, and the politics of globalization.

Acknowledgments

Speculations Transformations emerged from the "Baukulturatlas Deutschland 2030/2050" research project commissioned by and conducted in collaboration with the Federal Ministry for the Environment, Nature Conservation, Building, and Nuclear Safety (Bundesministerium für Umwelt, Naturschutz, Bau, und Reaktorsicherheit [BMUB]) and the Federal Institute for Research on Building, Urban Affairs, and Spatial Development (Bundesinstitut für Bau-, Stadt- und Raumforschung [BBSR]). We wish to thank all those who helped us in the realization of the project and of this publication.

Core Team: Marta Doehler-Behzadi, Michael Marten, Lars-Christian Uhlig

Participants in the Zukunftswerkstätten/ Workshops: Inke Arns, Thomas Auer, Christophe Barlieb, Heinz Beck, Stefan Bergheim, Tristan Biere, Nicolas Bourquin, Matthijs Bouw, Kai Braun, Anca Cârstean, Daniel Czechowski, Andreas Dittrich, Markus Eltges, Hagen Eyink, Peter Fazekas, Andreas Gebhard, Maja Göpel, Nicole Graf, Maria Grzegorzewska, Martin Haas, Ulrich Hatzfeld, Matthias Heumeier, Ludger Hovestadt, Markus Huber, Olga Maria Hungar, Ivo de Jeu, Juergen Klimpke, Petra Köpping, Sören Kube, Leona Lynen, Klaus Müschen, Norbert Palz, Julian Petrin, Lars Porsche, Tobias Preising, Fritz Reusswig, Matthias Rudolph, Marcus Schenk, Anke Schmidt, Julian Schubert, Adeline Seidel, Susanne Stauch, Antje Stokman, Gabriele Sturm, Niloufar Tajeri, Igor Torres, Kai Vöckler

Analytical Experts: Tanja A. Börzel, Heinz Bude, Frauke Burgdorff, Konrad Götz, Armin Grunwald, Klaus Hurrelmann, Michael Krautzberger, Fritz Reusswig, Ralf Schüle

International Experts: Maria Aiolova, Armen Avanessian, Stefano Boeri, Neil Brenner, Keller Easterling, Matthias Hollwich, Mitchell Joachim, Armin Linke, Chris Luebkeman, Kyong Park, Erik Swyngedouw, Peter Zellner

"Stadt von Übermorgen" Conference: Klaus Beckmann, Anne Katrin Bohle, Gerhard Bosch, Steffen Braun, Stefan Holl, Thomas Jocher, Claus Leggewie, Hilmar von Lojewski, Franz-Josef Radermacher, Stephan Reiss-Schmidt, Dirk Vallée, Johannes Weinand

Specialists Maps, BBSR: Rita Klütsch, Gesine Krischausky, Claus Schlömer

Local and Regional Experts: Hamburg Metropolitan Region – Barbara Engelschall, Katrin Fahrenkrug, Jörg Knieling, Michael Koch, Fred Niemann, Petra Pelster, Julian Petrin, Tobias Preising, Jakob Richter, Simona Weisleder; Kitzscher – Frank Amey, Andreas Berkner, Kai Braun, Sigrun Kabisch, Petra Köpping, Dieter Rink, Rainer Wünsche; Ludwigsburg – Albrecht Burkhardt, Peter Fazekas, Albert Geiger, Martin Haas, Christian Holl, Ulrich Pantle; Offenbach – Andrea l'Abbate, Loimi Brautmann, Erdogan Cavus, Tobias Kurtz, Marcus Schenk, Kai Vöckler; Saale-Orla-Kreis – Katja Fischer, Juergen Klimpke, Manfred Klöppel, Christine Kober, Sören Kube, Heike Ramon; Völklingen – Heinz Beck, Meinrad Grewenig, Knut Quinten, Igor Torres, Georg Winter, Michael Zimmer

Graphics/Layout: onlab – Nicolas Bourquin, Christian Lindemann, Benjamin Maibach, Laia Ortiz Sansano, Raphael Schön, Floyd E. Schulze, Thibaud Tissot, Signe Vej Ugelvig, Julie Vuagnoux

Illustrations: Xaver Böhm, Sebastian Lörscher, Ulrike Plassmann, Ann-Kathrin Radtke

Editing, Copyediting, Proofreading, Translation: Dörte Eliass, Christopher Jenkin-Jones, Cordelia Marten, Katrin Sauerländer, Emily Votruba

In addition to the people directly involved in the research project, many individuals and institutions have helped us over the past few years to look at the lived environment with different eyes, and to try out, refine, present, and publish our approach. We wish to thank them all.

Gunther Adler, *Arch+*, Andrea Augsten, Kristin Bartels, BBSR, BDA, Luis Berríos-Negrón, BMUB, BMW Guggenheim Lab, Verena Brehm, Tanmay Chakrabarty, Renato Cymbalista, Daimler AG, Pulak Promotesh Das, Marta Doehler-Behzadi, Sabine Drewes, Markus Eltges, Kristina Eschler, ETH Zürich, Hagen Eyink, Heiner Farwick, Lukas Feireiss, Katja Fischer, Ralf Fücks, Simon Gathercole, Ansgar Gessner, Roland Gnaiger, Saif ul Haque, Ulrich Hatzfeld, Ole Heidrich, Andrej Heinke, Heinrich-Böll-Stiftung, Lutz Henke, Laura Holzberg, Robert Kaltenbrunner, Gabriele Kautz, Franz Koppelstätter, Nikolaus Kuhnert, Agata Kurecki, Tristan Lannuzel, Tobias Leipprand, Kunstuniversität Linz, Sean Madden, Michael Marten, Eckard Minx, Keya Najmun Nahar, Christian Neuhaus, Anh-Linh Ngo, Maria Nicanor, Anne Niehüser, Reinhard Kannonier, Sabine Pollak, Lars Porsche, Nina Reckeweg, Marianne Reeb, Marcelo Rezende, Sanna Richter, Marcio Rosa D'Avila, Ashim Halder Sagor, Karin Sander, Anke Schmidt, Oliver Seidel, Martin Sobota, Stiftung Neue Verantwortung, Julius Streifeneder, Gabriele Sturm, Milo Tesselaar, Laleh Torabi, Lars-Christian Uhlig, Icaro Vilaça, Ute Weiland, Katharina Weinberger, Thomas Welter, Guilherme Wisnik, Andrea Zell, Lars Zimmermann